# OF THE PEOPLE,
# BY THE PEOPLE,
# FOR THE PEOPLE

# OF THE PEOPLE, BY THE PEOPLE, FOR THE PEOPLE

The Congress, the Presidency, and the Supreme
Court in American History

An Omnibus of three books
*The Congress, The Presidency,* and
*The Supreme Court*
(Revised and Updated)

By

## RICHARD B. BERNSTEIN

*and*

## JEROME AGEL

Wings Books
New York • Avenel, New Jersey

This omnibus was originally published in three separate volumes under the titles:
*The Congress*, copyright © 1989 by Jerome Agel and Richard B. Bernstein
*The Presidency*, copyright © 1989 by Jerome Agel and Richard B. Bernstein
*The Supreme Court*, copyright © 1989 by Jerome Agel and Richard B. Bernstein

This edition presents updated and revised texts of the original editions, whose series title was *Into the Third Century*. They have been completely reset for this volume.

This edition is published by Wings Books,
distributed by Outlet Book Company, Inc., a Random House Company,
40 Engelhard Avenue, Avenel, New Jersey 07001,
by arrangement with the authors.

Random House
New York • Toronto • London • Sydney • Auckland

Printed and bound in the United States of America

Library of Congress Cataloging-in-Publication Data
Bernstein, Richard B., 1956–
    Of the people, by the people, for the people: Congress, the Presidency, and the Supreme Court in American history / by Richard B. Bernstein and Jerome Agel.
        p.   cm.
    "Contains the books The Congress, The Presidency, and The Supreme Court."
    "This edition contains completely updated and revised texts of the original editions"—T.p. verso.
    Includes index.
    ISBN 0-517-09308-1
    1. United States—Politics and government.   I. Agel, Jerome.   II. Title.
JK31.B45 1993
320.973—dc20                                                              93-4628
                                                                              CIP

8 7 6 5 4 3 2 1

I dedicated the first version of this book to my mother, my first teacher, with love. That sentiment still stands.

I take the opportunity to dedicate this new edition, revised, expanded, and (I hope) improved, to my father, whose love, encouragement, and pride in me barely match my pride and love for him—and who counsels me, with gentle tact, to improve myself.

R.B.B.

. . . for Zachary Jerome Agel, who—if I may go out on a limb—will serve with distinction in all three branches of our national government.

J.A.

. . . that government of the people, by the people, for the people shall not perish from the earth.

ABRAHAM LINCOLN
Gettysburg Address
November 19, 1863

# CONTENTS

# INTRODUCTION

On March 19, 1993, a tall, quiet man from Colorado—who had labored more than thirty years in the service of his country without attracting much attention—made front-page news across the United States. Justice Byron R. White, whom President John F. Kennedy had named to the Supreme Court in 1962, announced that he would be retiring at the end of the Court's current session.

Justice White's announcement was noteworthy for several reasons. The only sitting member of the nation's highest court to have been named by a Democratic President, White's retirement gave President Bill Clinton the chance to name the first Democratic nominee to the Court in twenty-six years. A key member of the Court's center-right bloc, White had sparked legal controversy for twenty years with his votes against constitutional protection for abortion and sexual privacy and his tough stands on issues of criminal justice. His critics labeled him an unthinking right-winger; his defenders argued that he was a complex, at times unpredictable legal thinker who emphasized the demands of legal craftsmanship.

Justice White's resignation also signalled the possible end of conservative domination of the Court. Should other Justices—such as Harry A. Blackmun, John Paul Stevens, and Chief Justice William H.

Rehnquist—step down during Clinton's Presidency, Democrats would have the chance to shape a new, young, and vigorous moderate-to-liberal bloc that might have a chance to control the Court's direction for a generation. For this reason, conservative political activists vowed to subject any of Clinton's nominees to withering scrutiny, much as their candidates for the Court had been subjected to harsh examination by liberals in the 1980s and early 1990s.

President Clinton and his advisors sifted through hundreds of politicians and jurists. Many observers scolded the Administration for embarrassing potential nominees by "floating" their names and then ruling them out without explanation.

The criticism of President Clinton's hunt for a nominee was surpassed only by the praise his choice received. On June 14, 1993, eighty-eight days after Justice White announced his retirement, the President nominated Judge Ruth Bader Ginsburg of the U.S. Court of Appeals for the District of Columbia Circuit. Judge Ginsburg, who was named to the bench in 1980 by President Jimmy Carter, was the first Jewish Supreme Court nominee in nearly thirty years, and only the second woman named to the Court in American history.

Hailed by many as the Thurgood Marshall of the movement for women's rights, Ginsburg was born in the Flatbush section of Brooklyn, New York, in 1933. Educated at Cornell and at Harvard and Columbia Law Schools, she won election to both the *Harvard Law Review* and the *Columbia Law Review*. An eminent scholar and attorney who won five of the six women's-rights cases she argued before the Supreme Court, she was the first woman to become a tenured professor at Columbia Law School. Court observers agreed that Judge Ginsburg, who was widely known as a consensus-builder on the divided D.C. Circuit, was likely to win swift, and perhaps unanimous, Senate approval.

The retirement of a Supreme Court Justice is one of those rare moments that bring together all three key institutions of American government—the Congress, the Presidency, and the Supreme Court. Usually, these institutions go their separate ways, often cooperating and at times clashing over their overlapping spheres of responsibility and grants of power. These responsibilities and powers are the stuff of American constitutional government.

The people of the United States govern themselves under a Constitution more than two centuries old. It was written in the days of horse-drawn carriages and sailing ships, of powdered wigs and knee-breeches. Its authors, a few dozen men from twelve struggling states along the Atlantic Ocean, had never heard of personal computers or space satellites or nuclear reactors, of airplanes or railroads or automobiles.

The Constitution does not govern this country. "We the People of the United States" do that. We choose the people who will make our laws, enforce them, and resolve disputes arising under them. Our Constitution establishes three branches of government—the legislative, the executive, and the judiciary. Each of the three branches has the power to check or restrain the other two branches. The three branches have often worked together and, just as often, they have worked against one another. They are held in a delicate balance by the commands of the Constitution.

The Constitution is the core of the way we govern ourselves, but it is not the whole story—just as a human being is far more than the skeleton that gives him or her structure. Over the more than two hundred years since the Constitution was written and adopted, this system of government has developed and evolved. It has turned out to be strong enough to deal with national problems, flexible enough to adapt to changing times and conditions, and limited enough to avoid damaging our rights.

This book explores the histories of the three central institutions of American government. "Of the People" describes Congress, which represents the people through the House of Representatives and the Senate. "By the People" examines the Presidency, the only truly national political office established by the Constitution and chosen by the American people. "For the People" considers the Supreme Court, the capstone of the federal judicial system.

This book shows how each institution has developed over time, describes the key challenges that each institution has had to face, and introduces the men and women central to the history of our government.

## OF THE PEOPLE

# THE CONGRESS

All legislative Powers herein granted shall be vested in a Congress of the United States, which shall consist of a Senate and House of Representatives.

—Constitution of the United States
Article I, Section 1

*The Congress*

For Megan Hanford and Daniel Hanford . . . future leaders
of the rising generation.

R.B.B.

*The Capitol has been the home of the Congress of the United States since
1800. Its construction took more than a half century, and it has undergone
several extensive renovations. This aerial view also shows the Thomas Jefferson
Building of the Library of Congress, just behind the Capitol.*

# CHAPTER ONE

# INVENTING A LEGISLATURE

The system of government created in 1787 by the U.S. Constitution has three parts: the legislative branch, or Congress (composed of the House of Representatives and the Senate); the executive branch, directed by the President; and the judicial branch, headed by the Supreme Court.

Every American knows something about the Presidency, and more and more in recent years the Supreme Court has become part of our daily lives. But the Congress remains the unknown branch of our government. And most of the people who do know something about Congress do not see Congress in a flattering light. They are convinced that it is filled with politicians scheming to reward selfish interest groups and to keep themselves in office.

The problem is that most people do not appreciate the importance of the day-to-day grind of politics to the preservation of our liberties and the achievement of important national goals. The history of Congress shows the importance of politics in the development of our government and the nation it is to govern.

This part sketches the history of Congress, from its roots in the colonial and Revolutionary periods to our own time. It focuses on the place of Congress in our constitutional system. It also describes the three major functions and responsibilities of Congress: to make laws, or *legislate*; to discuss major national issues, or *debate*; and to *investigate* national problems, the workings of government, and the need for new laws.

There is a reason that Congress comes first in the Constitution (in Article I). The delegates to the Federal Convention who drafted the Constitution in 1787 drew on their experience of government during the American Revolution and on their memories of colonial government before the Revolution. In both cases, they were most familiar with legislatures.

Nearly two centuries passed between the establishment of the first permanent English settlement at Jamestown, Virginia, in 1607, and the American declaration of independence from Great Britain in 1776. During that period the colonists relied on their representatives in the colonial legislatures to protect their rights and defend their interests with the mother country. The colonial legislatures had two houses. The lower house was made up of representatives of the people. (In those days, that meant white male property owners, the only people allowed to vote.) The upper house was elected by the lower house, appointed by the royal governor, or elected by the lower house from candidates named by the governor.

The colonial legislatures modeled themselves on the British Parliament. The colonists thought of themselves as Englishmen with the rights of Englishmen, and their heritage was the history and heritage of Great Britain. Parliament had two houses: the House of Commons, which represented the voters, and the House of Lords, where the nobility took part in government. The American colonists admired the many courageous battles for the rights of Englishmen fought by the House of Commons against the Crown. They also appreciated the important role of the House of Lords as a balance between the Commons and the Crown. This history influenced the leaders of the Revolutionary movement in shaping new governments after the declaration of independence from England.

The American Revolution began as a disagreement between politicians in London and the colonists over how much authority Parliament had to make laws for the colonies—specifically, tax laws. The colonists claimed that under the unwritten English constitution, they could be taxed only by legislatures that they had a direct voice in choosing. The colonists were not represented in Parliament; therefore, Parliament could not impose taxes on them. Parliament replied that although the colonists could not elect anyone to Parliament, they were nevertheless represented because every member of Parliament had the duty to watch over the interests and defend the rights of every subject of the British Empire.

As disputes between the colonists and Great Britain increased, the colonists called meetings of delegates from all the colonies to discuss their common problems with Great Britain and what they should do about them. These meetings were called *congresses*. The Stamp Act Congress met in 1765, the First Continental Congress in 1774, and the Second Continental Congress beginning in May 1775.

It was the Second Continental Congress that took the critical steps leading to the Americans' decision to declare independence from Great Britain. In May 1776, that Congress adopted a resolution written by John Adams of Massachusetts calling on the colonies to adopt new forms of government—that is, to write new state constitutions. On July 2, 1776, that Congress adopted a resolution offered by Richard Henry Lee of Virginia declaring "that these united colonies are, and of right ought to be, free and independent States. "And two days later, on July 4, 1776, that Congress adopted the revised and edited Declaration of Independence, drafted by Thomas Jefferson of Virginia.

The Second Continental Congress was also responsible for the first charter of government of the United States of America. That summer and fall, the delegates wrangled over a draft prepared by John Dickinson of Pennsylvania. Not until a year later, in November 1777, did the delegates agree on a final version of this new charter: the Articles of Confederation. All thirteen states had to approve, or *ratify*, the proposed new charter to put it into effect; it was not until March 1781 that the last holdout, Maryland, ratified the Articles.

The Articles of Confederation created only one institution of government: the one-house Confederation Congress. The delegates did not create two houses for this new legislature of the United States because all previous congresses had had only one house. Also, as we shall see, the delegates kept most powers of government in the hands of the states. They did not see any need to establish a traditional form of government with checks and balances or separation of powers at the national level.

The delegates who drafted the Articles of Confederation were suspicious of strong central government, as most Americans were in this period. They believed that government should be placed as close to the people as possible. For these reasons, the government created by the Articles of Confederation was extremely weak.

The Confederation Congress could propose, it could resolve, it could issue requisitions (that is, demands to the states for money and supplies). But it had no power to tax the people directly, no power to regulate trade across state lines, and no power to make the thirteen state governments comply with its requisitions. It could handle foreign affairs and negotiate treaties, such as the Treaty of Paris of 1783 that ended the Revolutionary War, but it could not make the state governments obey the requirements of that treaty. It could issue instructions on relations with the Indians, but it could not prevent the states from cheating, robbing, or waging war on the Indians if they felt like it.

On June 28, 1783, a detachment of soldiers from the Continental Army marched on the Confederation Congress and stuck their muskets through the windows of the building in Philadelphia where Congress was meeting. They demanded that Congress make good on the back pay the soldiers were owed. The crisis was resolved, but the delegates were humiliated and never forgot the experience.

It might seem natural that so weak a government would be amended, or changed, as soon as people realized that there was a problem. But all thirteen state legislatures had to agree to adopt an amendment, and there was always one or another holdout state to go against the will of the other twelve. By the mid-1780s, the Confederation Congress seemed to be little more than a bad joke.

General George Washington was appalled. He had had to put up with a divided, angry, and confused Congress throughout the long Revolutionary War. As the former Commander-in-Chief of the Continental Army watched anxiously from retirement at his Virginia plantation, Mount Vernon, he realized that the affairs of the United States in peacetime were even more tangled and uncertain than they had been during the war. He exclaimed in one of his many despairing letters during the 1780s: "We are fast verging to anarchy and confusion!"

Other American statesmen were also trading disgusted observations about American politics. One of them was John Jay of New York. The veteran diplomat had been a New York delegate to the Second Continental Congress and President of that body for one year, and since the end of 1784 was Secretary for Foreign Affairs to the United States in Congress Assembled—the Confederation Congress. As Secretary, he had tried bravely to keep the United States on the board in the game

of power politics, but the Confederation Congress seemed too divided, too distracted, and too weak to back him up. More than practi-
cally anyone else in American politics, Jay knew the strengths and
weaknesses of the Articles of Confederation. In a letter to George
Washington, he suggested that the Articles needed a thorough overhaul, if not a replacement, and he stated the basic principle that such
an overhaul should follow: "Let Congress legislate—let others execute
—let others judge."

As John Jay, George Washington, James Madison, Alexander Hamilton, and their colleagues were writing back and forth about the
problems of the Confederation Congress and the United States, a
process was taking shape to promote just such an overhaul.

The first step was the Mount Vernon Conference of 1785, at which
Virginians and Marylanders amiably settled problems between the
two states, such as navigation on the Potomac River. The Virginians
were so pleased with the meeting that they suggested that all the
states send delegates to Annapolis, Maryland, in September 1786 to
discuss problems of trade and commerce under the Articles of Confederation.

The Annapolis Convention of 1786 did not fulfill the hopes of its
organizers. Only twelve delegates from five states showed up. They
were too few to make any serious proposals, but they did electrify the
country with their report. Drafted by young, combative Alexander
Hamilton, this report declared that the Articles of Confederation
were too weak and fragile to work as a plan of government. Hamilton's report urged that a new convention be called to meet in Philadelphia, Pennsylvania, in May 1787 to make the government of the
United States adequate to the needs of the Union. Several states
responded immediately to this call for action. Others waited for the
Confederation Congress to respond before acting.

Finally, on February 21, 1787, the Confederation Congress *did*
authorize what we now know as the Federal Convention. The delegates voted, however, to give the Convention only the authority to
propose amendments to the Articles of Confederation.

On May 25, 1787, the Federal Convention began its work in a
stuffy room on the second floor of the Pennsylvania State House—the
building we now call Independence Hall. The first action the delegates took was to scrap the Articles and start over, writing a totally
new charter of government: the Constitution of the United States.

Most of the Convention's work focused on designing the new legislature of the United States. The delegates decided to keep the name

*Congress.* They had to face two more issues: how Congress should be constructed and what powers it should have.

The first issue had to do with *representation*. Who should be represented: the people or the states? Under the old Continental and Confederation Congresses, each state had an equal vote. The delegates from the large states, such as Pennsylvania, wanted each state to have representatives allotted based on population, or wealth, or size, or some other "fair" system. The delegates from the small states, such as Delaware and New Jersey, resisted this idea. They feared that they would be swallowed up by the large states unless they had an equal vote. The fight dragged on all through June and into July. Finally, a compromise proposed by the Connecticut delegates Roger Sherman, William Samuel Johnson, and Oliver Ellsworth was adopted. Their idea is still built into the Constitution today.

Congress has two houses:

1. In the House of Representatives, the people of each state are represented. Each state gets a certain number of Representatives based on its population. Its members are elected by the people of each state to serve for two years. The House has the sole power to propose *money bills*—that is, appropriations and taxation measures. The House elects a presiding officer, called the Speaker of the House (a term borrowed from the British Parliament).

2. The Senate has two Senators from each state, preserving an equal vote for the large and small states. The Senators serve six-year terms. The Senate has the sole power to approve or reject treaties made by the President and to approve or reject the President's nominees for federal judgeships and executive offices. The Senate also works with the House in framing and revising proposals for laws, known as *bills*. The Vice President of the United States presides over the Senate's meetings and has the power to vote to break ties of that body. (The first Vice President, John Adams, holds the record for breaking ties; he did it twenty-nine times.) Under the Constitution of 1787, Senators were to be chosen by the state legislatures, which were free to authorize popular elections or to choose the Senators themselves. (This system lasted for over a century, until the Seventeenth Amendment, calling for the election of Senators by the people, was adopted in 1913.)

Another compromise the delegates adopted set the formula for representation in the House of Representatives: Each state would receive representatives based on the number of free inhabitants plus three-fifths of "all other persons"—a tactful way of saying *slaves*. This compromise was a concession to the Southern slaveholding states. They had threatened to walk out of the Convention if their states were not protected by such a compromise.

There was little fuss about the other issue, the powers of Congress. Congress was given a set of specific powers in Article I, Section 8 of the new charter. These powers amounted to far more than the Confederation Congress ever had. They included the power "to lay and collect Taxes, Duties, Imposts and Excises, to pay the Debts and provide for the common Defence and general Welfare of the United States"; "to regulate Commerce with foreign Nations, and among the several States, and with the Indian Tribes"; "to coin Money" and "to borrow Money on the credit of the United States"; "to establish Post Offices and post Roads"; to issue patents to inventors and copyrights to authors, composers, and artists to protect their rights to their works; "to raise and support Armies" and "to provide and maintain a Navy"; and so forth.

The delegates included a special clause at the end of Article I, Section 8: "To make all Laws which shall be necessary and proper for carrying into Execution the foregoing Powers, and all other Powers vested by this Constitution in the Government of the United States, or in any Department or Officer thereof." This clause has become known as the *elastic clause* because later Congresses and Presidents and the Supreme Court have found in it authority for all sorts of federal statutes, such as the civil rights laws, even though the statutes have no clear authorization in the listed powers of Congress.

The delegates intended Congress to play special roles in checking and balancing the two other branches of government, the Presidency and the Supreme Court. They provided that the President can name certain government officers and negotiate treaties with foreign nations "with the advice and consent of the Senate." They provided that Congress has the power to establish federal courts below the Supreme Court and to define the kinds of cases that the federal courts could hear.

But Congress does not have the power to adopt laws all by itself. Following British precedent and the constitutions of the states of New York and Massachusetts, the Constitution provides that *both* houses of Congress must pass a bill. Any bill passed by the House and Senate then goes to the President. He may sign it into law or return it "with his Objections"—that is, *veto* the bill. A vetoed bill goes back to the chamber that proposed it. If the bill is passed again by at least two-thirds of *both* the House and the Senate, Congress has *overridden* the

President's veto, and the bill becomes law. The President may also veto a bill by a more complicated means—if he takes no action on a bill for ten days after getting it, and Congress adjourns before that ten-day period is up, he has carried out a *pocket veto* of the bill.

The Constitution sets forth a special process, known as the *impeachment* process, by which Congress can remove from office "the President, Vice President and all civil Officers of the United States" who have committed "Treason, Bribery, or other high Crimes and Misdemeanors." In this process, the House *impeaches*, or accuses, the official in question, and the Senate conducts a trial of the official on the charges listed in the *articles of impeachment* adopted by the House. A two-thirds vote of the Senate is necessary to convict the official and remove him or her from office.

The delegates to the Federal Convention borrowed the impeachment process from British practice. Also, impeachment had been a favorite tool of the colonial legislatures to keep other government officials in line. Under the Constitution, if the President has been impeached, the Chief Justice of the United States presides over the Senate's trial; if anyone else has been impeached, the Vice President presides over the Senate's trial.

Finally, Congress has the principal responsibility for *amending* the Constitution. Under Article V, there are two ways to make formal changes in the Constitution. The more usual way is for Congress to propose an amendment to the states, by a two-thirds vote of both the House and the Senate. Three-fourths of the states must then ratify the proposed amendment to make it part of the Constitution. There is another way to amend the Constitution, also involving Congress, which has never been used: Two-thirds of the states must apply to Congress to call a special convention to propose amendments to the Constitution. Any amendments proposed by this convention must then be adopted by three-fourths of the states to become part of the Constitution.

On September 17, 1787, thirty-nine of the forty-two delegates to the Convention still present signed the Constitution and sent it by stagecoach to the Confederation Congress, which was sitting in New York City. After several days of argument and debate, Congress sent it on to the states on September 28. The states called special elections for *ratifying conventions*—bodies chosen by the voters for the sole purpose of voting to adopt or to reject the proposed Constitution.

The contending forces in the ratification controversy said and wrote surprisingly little about the proposed new Congress. The opponents of the Constitution—the Anti-Federalists—argued that the new Congress would be too small to ensure that all the people (about four million at that time) would be fairly represented. Some criticized the sweeping grants of power to Congress. Others denounced the compromises with slavery that gave "extra" representation to the slaveholding states. In *The Federalist*, a brilliant series of eighty-five newspaper essays written under the pen name Publius, Alexander Hamilton, James Madison, and John Jay defended the Constitution against these and other charges by the Anti-Federalists.

After ten months of often heated discussion, eleven state ratifying conventions voted to adopt the new Constitution. Unlike the Articles, the Constitution needed ratification by only nine states for it to go into effect. In October 1788, the dying Confederation Congress adopted procedures to help the new charter of government take effect.

# CHAPTER TWO

# "IN A WILDERNESS WITHOUT A PATH TO GUIDE US"

James Madison of Virginia was one of the most gifted politicians the United States has ever produced. He had served for several years in the Virginia legislature and the Confederation Congress. He had also been a principal delegate to the Federal Convention of 1787 and one of the most important leaders of the successful campaign to win adoption of the Constitution. He spent the fall and winter of 1788 mulling over the next steps that the country—and he—should take.

Madison wanted desperately to be a member of the House of Representatives in the First Congress. He was not pleased to discover that the Virginia legislature, led by the silver-tongued Anti-Federalist orator Patrick Henry, had put Madison's home town of Orange smack in the middle of an Anti-Federal legislative district or that his friend James Monroe, a popular Anti-Federalist, was planning to run against him. Madison and Monroe traveled throughout the district in the winter of 1788–1789, debating the issues before the voters of the region. Madison handily defeated Monroe and thus was ready to return to New York City, the first—temporary—capital of the United States under the Constitution.

When Madison arrived in New York, he discovered that few of his colleagues of either branch of the new First Congress had arrived. He looked over a list of the new Representatives and Senators. As was usual with the short, frail, pessimistic Virginian, gloom overtook him. He wrote to Thomas Jefferson that there were few men in either house of Congress who seemed likely to take on the burden of work that setting up a government would demand. He also wrote that the new Congress would be wandering "in a wilderness without a path to guide us." What Jefferson probably knew as he read the letter, and what actually happened, was that Madison, as usual, shouldered the burden of leading his colleagues in getting the government off the ground.

The Congress was the first branch of the new government to begin its work. It had to count the electoral votes from the states to determine who the first President and Vice President were to be, and it had to write the laws setting up the executive departments and the judicial system. On April 6, 1789, the House and the Senate had the necessary minimum number of members to do business—what legislators call a *quorum*. They met in joint session to count the electoral

Collections of the Library of Congress

*Representative James Madison of Virginia (1751—1836) was the leading member of the House of Representatives during the first four Congresses (1789 —1797). Among his many accomplishments was his primary role in the framing of the first ten Amendments to the Constitution, which we call the Bill of Rights.*

votes. They were the first Americans to learn officially that George Washington was the unanimous choice to be the first President and that John Adams, with the second greatest number of electoral votes, was elected the first Vice President. After sending messengers to Mount Vernon, Virginia, and to Braintree, Massachusetts, to inform Washington and Adams of the news, Congress got back to work.

The House of Representatives began a small political revolution by permitting anyone, even reporters, to attend its sessions. The Senate continued to meet behind closed doors, as most legislatures at all levels had done in the United States and in Europe. (We get most of what we know about the Senate in this early period from the diary of Senator William Maclay of Pennsylvania, a hard-bitten frontiersman who had nothing but scorn for secrecy, pomp, and pretense.) As a result, the people found the House much more interesting and had more respect for it.

The House quickly won the interest and favor of the people because it actually was getting work done. Rumors swept the capital and the country that the Senators and the Vice President were wasting their energies arguing about formal titles for officials of the new government. There was a good deal of truth to these rumors, and John Adams soon discovered that he was a political laughingstock.

The House took the lead in all but one major piece of legislation. It deferred to the Senate in the framing and the adoption of the Judiciary Act of 1789, the law that created the federal court system.

Unlike today's Congress, the First Congress did not rely on committees of its members to do most of its work. Most legislative business was carried out on the floor of each house. Every now and then, the House or Senate would appoint a *select* committee. Its members would go off, discuss the question "committed" to them, and report back to the full house. The select committee would then dissolve. Only gradually did the House and Senate come to appoint *standing* (permanent) committees of members to carry out certain regular functions. Standing committees did not become a central feature of the Congressional process until the early nineteenth century.

In the House, Representative Madison won general recognition as the leading member. The House had a presiding officer, the Speaker, but all the first Speaker, Frederick Augustus Muhlenberg of Pennsylvania, had to do was to preside over the meetings of the House. Under Madison's guidance, the House proposed bills setting up taxes and customs regulations, creating the executive departments of government, and, most far-reaching of all, proposing constitutional amendments.

In the ratification fight of 1787–1788, many Americans had demanded that the Constitution be amended to include a list of individual rights that the federal government could not violate. Under pressure from Jefferson, and his own growing belief that amendments were necessary, Madison took the lead in proposing such amendments and ramming them through Congress. Representative Fisher Ames of Massachusetts thought that Madison was just making a bid for popularity, but Madison was unshakable in his determination to win the day for his amendments. In September 1789, at the end of its first session, the First Congress finally agreed on twelve proposed amendments and sent them to the states for ratification. After slightly more than two years, ten of the twelve, which we call the Bill of Rights, became part of the Constitution. (The other two, concerning House membership and compensation to members of Congress, were not adopted then—but the proposed compensation amendment *was* ratified in 1992, becoming the Twenty-seventh Amendment.)

Madison also worked closely with President Washington. He helped to draft Washington's first Inaugural Address, then wrote the House's reply to the President, and finally wrote Washington's answer to the House's reply to the President's speech. The President respected Madison and valued his friendship and advice. Madison returned this respect. In those early days, the President and Congress worked in careful partnership.

In its second and third sessions, the First Congress turned its attention to the most pressing problem affecting the new government— debt. The United States and the states had run up staggering debts throughout the Revolution by borrowing money to pay for weapons, powder, uniforms, bandages, and other supplies for the Continental Army and to keep the Confederation going. How were these debts to be handled? Should the new nation try to pay them off? What could be done?

Congress had created the Treasury Department, and President Washington had appointed Alexander Hamilton as the first Secretary of the Treasury. Hamilton looked upon the debt crisis as a great opportunity to put into practice economic theories he had been working on for months. His economic policies, set forth in eloquent and closely reasoned reports, hit the First Congress like a bomb. The Senators and Representatives were astonished at his boldness.

Hamilton proposed that the United States assume the states' debts and consolidate them with the federal debt. He also proposed that Congress create a national bank to regulate the value of federal money and to stimulate investments. In a complex system of transactions, the debt would be turned into an engine to stimulate the economy, to strengthen the government of the United States, and to ensure that the commercial interests and the wealthy would become firm friends of the new government.

Hamilton's policies outraged many members of the House and Senate, who argued that he was "selling the government out" to the rich and powerful. Even James Madison, who had been Hamilton's friend and ally in the struggle to win adoption of the Constitution in 1787–1788, disapproved. Madison tried to lead the House in opposition to Hamilton's proposals but was defeated. A complicated series of deals between the Administration and Representatives and Senators from Pennsylvania and Virginia resulted in the adoption of Hamilton's programs in exchange for moving the capital to Philadelphia for ten years and then to a permanent site on the banks of the Potomac River between Virginia and Maryland. These clashes were important, for they marked the beginning of a development that no one had foreseen: the rise of political parties.

Washington, Madison, Hamilton, and their contemporaries feared and distrusted parties. They believed that parties were combinations of persons who did not have the general interest of society at heart and that these groups' pursuit of their own selfish interests could damage or even destroy a free, republican government. But these political leaders turned out to be wrong. Parties have become loose, broad-based coalitions of various sorts of people who have special interests to pursue but who also agree on general principles that the government should embody and goals that it should carry out. And parties soon became central to the way that Congress does its job.

# CHAPTER THREE

# DEBATE AND DISCORD

The great achievement of the First Congress (1789–1791) was to channel American politics within the matrix set up by the Constitution. For the next two decades, the new national political system also adapted itself to the growing system of political parties, and Congress had a major role in this process. Even so, the people and the politicians of the time only gradually accepted the idea that political parties were becoming necessary to the smooth working of government under the Constitution.

Two political parties emerged during the 1790s, the Federalists and the Republicans.

The *Federalists*—who were different from the supporters of the Constitution in the ratification contests of 1787–1788—supported a broad reading of the Constitution that would confer generous grants of power on the federal government. They enthusiastically argued that the "elastic clause" granted the federal government all powers and responsibilities not strictly forbidden to it by the Constitution. They also feared too much democracy, worrying that the horrors of the French Revolution might be unleashed in the United States. Because they were opposed to the excesses of the French Revolution, the Federalists favored either keeping the United States neutral in the rivalry and wars between France and England then taking place or actively allying with England. Washington, Adams, Hamilton, and John Jay were leading Federalists.

The *Republicans* believed that the Constitution should be read narrowly, to give the United States only those powers specifically mentioned in the Constitution. They disliked the Federalist reliance on the "elastic clause." The Republicans claimed that the Federalists favored some form of kingship, or monarchy, for America. The Republicans also applauded the French Revolution's overthrow of monarchy and made excuses for the excesses of the Revolution. They wanted the United States to honor its 1778 treaty with France, even though the French had executed Louis XVI, the king who had agreed to that treaty. Jefferson, Madison, Monroe, and George Clinton of New York were leading Republicans.

Party politics flared repeatedly in the halls of Congress. One controversy set major precedents for relations between Congress and the President in the matter of Congressional investigations. Federal land policy encouraged speculators to buy land in the Northwest Territories (present-day Ohio), where they had no business interfering with peaceful Indians. In late 1791 and early 1792, two detachments of federal soldiers sent to protect these speculators and settlers were cut to pieces by enraged Indians. Congress immediately called for an investigation, and the first House investigating committee was appointed. It asked President Washington to turn over papers and other records pertaining to the military missions that had ended so disastrously. The President and his advisers agreed to turn over some documents to the House committee but claimed the right to decide what documents should not be turned over, "the disclosure of which would endanger the public." Based on the documents the Administration did provide, Congress charged that corruption among the officials assigned to buy military supplies for federal troops was a major cause of the military disasters in Ohio. This accusation, aimed at the Treasury Department led by Secretary Hamilton, infuriated Hamilton and his supporters, and the first Congressional investigation helped to feed the split between the parties.

A second issue resulted in the first Presidential veto of a bill passed by Congress. President Washington received a highly technical compromise bill on reapportioning the House of Representatives (allotting seats in the House to states based on changing population) that seemed to be unconstitutional. He instructed Secretary of State Jefferson and Attorney General Edmund Randolph to work with Madison to prepare a veto message. Although some members of Congress were furious, there was no challenge to the veto. Washington's veto is notable also because it set a precedent for future Presidents to veto bills only on constitutional grounds—a precedent that lasted for nearly half a century.

A dispute about the Senate's way of conducting its business set another precedent. In 1793, when the Swiss-born Albert Gallatin of Pennsylvania was elected to the Senate, Federalist Senators began a campaign to oust him. They claimed that he had not been a citizen of the United States long enough to be a Senator. The Senate realized that if the proceedings on Gallatin took place behind closed doors, Gallatin's supporters could charge that a conspiracy had stolen his election. So the Senate opened its proceedings to the view of the press and the public for the first time. After the Senators voted to deny Gallatin his seat, they decided to continue meeting in public, as the House had been doing since 1789.

Animosity between Federalists and Republicans continued to grow through the balance of Washington's two terms as Chief Executive. Not even his unanimous re-election in 1792 could dampen party sentiment. The Whiskey Rebellion of 1794 gave Secretary Hamilton the chance to assert convincingly the authority of the federal government, but it also sowed seeds of discontent throughout the nation. In a message to Congress, President Washington denounced the activities of "democratic societies" for having helped to induce the farmers of western Pennsylvania to take arms against federal laws imposing taxes on distilling whiskey. The Federalists capitalized on Washington's outrage. The Republicans responded by reminding the Federalists that such societies had a constitutional right to organize and to publish their views.

When the treaty with Great Britain negotiated in London by Chief Justice John Jay (to normalize relations between the two countries) reached the United States in early 1795, bitterness between Federalists and Republicans reached all-time highs. Republicans charged that Chief Justice Jay had given away far too much to the British and that he was ignoring the interests of the South and the West in favor of the interests of New England and the Eastern seaports. Jay's role in this treaty made him one of the most unpopular men in the nation. It was said that he could walk at night from one end of the country to the other by the light of the fires burning him in effigy.

Even after the Senate ratified the treaty, the controversy contin-

*"Congressional Pugilists" describes the fight that took place on February 15, 1798, on the floor of the House of Representatives. Representative Roger Griswold (1762—1812) (Federalist-Connecticut), swinging a cane, kicks Representative Matthew Lyon (1750—1822) (Republican-Vermont), who grasps Griswold's arm and is about to strike him with the House fireplace tongs. Speaker Jonathan Dayton (1760—1824) (Federalist-New Jersey) looks on in amusement from the Speaker's chair. This rare political cartoon was published in Philadelphia, then the nation's capital, in 1798.*

ued. The House demanded that the President turn over papers relative to the negotiation of the treaty so it could decide whether to appropriate funds to help carry it out. Washington curtly informed the Representatives that these papers were none of their business. Ultimately, the Federalists won the day, thanks to the impassioned eloquence of Federalist Representative Fisher Ames. The former Speaker of the House, Frederick Augustus Muhlenberg, voted for the treaty even though he was a Republican. As a result, his angered brother-in-law stabbed him, and Muhlenberg lost his bid for reelection to the House.

Washington retired from the Presidency, sick at heart and exhausted by the violence of party politics. His Farewell Address, published in newspapers in September 1796, voiced his disgust at partisanship, which did nothing to endear him to the Republicans. The 1796 Presidential election did little to calm things down, either. The next four years, President John Adams's lone term in office, were the roughest yet for the new government.

Adams tried to walk a narrow line between the warring powers of Europe. But when French naval vessels carried out assaults on American ships, Adams sent a three-man delegation to Paris to try to stop the attacks. As Congress waited for news from France, tempers worsened. In fact, on January 1, 1798, Representative Matthew Lyon of Vermont, a frontier Republican, spit a stream of tobacco juice into the face of Federalist Representative Roger Griswold of Connecticut. After weeks of watching the House wrangle over its rules of discipline, Griswold literally took matters into his own hands and attacked Lyon with a hickory cane. Lyon picked up the House's fire tongs, and the two men whacked and swore at each other as other Representatives whooped and applauded. A motion to expel both men was defeated. But the Griswold-Lyon fight in the House suggested to worried Americans that partisan politics was getting so hot it might never cool down.

When news from Adams's representatives in France arrived in Philadelphia, the nation became furious. Corrupt French diplomats had declined to listen to the Americans' suggestions unless they first received bribes. The three Americans indignantly refused. Adams called for Congress to adopt defense measures and to back an undeclared naval war with France. Congress also passed—and the President signed—the Alien and Sedition Acts, harsh laws punishing criticism of the government. Federalists were delighted. Republicans, who expected to be the targets of these new laws, were cast into gloom. But the expected call for a congressional declaration of war never came.

Adams then realized that the French were willing to work matters out. And he discovered that his advisers were serving their idol and chief Hamilton rather than the President of the United States. In 1799, the President surprised the nation by opening new talks with the French; the next year, he cleaned out the "vipers" in his Cabinet. He saved the nation from a disastrous war but in doing so cost himself the election of 1800.

By this time, informal gatherings of party members in Congress—*caucuses*—selected the parties' Presidential and Vice Presidential candidates. The Federalists renominated Adams, but the split in the party was so serious that Hamilton and his colleagues schemed to bury the President in the electoral votes and elect Vice Presidential candidate

Charles C. Pinckney of South Carolina the new President. Hamilton's strategy backfired, however, and the Republicans triumphed.

The victorious Republicans had made a major mistake, however: They had not made sure that Thomas Jefferson, their Presidential candidate (and Adams's Vice President), would get more electoral votes than their Vice Presidential candidate, Aaron Burr of New York. The two men ended up tied with seventy-three votes each. Under the Constitution, the House of Representatives, voting by states, had the job of sorting out a tie vote in the Electoral College. It took the Representatives several weeks and thirty-six ballots to decide on Jefferson. Hamilton privately urged Federalist Representatives to vote for the Republican Jefferson, and Burr's continued silence persuaded the House that he was too ambitious to be trusted.

Jefferson's election, in February 1801, only two weeks before Inauguration Day (then in March), persuaded Congress to overhaul the Electoral College. Congress wrote the Twelfth Amendment, which requires the Electoral College to cast separate votes for Presidential and Vice Presidential candidates. This Amendment was ratified in time for the Presidential election of 1804. It was the first constitutional amendment proposed in the nation's permanent capital.

The new federal capital city, Washington, D.C., was "ready" in 1800, and the government moved glumly to the swampy, mosquito-infested, humid place. It was there that the Jefferson-Burr deadlock of 1800 was settled and that the nation and the world witnessed the first peaceful transition from one party to another under the Constitution. The Republicans had swept both the Presidency and Congress. They controlled both the Senate and the House, leaving the disgruntled Federalists ensconced in the judiciary.

President Jefferson worked closely at first with the new Speaker of the House, Nathaniel Macon of North Carolina, and with Macon's choice to head the important House Ways and Means Committee (the committee in charge of taxation bills), Virginian Representative John Randolph of Roanoke. Randolph was a distant cousin of the President, but the two men loathed each other. Randolph was eccentric to the point of mental imbalance, and other Representatives soon learned to fear the lash of his tongue.

Jefferson soon mastered a major change in the way that Congress did its business. As the ranks of the House and Senate swelled with Representatives and Senators from new states, Congress created standing committees. These committees acted almost as miniature legislatures, discussing and proposing bills, which were then debated and voted on by the full House and Senate. The creation of committees made the work of Congress somewhat more efficient. It also gave power to the Speaker of the House, who would pick the chairmen of the committees based on party loyalty. (The Senate elected its committees and chairmen by secret ballot, preserving the independence of its members.) Jefferson worked with committee chairmen, but he also chose informal "agents" from the ranks of the House and Senate to watch over Administration interests.

In the winter of 1801, the outgoing Federalist Congress had created dozens of new federal judgeships, and President Adams had appointed Federalists to these posts. A wrangle over one of these appointments led to the first decision by the Supreme Court striking down an act of Congress as unconstitutional—an exercise of *judicial review*. The 1803 case of *Marbury v. Madison* focused on a technical point of the jurisdiction of the Supreme Court in a section of the Judiciary Act of 1789, but President Jefferson and his Republican colleagues in Congress realized that the decision had far-reaching significance. They were outraged by Chief Justice John Marshall's claim that the Court had the power to strike down a statute as unconstitutional. They also resented that the Federalists had planted themselves in the federal courts. They determined to wage war on the Federalist judiciary. Their chosen weapon was impeachment.

Congress targeted a senile, drunken New Hampshire federal district judge, John Pickering. He never knew what hit him. The House impeached him, and the Senate removed him from office. Nobody could explain what his impeachable offense was. One Republican in the House declared that impeachment was simply an inquiry by Congress whether a federal office might better be filled by someone other than the current official.

The House then went after old, fat Samuel Chase, a Justice of the Supreme Court. He had enraged Republicans by his gleeful conduct of trials for violations of the hated Sedition Act. Chase was impeached by the House, but the Senate trial in 1805 was another matter. For one thing, Representative John Randolph of Roanoke, the "manager" (that is, prosecutor) of the Chase impeachment, was erratic and undependable. For another, Vice President Aaron Burr presided over the trial. Burr had never overcome Jefferson's distrust of him following the election of 1800. He also had disgraced himself and destroyed his career by killing Alexander Hamilton in a duel. But Burr was determined to conduct the trial of Justice Chase honorably and fairly. He managed the Senate trial so well, in fact, that he won approval of all but his bitterest foes. The impeachment process was stopped dead when the Senate acquitted Justice Chase on March 1, 1805. Three days later, Vice President Burr made a farewell speech to the Senate: "This House, is a sanctuary; a citadel of law, of order, and of liberty; and it is here, in this exalted refuge, here, if anywhere, will resistance be made to the storms of political phrensy and the silent arts of corruption; and, if the Constitution be destined ever to perish by the sacrilegious hands of the demagogue or the usurper, which God avert, its expiring agonies will be witnessed on this floor."

In President Jefferson's second term, Representative John Randolph of Roanoke was toppled from power as the chairman of the House Ways and Means Committee. His long-suffering colleagues had grown impatient with Randolph's sloppy methods of running the committee and his increasingly strange behavior. Speaker Macon bowed to pressure from the rank-and-file members and appointed another House member to the chairmanship. The enraged Randolph drew around himself a group of like-minded Representatives and bedeviled Jefferson and his successor, James Madison.

Randolph's faction contributed to the difficulty that Congress and Madison had with each other in Madison's first term. Neither house had strong leadership, and the President was not providing guidance, either. As the government floundered, the United States drifted toward war with Great Britain over British attacks on American shipping during its wars with Napoleonic France.

The leadership question in the House was settled as if by a stroke of lightning at the end of 1811. Henry Clay of Kentucky, who had served briefly in the Senate (though he was several months too young) and had made a prodigious reputation for himself as an orator and political wheeler-dealer, entered the House as a freshman member and on the first day captured the Speakership. Clay became one of the most vigorous, able, and dynamic Speakers in the history of the House. He once explained his methods: "Decide, decide promptly, and never give your reasons for your decision. The House will sustain your decisions, but there will always be men to cavil and quarrel about your reasons."

The free-living, hard-drinking Speaker and a group of other young Representatives from the South and West agitated fiercely for war against Great Britain. They wanted to punish slurs on national honor and to acquire Canada for the United States. One of these "war hawks" was John C. Calhoun, a brilliant, humorless Representative from South Carolina. Because of the war hawks' pressure and because he believed that war with England was necessary to defend the Constitution, President Madison asked Congress for a declaration of war in 1812. Congress swiftly gave him what he—and they—wanted.

The War of 1812 was a mixed bag for the United States. After a series of early naval victories, the U.S. Navy found itself bottled up in American harbors by an unbreakable British blockade. On land, advantages seesawed back and forth. The most humiliating moment came in 1814, when the British landed a force that burned Washington, D.C. Legend has it that their commanding officer stood on the Speaker's chair in the Capitol and asked his men, "Shall this citadel of Yankee democracy be burned?" Congress returned to find that the Capitol was a smoke-blackened ruin. The British had stolen or destroyed the mace of the House, the symbol of its official dignity. The Senate wing was nothing but piles of timber and ash. Rebuilding began at once, but the damage to the pride of Congress and the nation took longer to heal.

Congress was in a state of shock. Its members could not agree on even the most necessary measures. The government was all but paralyzed. New England legislators such as Representative Daniel Webster of New Hampshire talked angrily of the possibility that their states might leave the Union to end their role in the useless war.

With the end of the war in early 1815, however, the nation and Congress recovered some measure of spirit and enterprise. A new generation of leaders was emerging. Its chief members were Clay, Calhoun, and Webster.

# CHAPTER FOUR

# THE AGE OF GIANTS

For three decades, from the 1820s to the 1850s, Henry Clay, John C. Calhoun, and Daniel Webster dominated American politics. They had begun their careers in the House of Representatives. But it was not until all three men entered the Senate that the "golden age" of American legislative politics began.

This new age also witnessed major changes in political parties and the political process. The end of the War of 1812 brought with it the disintegration of the Federalist Party. But the Republican Party did not long survive its old adversary. It split into several factions during the 1824 election. John Quincy Adams of Massachusetts, President James Monroe's Secretary of State and the son of former President John Adams, was the standard-bearer of the National Republicans. General Andrew Jackson, a military hero of the War of 1812 and of many skirmishes with Indians, was the candidate of a group that began to call itself Democrats. The Congressional Republican caucus named Treasury Secretary William Crawford its candidate, but Crawford suffered a series of strokes, which left him crippled and nearly blind. (Crawford was the last Presidential candidate named by a Congressional caucus.) And Speaker of the House Henry Clay was a candidate as well.

The four candidates so divided the electoral votes that no one man received a majority, and the election landed in the House. Clay threw his support to John Quincy Adams, who thus was able to edge out the front-runner, General Jackson. When President Adams chose Clay to be his Secretary of State, Jacksonians charged that a "corrupt" bargain had taken place. Four years later, they triumphantly swept Adams out of the White House and Jackson in. The opposition to Jackson reorganized as a new political party to counter Jackson's Democrats. They called themselves the Whigs, taking the name from the old English political party associated with the defense of political liberty.

Congress adjusted itself to this new party system. The House of Representatives and the Senate had begun to work out a rough division of roles. The House tended to direct the grinding business of legislation, and the Senate emerged as the forum of debate. Meeting in a chamber with superb acoustics, Senators could hold their colleagues and packed galleries of visitors spellbound for hours or even days. Oratory in the first half of the nineteenth century was as entertaining as a hard-fought World Series or popular television program can be today. And the "great triumvirate," as historian Merrill Peterson has dubbed Clay, Calhoun, and Webster, were the greatest of the Senate's orators.

Clay, Webster, and Calhoun had weighty subjects to hold forth on. President Andrew Jackson's fiery temper and rough-edged brand of politics were lightning rods for Senatorial criticism. He was not willing to defer to Congress, as his predecessors had been. He was his own man and ruthlessly used the powers of the Presidency to advance his own agenda and to hammer at Congress when it stood in his way. "Old Hickory" discarded the precedent, established by George Washington, of limiting the use of the Presidential veto to constitutional grounds. Jackson vetoed bills merely because he disagreed with them, and he made his vetoes stick. He resisted Congressional attempts to censure him, and he took delight in skewering his enemies in the House and the Senate.

Another issue worthy of these great debates was slavery. The delegates to the Federal Convention had sidestepped the problem, hoping it would fade away on its own. But slavery persisted—a smoldering bomb waiting for the moment to explode. Henry Clay helped to defuse the first such potential explosion by hammering together the Missouri Compromise in 1820. Under the Missouri Compromise, Missouri was allowed to enter the Union as a slave state, and Maine, once part of Massachusetts, came in as a free state. These two new states preserved the balance of power in the Senate between free states and slave states. A line drawn across the rest of the Union at latitude 36° 30′ North marked off the regions where new states would be free (north of the line) or slave (south of the line), again to preserve the balance of power.

A third great issue was the character of the Union. Was the Constitution the creation of the states? Did a state have authority to decide which federal laws would be valid within its borders and which would not? Did a state have the right to choose to leave the Union? Southern Senators such as Robert Y. Hayne of South Carolina answered these questions "Yes." In a major speech on the floor of the Senate in 1830, Hayne voiced the "state sovereignty" theory of the Constitution shared by Calhoun and other Southerners. By this time, Calhoun had become Vice President under Jackson. (He had also been John Quincy Adams's Vice President.) He could take no part in the debate, but he nodded approvingly as Hayne addressed the Senate. In response to Hayne, Daniel Webster, now a Senator from Massachusetts, made a powerful and eloquent plea in favor of "the people's Constitution." The Constitution, Webster declared, was created by the People of the United States; by adopting it, the People created both a national government superior to the states and a permanent Union.

Senators Hayne and Webster revived a dispute, going back to the framing of the Constitution in 1787, that would persist for decades. Soon, however, Hayne stepped aside as the spokesman for state power in favor of his hero, John C. Calhoun. Calhoun resigned from the Vice Presidency in early 1832 to protest President Jackson's unflinching support for federal power against the "rights" of South Carolina. The South Carolina legislature promptly elected him to the Senate to speak for its interests and to argue for the "state compact" theory of the Constitution.

The House, too, had its say about such issues as slavery and the Union. Former President John Quincy Adams had broken precedent by returning to public life in 1830 as a Whig Representative from Massachusetts. He soon emerged as a vigorous defender of the *right of petition.*

Americans of all points of views had long sent petitions to Congress setting forth their hopes for legislation, their goals for national development, or their attacks on national policy. Fearing the divisive effect of the slavery issue, the House leadership proposed a rule barring any member from presenting a petition having to do with slavery. Adams fought a lonely and energetic eight-year campaign in the

House against this "gag rule," claiming that it violated the First Amendment. He finally triumphed, despite at least one attempt by the House to censure him.

But it was the Senate that tended to attract popular attention, and it was the three great men of their time who were most interesting to the nation. Each man represented one of the three great sections of the nation: Clay, the West; Webster, the North; and Calhoun, the South. Clay was known as the "Great Compromiser," for his role in pulling together the Missouri Compromise that saved the Union in 1820. He also became known for his dream of the *American system*—a vast network of roads, bridges, and other internal improvements paid for by the federal government and intended to help knit the Union together and to foster the growth of American industries to compete with Europe. Webster, allied with Clay in his campaigns for internal improvements, was also known as the defender of the Union. Calhoun, the voice of the South and its greatest intellectual strategist, hammered home his theory that the Constitution was—and had to be —a compact among the states, not a charter of government adopted by the people of the United States.

The Union in this period was like a fragile piece of china balanced on a knife's edge. Men of all political stripes watched it cautiously, shuddering at each tremor of the ground. It was in the halls of Congress that each new tremor was most carefully monitored, and where each new crisis was faced.

Even issues that did not on the surface have a clear connection to slavery and the Union could ignite the powder keg. Most disturbing was the matter of acquiring new territory. Each such acquisition raised the question of how the territories would be organized: Would they become free states or slave states? Northerners asked whether a push to acquire territory, by purchase or the threat of force or even war, was simply a bid to get more territory in which slavery could be expanded. Southerners retorted that Northern opposition to the acquisition of more territory clearly showed Northern hostility to slavery by choking off needed room for growth.

The Mexican War of 1846–1848 became the most sensitive territorial issue by far. The Whigs opposed the war with great bitterness, denouncing it as robbery. A young first-term Representative from Illinois named Abraham Lincoln implied that President James K. Polk (the only Speaker of the House ever to be a successful candidate for President) had deliberately provoked war with Mexico. Other Whigs joined in. (John Quincy Adams suffered a fatal stroke on the floor of the House in early 1848 as he waited impatiently to speak against the war.) The Whigs also raised the antislavery issue. Representative David Wilmot of Pennsylvania attached to a necessary appropriations bill a provision barring the spread of slavery into any territories acquired as a result of the war. The Wilmot Proviso, as it was called, resurfaced again and again but always met defeat. Still, each reappearance raised the dread issue of slavery.

One consequence of the growing importance of the slavery issue was a change in the method of organization of the Senate. Senators had elected their committees and their committee chairmen by secret ballot. In December 1846, it was agreed that party caucuses would choose the members of the committees and that the Senate would accept these arrangements. This was the seed of the *seniority system:* Senators who had served longest would get first choices of committee assignments. It was also a way for the leadership of both parties to

Collections of the Library of Congress

Senator Henry Clay (1779—1852) (Whig-Kentucky) holds his colleagues spellbound during his memorable appeal for a compromise on slavery. Senator Daniel Webster (1782—1852) (Whig-Massachusetts) sits at the left, holding his head. Senator John C. Calhoun (1782—1850) (Democrat-South Carolina) stands third from the right. Clay, Webster, and Calhoun were known as the Great Triumvirate.

control the assignment of Senators to committees that might have explosive consequences for the slavery issue.

At the end of the Mexican War, the United States acquired for $15 million—by the Treaty of Guadalupe Hidalgo—more than half of Mexico's territory: a vast area of the present Southwest from Texas to California, which included most of what is now Colorado, Utah, Nevada, New Mexico, and Arizona. This new territory, and the recurrent threat of the Wilmot Proviso, led to one of the greatest periods in the history of the Senate. On February 5 and 6, 1850, Henry Clay, now seventy-three years old, began the debate with a set of compromise proposals designed to save the Union. He suggested that the Republic of California join the Union as a free state. (Its constitution already prohibited slavery.) He also proposed a series of concessions demanded by Southern Senators as the price for California's admission to the Union.

On March 4, John C. Calhoun, speaking for the die-hard Southern Senators, replied to Clay. The "Iron Man" was emaciated, racked with tuberculosis, and too frail to give his own speech. His eyes burned somberly as he listened to Senator James M. Mason of Virginia read his address. Calhoun offered no quarter to Clay or to anyone else from the North or West. His last speech was an unbending call for Southern unity. Every last Southern condition for compromise must be met. Calhoun rejected Clay's compromise proposal and threatened that the Southern states would leave the Union, or *secede*, if his terms were not met.

Three days later, Daniel Webster arose to reply to Calhoun and to endorse Clay's compromise plan. The "Seventh of March" speech is now regarded as Webster's greatest, but at the time he gravely injured his standing in the eyes of Northern abolitionists (who wanted to end slavery). Point by point, Webster explained and endorsed Clay's compromise proposal and sadly rejected Calhoun's threats of disunion. He set the tone of his speech with his opening lines: "I wish to speak today not as a Massachusetts man, nor as a Northern man, but as an American. . . . I speak today for the preservation of the Union. 'Hear me for my cause.' "

Within four weeks, Calhoun was dead, the first of the Great Triumvirate to pass from the scene. He was spared one of the ugliest and silliest scenes in the history of the Senate. Senators' tempers had become so frayed that many carried knives, small pistols, and other weapons for self-defense. Senator Henry S. Foote of Mississippi, a short, violent-tempered man, had gotten into a wrestling match with one Northern Senator and had threatened to hang another. Tall, bluff Senator Thomas Hart Benton of Missouri, who was a much greater man and Senator than he appears to be in this incident, had frequently mocked Foote's readiness to fight duels. In an angry exchange of words, Benton kept advancing on Foote. Foote suddenly drew a pistol. Benton bellowed, "Let him fire! Stand out of the way! Let the assassin fire!" Other Senators separated Benton and Foote, and the Mississippian explained that he had assumed that the Missourian was armed.

By the end of September, the several bills making up Clay's Compromise of 1850 were finally voted into law and signed by President Millard Fillmore. Within two years, both Clay and Webster were also dead. An age of giants had come to an end. It seemed at first that the giants had taken the spectre of disunion over slavery to the grave with them, but such was not to be the case.

# CHAPTER FIVE

# THE HOUSE—AND SENATE—DIVIDED

In the 1850s, the Whig Party faded away, disintegrating as completely as had the Federalists in the late 1810s. A short-lived Free Soil Party, whose platform opposed slavery, gave way to an organization that brought together Free-Soilers, abandoned Whigs, and other politicians bent on preserving the Union and opposing the "slavocracy." They called themselves the Republicans, after the old party founded by Jefferson and Madison in the 1790s. They claimed to be the true heirs of the Jeffersonian commitment to the rights of human beings (although Jefferson and Madison had owned slaves). By 1856, the Republicans had become a permanent political force.

The issue of slavery became ever more divisive in the 1850s. Many political observers feared that the successors of Clay, Calhoun, and Webster lacked the will or the ingenuity to carry on the process of compromise.

In 1854, the territories of Kansas and Nebraska hovered on the brink of statehood. Would they enter the Union as free states or slave states? The controversy focused on Kansas because it was below the old line drawn by the Missouri Compromise and thus ordinarily would be classified as a slave state. But nobody believed that this mechanical solution would work. Abolitionists in the North and West squared off against proslavery agitators in the South and pro-Southern "dough-face" Democrats in the other sections.

Senator Stephen A. Douglas (Democrat-Illinois) was at the storm center of the Kansas crisis. The tiny, pugnacious man had been nick-named "the Little Giant" because of his ferocious speaking style. He thought he had the answer, and he was ambitious enough to hope that it would propel him into the Presidency.

Douglas argued that Congress could not—and should not—impose a solution to the Kansas crisis. Why not let the people of the territory decide the issue for themselves by majority vote? Douglas called this solution *popular sovereignty*. It sounded simple, and it sounded as if it were a principled solution. But there was a problem. Both proslavery and antislavery organizations mustered hundreds of like-minded set-tlers to the Kansas territory to stack the outcome of the election. Outbreaks of violence, including bloody massacres of unarmed set-tlers, made all previous disputes over slavery look like tea parties.

The halls of Congress once again saw real and threatened blood-shed. Members of the House and Senate who knew their Shakespeare even feared that one of their number might be murdered in the Capi-tol, just as Julius Caesar had been murdered by Senators in Rome nearly two thousand years before. The fate of Senator Charles Sumner seemed to bear out these concerns.

Sumner, a Massachusetts Republican, was a great orator who fiercely opposed slavery. In a speech to the Senate on the subject of "Bleeding Kansas," he went out of his way to attack Southern Sena-tors who were members of the "slave oligarchy." Among Sumner's targets was the absent Andrew P. Butler of South Carolina. Butler's nephew, Representative Preston Brooks, swore vengeance on Sumner.

On May 22, 1856, Brooks and a South Carolina colleague, Repre-sentative Laurence M. Keitt, entered the Senate Chamber. Members of each house regularly visited each other's chambers, so no one took much notice. Both Brooks and Keitt had wooden canes in hand. The Senate had adjourned for the day, and Sumner was writing at his desk. He did not notice the two Representatives approaching him from behind. Brooks raised his cane and slammed it down again and again across the Senator's head and shoulders. Keitt stood guard, brandishing his cane to prevent any other Senator from coming to Sumner's aid. Sumner struggled helplessly, but his long legs were held in place by his desk, and he could not get out of the range of Brooks's murderous assault. Finally, with a convulsive effort, Sumner ripped his desk from where it was bolted to the floor and collapsed across its top.

Brooks and Keitt walked from the Senate Chamber, shaking hands with several Southern Senators on the way out. Other Senators carried Sumner's senseless body from the chamber.

Sumner was so badly injured by the attack that he could not return to the Senate for two years. The Massachusetts legislature refused to select a replacement; Sumner's seat would be waiting for him whenever he was strong enough to return. Brooks received congratulations from all over the South and several canes to replace the one he had broken over Sumner's back. The Democratic leadership in the Senate blocked any investigation of the incident. In the House, Republicans moved to expel Brooks and Keitt, but the motion did not get the two-thirds vote needed for adoption. Brooks and Keitt nonetheless resigned, only to be re-elected in triumph.

"Bleeding Kansas" dominated American politics. Even the Supreme Court tried to solve the slavery issue. But the attempt to transform the issue into a constitutional question (and settle it by a final decision of the Justices) backfired. The *Dred Scott* decision held that slavery was protected by the Constitution and that Congress could not interfere with it anywhere in the United States. Southerners were delighted, but Northerners were outraged. Moderates on the issue piously begged the nation to uphold the Court's decision but refused to comment on the merits of the decision.

The outcome of Senator Douglas's "popular sovereignty" proposal was predictable: two governments in Kansas—one favoring slavery, the other opposing it. Each claimed to be the legitimate state government. Each government had its supporters in Congress. By now, Douglas realized that his bid to solve the slavery question had failed completely. He denounced the proslavery government and its "constitution" as "a trick, a fraud upon the rights of the people." But he failed to defeat the proslavery forces led by the unbending Senator Jefferson Davis (Democrat-Mississippi). Davis rammed through the Senate a bill admitting Kansas to the Union as a slave state.

When the House got the Senate bill, the Representatives got into shouting matches, fist fights, and even a full-fledged brawl. The members rejected the Senate bill, and leaders of the House and Senate began a long but fruitless quest for a compromise. The Kansas matter simmered without a solution until after the Civil War broke out, in 1861.

In 1858, Senator Douglas found himself in the political fight of his life. He was running for another term in the Senate against Republican challenger Abraham Lincoln, a Springfield lawyer and former

Representative. The state legislature elected Senators, but the outcome of its vote was a strict party matter. Lincoln and Douglas agreed to debate each other several times throughout Illinois. The debates were dominated by slavery, Kansas, and *Dred Scott*. They became hugely popular events, attracting hundreds of spectators and coverage by the newspapers. The Democrats carried the state legislature, and Douglas was re-elected. But the debates made Lincoln a national figure and a major contender for the Republican Presidential nomination in 1860. They also injured Douglas's hopes for the Presidency. The Little Giant was hard-pressed to explain how he could support popular sovereignty and yet endorse the Supreme Court's *Dred Scott* decision. Southern Democrats were furious with him, and Northerners grew to distrust him.

By 1860, Congress was stalemated between North and South. National attention focused on the Presidential election. The Democrats split into three factions. Proslavery Democrats settled on Senator John C. Breckinridge of Kentucky. Northern antislavery and moder-

Illinois State Historical Library

*No photograph exists showing any of the seven Lincoln-Douglas Senatorial debates in Illinois, which dominated national politics in the summer of 1858. In this artist's reconstruction, Republican challenger Abraham Lincoln (1809—1865) stands at the podium, with Democratic incumbent Senator Stephen A. Douglas (1813—1861) seated (second from left). The debates presented a thorough discussion of the great issues of slavery and the Union. Although the Democrats kept control of the Illinois legislature and re-elected Douglas, the debates made Lincoln a major national political figure.*

ate Democrats rallied behind Stephen Douglas. And old-line politicians who still wanted to compromise the slavery issue endorsed former Senator John Bell of Tennessee, who ran on the Constitutional Union ticket. Abraham Lincoln became the Republican Presidential candidate as his managers outmaneuvered the abolitionist front-runner, Governor William Seward of New York, in the nominating convention in Chicago, Illinois.

The three-way Democratic split handed the election to the Republicans. Lincoln swept the electoral votes but got only a plurality of the popular vote (that is, he got more votes—40 percent—than any other candidate but fewer than half of the total). Southern politicians feared what would happen once Lincoln became President. Southern states talked about seceding from the Union. President James Buchanan timidly declared that no state had the right to secede but that the federal government could not prevent a state from seceding if it

Collection of L. Allen MacLean

*Jefferson Davis (1808—1889) (Democrat-Mississippi), a former Secretary of War, took part in the first parade of Senators from the eleven seceding Southern states out of the upper house in early 1861. He helped to set up the "Confederate States of America" and served as the Confederacy's only president. After the Civil War, Davis was held in chains in a federal military prison (1865—1867). He was given a hero's funeral in New Orleans in 1889.*

chose to do so. (He was like the driver of an automobile who, seeing that an accident is about to happen, takes his hands off the steering wheel and closes his eyes.)

Congress tried desperately to prevent the developing crisis, but all efforts at compromise conventions failed. In January 1861, five Southern states voted to leave the Union. On January 21, five Southern Senators dramatically filed out of the Senate Chamber. The last to leave was Mississippi's Jefferson Davis, who addressed his colleagues: "I am sure I feel no hostility toward you, Senators from the North. I am sure there is not one of you, whatever sharp discussion there may have been between us, to whom I cannot now say, in the presence of my God, I wish you well." As Davis walked from the chamber, Senators and onlookers wept quietly.

What did secession mean? other Senators and Representatives wondered, as one by one their Southern colleagues left for home. Was this just another Southern power play? Most politicians, including President-elect Lincoln, were not sure whether to take seriously the newly organized "Confederate States of America," whose president was Jefferson Davis. In fact, the depleted Congress carried on business as usual for three months, relying on the absence of the Southern members to push through tariff bills and the bills admitting Kansas as a free state.

President Lincoln warned the South in his First Inaugural Address, on March 4, that he would be true to his constitutional duty to preserve the Union. Confederate forces demanded that the federal government abandon all its military posts in the seceded states. Lincoln refused.

The symbol of the confrontation was Fort Sumter, in the harbor of Charleston, South Carolina. On April 12, 1861, Confederate units fired on Fort Sumter. These were the opening shots of the Civil War. Because the old Congress had adjourned on March 4 and the new Congress was not scheduled to convene until fall, Lincoln considered himself free to make federal policy on the secession crisis. He issued a call for 10,000 volunteer soldiers and summoned federal soldiers to defend the capital. The first units to arrive were housed in the Capitol's basement. The building soon filled with the smell of bread baking to feed the troops.

Lincoln then called Congress to a special session to begin on July 4. On that date, he reported on the measures he had taken against the South, and Congress endorsed his policies. At first, the two branches worked in harmony, but signs of trouble were on the horizon.

Many Senators and Representatives denounced the Administration for being slow, hesitant, and lackadaisical. They had gone off to watch the first major battle of the war, at Bull Run, Virginia, as if they were going to a picnic. But the Confederate soldiers routed the Union forces, and the Congressional onlookers had to flee for their lives. A later battle claimed the life of the popular Oregon Senator Edward Baker, who had enlisted as a Major in the Union Army. Baker, a Republican and a close friend of the President, was shot dead on the field as horrified friends and colleagues looked on. Other critics in Congress were angry because Lincoln would not declare that the Union's war aims were to destroy slavery.

The President answered his critics. He pointed out that he was trying his best to force the Union commanders to fight rather than sit idly by but that it was tough and frustrating work. He also responded to abolitionist criticisms of his war aims. Lincoln's goal was to preserve the Union—whether he had to free all the slaves or none of the slaves to do it. He insisted that it was not yet time for abolition.

The recovered Senator Charles Sumner was not satisfied. Representative Thaddeus Stevens (Republican-Pennsylvania) was angered by what he saw as Lincoln's moral and military weaknesses. They spoke on behalf of a loose, quarrelsome collection of Republicans and War Democrats that some historians have lumped together as the Radicals.

The House and Senate formed the Joint Committee on the Conduct of the War, which made useful contributions to the war effort by investigating and exposing corruption in the War Department's supply operations. The President heeded the results of the Joint Committee's investigations. He replaced his Secretary of War, Simon Cameron, with War Democrat Edwin M. Stanton, a ruthless, brilliant lawyer and administrator. Stanton cleaned up the department and loyally supported the President. But the Joint Committee's other investigations, reports, demands, and suggestions soon vexed and exhausted the Administration.

As the war dragged on, Congress kept pressure on Lincoln to emancipate the slaves and abolish slavery. The House adopted a constitutional amendment to achieve these goals, but it died in the Senate. Meanwhile, the more cautious Lincoln maneuvered events so that he could act when the time was right. As the Union Army moved toward victory, another source of controversy between Congress and the President sprang up: What policy should the government adopt toward the Southern states that had tried to leave the Union? Lincoln wanted to crush the Confederacy, which he called a criminal conspiracy against the Constitution. But he disagreed with Radicals in Congress who wanted to break the South's political power and treat the region like a conquered foreign enemy. In his Second Inaugural Address, in 1865, Lincoln proposed a more lenient policy designed "to bind up the nation's wounds."

The skirmishing between Lincoln and the radical wing of his party ended abruptly less than a week after Confederate General Robert E. Lee surrendered the Army of Northern Virginia to Union General Ulysses S. Grant at Appomattox Court House in Virginia. Lincoln was murdered while attending a play at Ford's Theatre in Washington, D.C. This first Presidential assassination plunged the nation into grief. But Radical Republicans quickly saw that the assassination gave them the opportunity to impose harsh Reconstruction policies on the defeated South.

Congress got its way for the most part. It rammed through three constitutional amendments that abolished slavery (the Thirteenth Amendment, 1865), made the federal government supreme over the states in a reworking of federalism (Fourteenth Amendment, 1868), and barred discrimination against voters on the basis of race (Fifteenth Amendment, 1870). Secretary of War Edwin Stanton directed the Army's occupation of the South. The Army oversaw the defeated states' governments and established a Freedmen's Bureau to help the freed slaves.

The new President, Andrew Johnson of Tennessee, soon clashed with Congress. Johnson, the only Southern Senator who had remained loyal to the Union, was a War Democrat who nonetheless was sympathetic to the Southern whites and did not believe in racial equality. He fought the Reconstruction policy supported by Congress. He vetoed many major Reconstruction bills, only to see them reenacted over his veto. He then ignored or defied these laws. An outraged Thaddeus Stevens proclaimed: "Though the President is Commander-in-Chief, Congress is his commander; and, God willing, he shall obey. He and his minions shall learn that this is not a Government of kings and satraps, but a Government of the people, and that Congress is the people."

The final straw came in 1867 when Congress adopted the Tenure of Office Act. The measure required the President to get the Senate's approval before he could fire any government official whose appointment was made with the consent of the Senate. The First Congress had rejected this view in 1789, believing that the President had the right and the responsibility to fire officials on his own. Congress revived this notion to prevent President Johnson from firing Cabinet officers and other government officials who agreed with Reconstruction. Johnson defied Congress by firing Secretary of War Stanton even after the Senate had refused his request.

When Congress received word from Stanton, who had barricaded himself in his office in the War Department, the House voted to impeach the President. It appointed a seven-member special committee led by Thaddeus Stevens to draft charges, or *articles of impeachment*. Some of the charges in the eleven articles they adopted were silly, but several were well grounded in Johnson's defiance of Congress. The Tenure of Office Act crisis was the centerpiece of the impeachment effort. It did not matter that the President had only a year left in his term of office or that neither the Democrats nor the Republicans would renominate him. It was the principle that counted.

The House adopted the articles of impeachment and sent them to the Senate. The House special committee served as the managers of the impeachment before the Senate. As required by the Constitution, the Chief Justice, Salmon P. Chase, presided over the trial. Chase was a Radical Republican who nonetheless valued the rule of law. He presided over the Senate's trial with dignity and fairness, in part because he recalled the example of Vice President Aaron Burr's conduct six decades earlier during the Senate's trial of Justice Samuel Chase (no relation). The managers of the impeachment claimed that an impeachable offense was whatever the House and Senate defined it to be. President Johnson's lawyers argued that an impeachable offense had to be something serious for which you could be indicted and convicted in a court of law. Neither side prevailed clearly.

The visitors' galleries in the Senate were packed every day of the trial. Each day, two men carried the seventy-six-year-old Thaddeus Stevens into the Chamber because he was too weak to walk in with his fellow Representatives. On May 16, 1868, the Senate voted on the charges against the President. As the roll call proceeded, it became clear that twelve Democrats and six Republicans were agreed that impeachment was a legal matter, not just a political tug-of-war. They voted to acquit the President. These eighteen Senators were one-third of the Senate. The Constitution requires a two-thirds vote to convict and remove an impeached official. Thus, the pro-impeachment forces could not afford to lose a single vote. Republican Senator Edmund G. Ross of Kansas waited silently for his name to be called. As he later described it, "I looked into my open grave." When his turn came, Ross answered firmly, "Not guilty." He had saved Johnson, and he had destroyed his own political career.

If the Senate had convicted the President and removed him from office, many historians suggest that the whole balance of our constitutional system would have been altered. Ross and the six other Republican Senators believed that the Presidency itself was at risk. They voted not to save Andrew Johnson, but to save the constitutional system of separation of powers and checks and balances.

Both Congress and Andrew Johnson were relieved when he left office in early 1869. Johnson even left town before Ulysses S. Grant's inauguration. In 1875, Johnson returned to Washington as a Senator representing his home state of Tennessee, but it had taken fifty-five ballots by the Tennessee legislature to make it happen. The only President besides John Quincy Adams to serve in Congress after his Presidency, Johnson died of a stroke less than five months after taking his seat in the upper chamber.

# CHAPTER SIX

# CONGRESS IN THE GILDED AGE

In 1869, Republican Ulysses S. Grant, the foremost military hero of the Civil War, took office as the eighteenth President of the United States. Nicknamed "Unconditional Surrender" Grant for his uncompromising tactics during the war, he belied his reputation for toughness within months of his inauguration. Leaders of his own party in Congress clipped his wings ruthlessly when he tried to think and act for himself in setting policy and making appointments to federal offices. Grant's surrender to Congress set the pattern for relations between the two branches for nearly a generation.

During Grant's two terms, corruption dominated American politics. Officials at all levels of government sold their influence, their judgment, and their votes. Scandals surfaced almost monthly. Congress suffered more from corruption and scandal than any other institution of government. Even the handsome, articulate Speaker of the House, James G. Blaine of Maine, was making deals with railroads and other powerful economic interests to get loans and other favors in return for his vote and support.

Even worse, the sleaziness of Congress seemed incurable. Congressional "investigations" concealed at least as much as they were supposed to reveal. Although some notorious wrongdoers were caught and punished, others flourished.

National politics drifted. In Congress, the House took a back seat to the Senate, which quickly won the reputation of being a "millionaire's club." Wealthy men were able to bribe their way into "the nation's greatest deliberative body." It was easier to bribe a few dozen state legislators to get oneself—or a reliable stooge—into the Senate than to bribe voters to get oneself elected to the House. Public policy was made in fits and starts—if a Senator was interested enough to focus on a national problem and was able to rally enough of his colleagues to push a bill through.

During this period, agitation began, chiefly in the Midwest and West, for a constitutional amendment mandating direct election of Senators by the voters of each state rather than by the easily corruptible state legislatures. Many states already had direct-election systems, and others had enacted laws requiring their legislatures to follow the will of the people as expressed in nonbinding elections. But it would require a constitutional amendment to force *all* the states' legislatures to give up their power to choose Senators. This campaign lasted for four decades.

The fate of Republican Charles Sumner illustrates what happened to Senators who took the nation's business seriously. Still revered as the martyr of "Bleeding Kansas," Sumner was chairman of the Senate Foreign Relations Committee. He smelled corruption in a treaty that came before his committee and scuttled it—even though it was supported by President Grant. The President was relying on a trusted secretary, Orville Babcock, who had pushed the treaty in order to line his own pockets. Babcock schemed with the Republican leadership in the Senate to remove Sumner from his chairmanship. They "explained" that the committee and the Senate needed a chairman who could work closely with the Administration—that is, someone who would not make waves. The loss of his chairmanship was a terrible blow for Sumner. He died three years later, in 1874.

The nation's politics hit bottom in 1876. In the Presidential election that fall, Governor Samuel J. Tilden of New York, the Democratic Presidential nominee, faced Governor Rutherford B. Hayes of Ohio, the Republican candidate. (Hayes had been a compromise choice, selected instead of Speaker Blaine because Blaine had made powerful enemies in the party—enemies who were as corrupt as he was but who could not stomach his arrogance.) For the first time since the John Quincy Adams election over fifty years earlier, a Presidential election did not end with Election Day.

Tilden apparently had won, but Republicans challenged the results in three Southern states—Louisiana, Florida, and South Carolina—with nineteen electoral votes. With these three states up in the air, Tilden needed only one of the nineteen electoral votes to become the nineteenth President; Hayes needed them all.

Congress named a bipartisan Electoral Commission to sort the matter out. The commission included five Senators, five Representatives, and five Justices of the Supreme Court. Seven commissioners were Democrats, and seven were Republicans. Independent-minded Justice David Davis of Illinois, a long-time friend of the late President Lincoln, held the deciding vote. Illinois Republicans decided to take no chance that Davis would vote for Tilden, and they quickly elected him to the Senate. Davis felt that he had to accept the new post; thus, he had to resign from the Court and the commission. The Republican Justices then picked a loyal Republican from their ranks to replace Davis, and the commission voted, eight to seven, to give all nineteen disputed electoral votes to Hayes.

To prevent a challenge to the commission's report on the floor of Congress, Republican political leaders struck a deal with Southern Democrats. We may never know all the elements of this deal. The parties to it buried the evidence so well that even now historians cannot agree on what its terms were. We *do* know that the Southern Democrats wanted an end to the hated Reconstruction policy. They wanted to take back their state governments from the Army, Northern *carpetbaggers* (men who journeyed to the South to build new political careers for themselves based on black voters' support), and the freed slaves. The Republicans wanted Hayes in the White House. They did not care that ending Reconstruction and pulling federal soldiers out of the Southern states would leave the freed slaves without protection against their former masters. Both sides got what they wanted, and Congress voted to confirm the decision of the Electoral Commission.

The Republicans in Congress stole the Presidency from Samuel Tilden. The people had spoken, but that did not matter. Corruption had triumphed over democracy. The highest office in the land had been sold to the highest bidder—for the Democrats had been bidding, too.

The great American writer Mark Twain could not conceal his disgust with American politics in general, and with Congress in particular. He once described Congress as the nation's only identifiable "criminal class." He and his friend Charles Dudley Warner wrote a novel about postwar American life. Their title for the book, *The Gilded Age*, described their time as splendid in appearance but rotten under the glittering surface. Historians have adopted "the Gilded Age" as the standard nickname for this period.

But there were some glimmers of hope, and from a surprising source —the Presidency. President Hayes was an honest man who had had nothing to do with the wheeling and dealing that put him in office. He was interested in reforming the government—in particular, the way that jobs were filled in the executive branch. He disliked the use of political patronage by members of Congress to staff such agencies as the Post Office and the various Collectors of Customs; the country was getting political hacks, not the best people, for vital government jobs. Hayes favored a new system for hiring people to work for the federal government—*civil service*. In a civil service system, candidates for government jobs take examinations that measure whether they are qualified for the jobs they seek. Only those people who are most qualified get government jobs.

The Grant Administration had begun some feeble, tentative experiments with civil service, but Hayes was more enthusiastic about the issue. His push for civil service reform angered powerful Republican politicians, such as New York's Senator Roscoe Conkling, who with his cronies used government jobs to reward friends and punish enemies. They still believed in the *spoils system* (to the victors—in war and in politics—belong the spoils) made notorious a half-century before under President Andrew Jackson. Conkling and other Senators saw Hayes's program as a direct threat to their political power. Hayes managed to persuade Congress to enact a limited civil service bill, but Conkling skillfully cut back on its reach.

Conkling's victory turned to ashes during the next Presidential term—1881–1885. Hayes was out of the running for the Republican nomination. After a failed effort by the bosses to get the convention to nominate a willing former President Grant, just back from China, for an unprecedented third term, the leading contenders for the nomination were Blaine and Conkling. These men were leaders of the *Stalwart* faction of Republicans—loyal party members who did not approve of such newfangled ideas as civil service reform. Blaine and Conkling battled to a standstill. In desperation, the delegates seized on handsome, popular James A. Garfield of Ohio. Garfield, who has been thus far the last successful Presidential candidate to emerge from the House of Representatives, was a former chairman of the new and powerful House Appropriations Committee. He had made his reputation by leading an attempt to bring system and honesty to the process of writing and passing bills to finance the government. A brilliant orator, he was the candidate of the reform, or *Mugwump*, faction. (It is uncertain where the word *Mugwump* came from. Some say that it was a Native American word meaning "great chief." Others claim that a Mugwump was someone who wants to be on both sides of an issue; his "mug" is on one side of the fence and his "wump" is on the other side.)

Garfield, an indecisive, timid man, was easily intimidated by Blaine and Conkling. The two great Republican powerbrokers forced the nominee to accept a Stalwart, the fashionable Chester A. Arthur of New York, as his running mate. Garfield defeated the Democratic candidate, General Winfield S. Hancock, but found no joy in his victory. He was pulled back and forth over government appointments between Blaine, his new Secretary of State, and Senator Conkling.

At this time, the Senate was evenly divided between Democrats and Republicans, with two independent Senators holding the balance. The Republicans, led by Conkling, managed to persuade one of the independents to vote with them to break the deadlock in order to confirm the President's appointees. But Garfield selected advisers from among the ranks of the Republican Senators, reducing his party's strength in the Senate. Seeing an opportunity to keep control of the Senate, the Democrats tried a "squeeze play." Garfield, too, saw a chance to try to assert himself. He refused to accept Senator Conkling's candidate for the office of Collector of Customs of the Port of New York, the post that Vice President Arthur had held before the election. Conkling and his New York colleague, Thomas Platt, resigned in a dramatic move in May 1881. They claimed that the President had violated the old and honorable tradition of "Senatorial courtesy"—the practice of consulting a state's Senators in appointing federal officials serving in that state. Conkling and Platt confidently expected to be returned to office, but the New York legislature had other ideas. As they debated the issue of re-electing Conkling and Platt, other events intervened.

Five months after he took office, the President wanted to take a brief vacation. Walking with Secretary Blaine through the waiting room of a Washington, D.C., railroad station, Garfield was shot twice in the back at point-blank range. His assassin, Charles J. Guiteau, was a deranged man who had long sought a government job. Guiteau surrendered himself to police at the scene, grandly declaring, "I am a Stalwart and Arthur is President!" Guiteau had acted on his own, but the incident disgraced the Stalwarts in American politics. Worse tidings for that faction were just over the horizon.

When Garfield died two months later, in terrible pain, one of the Vice President's friends exclaimed, "Chet Arthur President? My God!" Conkling expected to be able to rule the new President, who owed his entire career to him. But Conkling suffered a terrible shock. President Arthur was a new man—almost unrecognizable to those who had known him in New York City as the easy-going Collector of Customs. He adopted civil service as his personal cause and fought to extend President Hayes's reforms to cover many more government jobs in the executive branch. Like Hayes, Arthur was not given his party's nomination for a second term, but he could take comfort that he had achieved his goals.

Arthur's successor, another New Yorker, Grover Cleveland, was the first Democratic President since the disgraced James Buchanan had left office in 1861. Cleveland quickly tangled with Congress over the "private bills" that members of Congress introduced to award government pensions to Civil War veterans and their families. Such private bills usually got speedy treatment from Congress, and previous Presidents had signed them as a matter of course. But Cleveland suspected that most private pension bills were frauds on the public, and he read each one carefully. He vetoed one bill on the grounds that the deceased veteran died from drowning when his buggy overturned in a stream; his widow had claimed that an obscure war injury had been the cause of the fatal accident. A second bill fell to Cleveland's veto because the applicant had served in the Army for only three days in March 1865 without seeing action except for a bout with the measles; the applicant had sought a pension fifteen years later because his "war measles" supposedly had affected his vision and had settled in his spinal column. Most of the nearly six hundred vetoes that Cleveland racked up in his eight years as Chief Executive rejected these private pension bills, and often the President explained his reasons for vetoing the bills with stinging sarcasm. More important, he made the vetoes stick.

In the 1880s and 1890s, the nation was troubled by two major economic issues. Republicans favored tariffs, or taxes on imports, to protect American manufacturers; Democrats argued for free (that is, unrestricted) trade, forcing American businesses to compete with those overseas for the domestic market. The other issue had to do with the nation's currency system. Midwestern and Western farmers facing ruin from debts they owed to Eastern financial interests wanted a way to pay off these debts easily. They wanted the government to inflate the currency and advocated issuing sixteen silver dollars for every gold-backed dollar in circulation. "Gold Democrats" and Republicans opposed the farmers' demands for "free silver," fearing that such inflation would destroy the economy. Congress wrestled with the currency issue throughout the last years of the nineteenth century, repeatedly rejecting the free silver cure-all endorsed by such Democrats as William Jennings Bryan, the perennial Democratic Presidential candidate.

Meanwhile, veteran legislators worried about the growing chaos in the House. The rapidly growing number of standing committees created a set of petty empires, with each committee chairman his own petty emperor. The chairmen often squabbled with one another about who would bring a given piece of legislation to the floor. The resulting disputes strangled the House's methods of doing business. Speaker Samuel J. Randall (Democrat-Maine) tried to focus the process of bringing bills to the floor by giving increased authority to the Rules Committee, but he had only modest success. Other problems facing the House included the members' use of motions for adjournments and quorum calls (both of which required full roll-call votes) and their practice of leaving the floor to deprive the House of a quorum so that it could not do business. These practices abused the rules of the House to delay the process of debating and passing bills. Only a strong Speaker could restrain these abuses and do something to reform the House. Just such a man was on the horizon.

In 1889, the Republican majority in the House elected a new Speaker, Thomas Brackett Reed of Maine. Reed soon won the nickname "Czar" Reed (after the absolute ruler of Russia) for his vigorous use of his office's authority to reform the House. He announced that he would no longer recognize motions that he deemed "dilatory" or time-wasting. He also announced that he would not tolerate members' attempts to shut down the House by depriving it of a quorum. The test came in a dispute over the election of a Representative from West Virginia. The House vote was 161 Republicans to 5 Democrats, with another 165 Democrats abstaining from voting although they were on the floor of the House. Reed commanded the Clerk to call the roll *and* to record the present but nonvoting Representatives as present, no matter what they said. One Democrat shouted, "I deny your right, Mr. Speaker, to count me as present." Reed replied: "The

Collections of the Library of Congress

" 'Czar' Reed is ready." This political cartoon lampoons Speaker Thomas Brackett Reed (1839—1902) (Republican-Maine), who was known as the "Czar" because of his iron-willed control of the proceedings and business of the House of Representatives. Reed was the framer of the "Reed rules," the core of the modern system of legislative procedure used by the House.

Chair is making a statement of fact that the gentleman from Kentucky is present. Does he deny it?" The debate continued for three days. When some Representatives tried to leave the chamber, the Speaker ordered the doors locked. (This did not stop one Representative, who kicked down a locked door and thereafter was known as "Kicking-Buck" Kilgore.) Reed's tactics prevailed.

Reed took another giant step toward bringing order to the House by rewriting its rules. He had the power to do so because he was the Chairman of the Rules Committee and Speaker at the same time. The Rules Committee already had won the authority to control which committees got which bills. Under the "Reed rules," the committee handling a particular bill could establish the guidelines for the House's consideration of that bill when it arrived on the floor. This enabled "Czar" Reed and his allies, Joseph Cannon of Illinois and William McKinley of Ohio, to control the business of the House. The Democrats fumed at Reed's high-handed tactics but were helpless to oppose them.

Reed ruled with an iron hand, resigning from the House in 1899 only because he opposed the foreign policy (including the Spanish-American War) of an old friend and former colleague, William McKinley, who was now President. Reed's eventual successor, in 1903, was Joseph Cannon, nicknamed "Uncle Joe." Cannon delighted in the tradition of the strong, autocratic Speaker, pushing his authority far beyond even Reed's hopes for the office. For example, Cannon asserted the right to pass on every bill introduced in the House, no matter how essential or petty it was. He appointed every member of every House committee. As his mentor, "Czar" Reed, had done, Cannon kept a tight grasp on the chairmanship of the all-powerful House Rules Committee. But Cannon's day was past, though he did not recognize it. At the dawn of the twentieth century, he was a relic of the Gilded Age. He soon would have to confront a new style of politics and an active revolt against his dominance of the House.

The Senate had adopted methods similar to Reed's and Cannon's for bringing its business, including the chairmanships and staffing of its committees, under the strict control of the majority party's leadership. But the "old guard" who ran the Senate in this period, like their counterparts in the House, were about to suffer a bruising confrontation with a new age in American politics.

# CHAPTER SEVEN

# THE PROGRESSIVE ERA TRANSFORMS CONGRESS

Historians call the period beginning in the 1890s and continuing until the United States entered the First World War in 1917 the Progressive Era. A wide range of political, economic, legal, and social reformers enlisted under the Progressive banner; they wrote and published and campaigned to reform the United States from top to bottom. Relations between management and labor; the quality of foods, drugs, and other consumer goods; conditions of life in urban slums and factories and on farms; the problems of the millions of immigrants; abuses of economic power; and political corruption and inefficiency—all these subjects were grist for the Progressives' mills.

Congress led the list of Progressives' complaints about the national political system, so Congress felt some of the earliest effects of Progressivism. Also, because the Progressives believed that many of the problems they sought to cure were national problems requiring national solutions, Congress had to deal with their demands for answers.

One of the most important goals of the Progressive movement was the adoption of an amendment to the Constitution requiring that Senators be elected by the people directly instead of by state legislatures. The campaign for this amendment to the Constitution finally

*The tyrannical Speaker Joseph G. Cannon (1836—1926) (Republican-Illinois)*
*was even more autocratic than his mentor, "Czar" Reed. Known as "Uncle*
*Joe" (perhaps because of his resemblance to "Uncle Sam," the legendary*
*national symbol), Cannon ruled the House so arrogantly that he provoked a*
*full-scale rebellion against his authority. This 1905 photograph shows Cannon,*
*at the peak of his power, presiding over the House.*

succeeded in 1913. In large part, its success was due to the exposure of
the corruption and inefficiency of the old Senate.

In 1906, two Senators were convicted of accepting bribes to interfere in the work of federal agencies regulating interstate commerce.
This scandal outraged journalists and publishers such as William Randolph Hearst. He ordered his newspapers to conduct a full-scale investigation of what he called "The Treason of the Senate." The exposés
shocked the nation. For the first time, the American people began to
realize how powerful the Senate was in the constitutional system and
how fraud, incompetence, and corruption had stained the state legislatures' election of Senators and the Senate's conduct of its business.

Many states found themselves unrepresented in the Senate for weeks or even months as their legislators wrangled, wasted time, and even got into fistfights with one another.

In 1912, the House and the Senate approved the proposed Seventeenth Amendment providing for direct election of Senators. Senator William Borah (Republican-Idaho) was the Progressives' hero due to his skillful and tactful guiding of the proposed amendment through the Senate. The Amendment was ratified by the states in 1913. This great symbolic victory heralded a new era in the Senate. As Senators were compelled to undergo the fatigue and stress of political campaigns, they also were forced to learn about the interests and needs of the people they were to represent. The Senate thus grew to reflect the condition of the nation and its people.

The House, too, felt the winds of change. In 1909, Republican Representative George W. Norris of Nebraska stepped forward to lead a challenge to Speaker Cannon. Cannon had continued to rule the House with inflexible hostility to any reform legislation and with an eye to preserving his own authority. Norris led a group of like-minded Progressive Republicans who allied themselves with the Democrats seeking to defeat Cannon's bid for another term as Speaker. The move failed, but the vote was extremely close. Cannon narrowly beat back another Progressive attempt to reform the procedures of the House by stripping him of his chairmanship of the Rules Committee and his power to appoint committee chairmen. But the Progressive Republicans saw that time was on their side. On March 17, 1910, Norris tried again. He offered a proposal to revamp the Rules Committee, to permit its members to elect their own chairman, and to bar the Speaker from membership on the committee. Cannon kept the House in session for twenty-nine straight hours, trying to shore up his support for a final confrontation with Norris. But on March 19, when he ruled Norris's motion out of order, the full House stunned the Speaker by overruling his decision. Norris's motion passed, and the Speaker lost his beloved Rules Committee. It was a major victory for Progressivism and a shattering defeat for Cannon.

Slowly the House began to reshape its procedures and methods of doing business. The process quickened in 1911 when the Democrats had control of the House and sought to undo the legacy of "Czar" Reed and "Uncle Joe" Cannon. The House shifted power from the Speaker to the party leadership. The Majority Leader of the House of Representatives became a new power broker, and the power of the Committee on Ways and Means (the House committee that considers tax bills) began to grow as the Rules Committee's wings were trimmed.

In both the House and Senate, the Democratic and Republican parties were divided into Progressive and conservative blocs. In 1912 and 1913, Democrats allied with Republican Progressives to use Congress's power of investigations to probe the power of concentrated wealth in American society. Chaired by Representative Arsène Pujo (Democrat-Louisiana), this special committee called such leading financiers as J. P. Morgan and grilled them about their holdings, their economic and political power, and their control of the American economic system. The Pujo Committee's report aroused national indignation, and the Democrats vowed to make its findings part of their agenda.

Conservatives still sought to frustrate the legislative programs of Presidents Theodore Roosevelt and Woodrow Wilson, but the two Presidents fought back, managing to wrest some of their most cherished reforms from a reluctant Congress. Such bills as the Pure Food and Drug Act of 1906, the Clayton Anti-Trust Act of 1914, and the Federal Reserve Act of 1914 (the fruit of the Pujo Committee's investigations) were the results of a newly aggressive Presidency.

Roosevelt began the process of trying to set the nation's political and legislative agenda, and Wilson built on his work. In fact, in his first term, Wilson maintained close but secret ties with Representative John Nance Garner (Democrat-Texas), who regularly fed the President political gossip and information about his support and opposition in the House. And Wilson became the first President since John Adams to appear before a joint session of Congress.

President Wilson had a firm base to build on for his knowledge of Congress. In 1885, when he was not yet thirty years of age, he had written his Ph.D. dissertation on Congress. Published later that year as *Congressional Government*, Wilson's pathbreaking book introduced its readers to an institution they barely knew and also introduced the nation to a brilliant student of American public affairs. For the most part, the President demonstrated that he still understood Congress and how to work with that body.

President Roosevelt had always had his greatest successes in duels with Congress over foreign policy. President Wilson was not so fortunate. When the First World War broke out in Europe, in 1914, most Americans wanted the United States to stay out of it. In the 1916 Presidential election, Wilson narrowly won a second term with the slogan "He Kept Us Out of War." But he knew that the war in Europe was worsening and that American interests were being endangered. In particular, Germany's indiscriminate use of a new weapon of war, the torpedo-firing submarine, threatened American shipping and American lives. The Germans had agreed to follow strict rules governing the use of submarine warfare, but Wilson worried that they would change their minds.

The President proposed early in 1917, in the last days of his first term, that the United States arm merchant ships traveling to and from Great Britain and France. The bill stalled in the Senate, where several Senators, led by Progressive Republicans William Borah and George W. Norris, conducted a *filibuster* against it until the Senate adjourned. (A filibuster is a long, drawn-out debate in which opponents of a measure keep control of the floor of the Senate—that is, the right to address the body—as long as they can. They make use of the Senate's long tradition of freedom of debate to retain the floor; even one Senator can conduct a filibuster if he can keep talking and if he has friends on the floor who will give him a few minutes to rest every now and then.) Wilson was infuriated by the Senators' filibuster, declaring: "A little group of willful men, representing no opinion but their own, have rendered the government of the United States helpless and corruptible." Senator Norris retorted, quoting Wilson's own book on Congress: "It is the proper duty of a representative to look diligently into every affair of government and to talk much about what he sees."

The President rallied his supporters to make a major change in the Senate's rules governing debate. The Senate adopted a new *cloture rule* under which it could shut off debate if two-thirds of its members vote to adopt a petition, supported by at least sixteen Senators, to end debate.

The filibuster controversy was forgotten on April 2, 1917. In a dramatic gesture, the President appeared before a joint session of Congress to announce that Germany had resumed unrestricted submarine warfare against American shipping. He asked for a declaration of war, pledging that the United States was not interested in territorial gain or the other spoils of war. The House and the Senate debated the measure for four days and voted to declare war by overwhelming majorities. One opponent of the measure was Representative Jeannette Rankin (Republican-Montana), the first woman elected to the House. She was defeated for re-election in 1918.

Democrats and Republicans in Congress joined ranks to support the Wilson Administration's war effort. This bipartisanship had its

Collections of the Library of Congress

*Jeannette Rankin (1880—1973) (Republican-Montana), the first woman elected to the U.S. House of Representatives, was an advocate of women's suffrage and pacifism. This 1916 photograph shows her in the year she was first elected to the House. She was the only member of Congress to vote against American entry into the First and Second World Wars.*

less fortunate side. Congress adopted, for the first time in over a century, federal laws restricting freedom of speech and press. The Sedition Act of 1918 prohibited speaking or publishing that might endanger the war effort. This law severely damaged civil liberties in the United States and subjected to arrest and exile hundreds of foreign-born Americans and aliens seeking U.S. citizenship.

In 1918, the President destroyed the bipartisanship brought into being by the war—he urged the voters to return a solid Democratic Congress. Republicans were angered by what they saw as the President's violation of the ground rules of wartime politics, and the voters handed the Democratic President a stinging defeat, electing a Republican House and Senate.

On November 11, 1918, the signing of a truce, or *armistice*, brought joyous celebration of the end of the war throughout the world, and politicians turned their minds to the making of the peace. Again, Wilson erred by renouncing bipartisanship. Instead of appointing prominent Republicans to join him in the American peace delegation, he shut them out. Powerful figures such as Republican Henry Cabot Lodge of Massachusetts, chairman of the Senate Foreign Relations Committee, neither forgave nor forgot the snub. And the Midwestern Progressive Republicans who resented the war, such as Borah and Norris, were not inclined to support the President, either.

Wilson's miscalculation looks even greater when we remember that whatever treaty the President helped to negotiate at the Versailles Conference (at the old French royal palace of Versailles, just outside Paris) had to be approved by two-thirds of the Senate. Word of the Treaty of Versailles leaked back to the United States. Disappointed Democrats and vengeful Republicans alike were startled. Wilson apparently had abandoned all but a handful of his idealistic war aims, the "Fourteen Points." He had endorsed the efforts of the other victorious nations (Britain, France, Italy, and Japan) to carve up the old colonial empires of their defeated opponents (Germany and Austria-Hungary) and to inflict harsh and humiliating punishment on the "aggressor nations." Borah, Norris, and other like-minded Midwesterners, whose constituents included large blocs of German-American voters, were not likely to support this treaty. Moreover, Wilson's ultimate dream, an international peacekeeping organization called the League of Nations, terrified several Senators. They asked troubling questions: Would this League respect American independence? Would it become some sort of supergovernment? Could the Senate adopt this treaty under the Constitution?

The Chief Executive returned home, having convinced himself that the treaty was not just the best that he could get but the best treaty ever. He brushed aside the worries of the Senate and challenged it to reject the treaty that, he declared, carried the hopes of the whole world for an end to all wars. Senator Lodge met the challenge. He did not respect Wilson's learning (after all, he had received Harvard's first doctoral degree in political science, in 1876, nearly a decade before Wilson received *his* Ph.D. from Johns Hopkins). He was the senior Republican in the Senate and its most respected member. He had managed to win some minor concessions from the President, and when Wilson made a personal appearance before the Senate to present the treaty for its consideration, Lodge had escorted him onto the floor. Now he warned the President that the treaty was not likely to pass—at least not without revisions.

Senator Lodge proposed that the Covenant of the League of Nations (the proposed world organization's founding document) be detached from the treaty. Wilson rejected this idea indignantly. Lodge and other Republicans also proposed four major and more than forty minor revisions and amendments. Democrats and Republican "mild reservationists" beat back most of these, but it was becoming clear that the treaty would fall short of the two-thirds vote needed for adoption.

President Wilson decided to go over the heads of the Senate to the American people. He set out on a twenty-nine-city cross-country speaking tour, traveling by railroad. In the middle of this tour, he had a physical breakdown, and a couple of weeks later, in October 1919, he suffered a severe stroke in the White House. The President was crippled—some said as crippled as his treaty. On November 7, Lodge presented the treaty to the Senate with fourteen "reservations" (usually called the *Lodge Reservations*). The Senate decisively rejected the treaty—the first time in American history that it had refused to ratify a treaty. This rejection was due in part to Wilson's plea from his sickbed to his supporters to reject a watered-down treaty. Five months later, in March 1920, the Senate again voted on the treaty. This time it received a majority but less than the two-thirds vote needed to ratify.

The treaty fight broke the President and reasserted the independence of the Senate. Partly as a result of Wilson's stubbornness, the Democrats lost control of the Presidency in the 1920 election. For the first time in nearly a century, a sitting Senator—the obscure Warren

G. Harding of Ohio—was elected to the Presidency. After the bold leaps of the Progressive Era and the stresses and strains of the war years, the nation—and Congress—settled down to what they hoped would be a period of quiet.

# CHAPTER EIGHT

# FROM BOOM TO BUST

The American humorist Will Rogers once observed that after a period of great political change and controversy, the American people like "to sleep it off for a while." The 1920s were one such period. But the character of the 1920s was shaped by one last Progressive measure.

Many of the Progressives urged social as well as political reform, and one of their favorite targets was "the evils of strong drink." For most of the nineteenth century and well into the twentieth, reformers campaigned against alcohol. Some advocated *temperance*—getting the people to give up or cut down their drinking on their own. Others believed that only *prohibition*—an outright ban on the manufacture and sale of alcoholic beverages—would work. In 1919, Congress proposed to the states the Eighteenth Amendment, which prohibited the manufacture or sale of virtually any kind of hard liquor, wine, or beer. Congress also adopted the Volstead Act, a law designed to put "the noble experiment" of Prohibition into effect. In 1920, with the ratification of the Eighteenth Amendment, the United States went from "wet" to "dry."

Prohibition may have been a noble experiment, but as an experiment it was a dismal failure. Millions of Americans willingly became lawbreakers because they would not give up alcohol. Criminals such as "Scarface" Al Capone founded huge empires on the demand for illegal, or *bootleg*, alcohol. Smugglers brought in whiskey, Scotch, brandy, and other hard liquor from overseas, evading U.S. Coast Guard patrols. Other enterprising criminals learned to make their own liquor, distilling such beverages as "bathtub gin." Homemade liquor was often dangerous to drink because its manufacturers were not particular about the ingredients they used to make their products. Illegal bars and clubs, called *speakeasies*, flourished throughout the United States. The government could not keep up with those who were willing to violate the law, and many authorities turned a blind eye—for a price. Instead of increasing the virtue of the American people, Prohibition made the United States a nation of lawbreakers.

The First World War had focused the nation's politics in Washington, D.C., and Congress discovered that its old methods of doing business were inadequate to the new century. The Senate reorganized itself, cutting down on the number of its committees to promote efficiency in dealing with proposed bills. Congress and President Harding also worked together to rethink the way that the budget of the United States should be drawn up. (A *budget* is an itemized list of the sources and amounts of money the government expects to receive, and the ways and amounts that the government expects to spend.) In earlier years, each institution and government agency would submit its own budget request to Congress, which would pass these bills piecemeal. Congress passed and President Harding signed the Budget and Accounting Act of 1921. For the first time in American history, the President was to submit a *unified* budget—a single proposal covering all parts of the government and all sources of revenue. To help him, Congress created the Bureau of the Budget. The House also decided that all bills for spending money should be handled by one committee, the Appropriations Committee, to avoid wasting time and to give Congress a full picture of how the government was spending its money.

As the 1920s began, the Republican majorities in the House and Senate largely carried on business as usual, and the passive President Harding followed their lead. Harding's Administration included some first-rate officials, but at least as many were mediocre or incompetent, and some were outright crooks. One of the crooks was Senator Albert B. Fall of New Mexico, a clever, grasping man whom Harding named to head the Department of the Interior. Fall used his position to launch what became one of the most famous corrupt deals in American history.

The Navy Department had charge of vast oil fields, called oil reserves, in the Western states. These oil reserves were insurance that the U.S. Navy would have reliable supplies of fuel to power its ships. No one could drill on these oil reserves without a license from the government. Secretary Fall persuaded his dimwitted colleague, Navy Secretary Edwin Denby, to transfer control of the oil reserves to the Interior Department. Then Fall cheerfully pocketed bribes from oil companies in exchange for licenses to drill on the oil reserves. The two reserves at the heart of the scandal were Elk Hills, Nevada, and Teapot Dome, Wyoming.

The Teapot Dome affair was only the most blatant of the many scandals that plagued the Harding Administration. The President was personally honest but had made the mistake of trusting the wrong people. The strain of realizing just how serious a problem he faced was too much for him.

After Harding's sudden death in California in 1923, the signs of corruption were too obvious to ignore. Senator Robert LaFollette, a Wisconsin Republican and a leader of that party's dwindling Progressive wing, urged his friend and colleague Democrat Thomas Walsh of Montana to conduct an investigation. Walsh was a former prosecutor who knew how to uncover evidence of wrongdoing. He pressed his investigation, indifferent to the avalanche of public criticism. At first, most Americans believed that the Democrats were just looking for an issue to use against the Republicans in the 1924 Presidential election. But Walsh uncovered too much evidence that the Teapot Dome scandal was real and serious. At the same time, the other Montana Senator, Democrat Burton K. Wheeler, launched his own investigation. His target was Attorney General Harry M. Daugherty, who was taking bribes in return for refusing to enforce the Volstead Act against bootleggers. Fall and Daugherty were forced to resign. Fall became the first Cabinet member to go to prison; Daugherty escaped a jail term by pleading ill health. The Teapot Dome investigations ultimately led to two Supreme Court decisions upholding the power of Congress to conduct investigations and to require witnesses to appear before it. These cases confirmed the continuing importance of Congressional investigations in informing the nation about problems of government and society.

Congress itself was not immune from charges of corruption and wrongdoing. The Senate conducted investigations of several of its own members whose election campaigns were marred by excessive spending and, in some cases, corruption. These charges, and the Harding Administration scandals, led to enactment of the Federal Corrupt Practices Act of 1925. This law was a step in the right direction but in later years proved to be a "toothless tiger."

The nation in the 1920s seemed to be experiencing a remarkable period of growth and prosperity—what stockbrokers called a "boom." But not everyone felt that things were booming. Labor unions had to fight for their very existence against strong-arm tactics by industrialists such as Henry Ford. Farmers were hard-pressed to meet mortgage payments on their farms and equipment. Veterans of the First World War had to lobby Congress persistently for payment of the "bonus" promised them when they were mustered out of the armed forces. For the most part, Congress and the Republican Presidents of the 1920s— Harding and Calvin Coolidge—did little about such problems, and Congress followed their lead.

As Presidents Harding and Coolidge followed a policy of passive leadership and Congress was preoccupied with its own concerns, worried economists noted a growing instability in the American economy. Thousands and thousands of ordinary Americans—retirees, schoolteachers, salesmen, and so forth—were plunging recklessly into the stock market, seeking to make huge profits. At first, they did. At that time, one could call a stockbroker and buy a large quantity of stock *on margin*—by putting up only a small part of the stock's value. Then the investor would wait for the right time to sell, collect the (increased) purchase price, and pay the broker the balance of the original sum he or she had promised to pay for the stock in the first place. Meanwhile, the company paid out part of its profits (in *dividends*) to its stockholders, and everyone was happy. Eager would-be investors plunged themselves into debt to brokerage houses for tens of thousands, or even hundreds of thousands, of dollars. The leading figures in the economic world did the same, on a much larger scale.

Could this ballooning stock market last? If the market finally went "bust," what effect would it have on the economy as a whole? Although many economists began to ask these questions more and more pointedly, no leading political figures ever did. President Coolidge saw no reason to advise caution, and his successor in 1929, the widely respected Herbert Hoover, confidently declared that the United States was about to win the final battle against poverty.

Four dismal weeks in October 1929 changed all that. The bottom fell out of the market, plunging the New York Stock Exchange into panic. Billions of dollars of "paper value" vanished into thin air. The crash at first seemed to have little effect beyond shattering the dreams and careers of the unlucky speculators who had not unloaded their holdings in time. But the ripples spread throughout the economy. Corporations depend upon their stock's value in all sorts of ways. They can borrow money to finance expanding or revamping their facilities and issue new shares of stock to raise new money, or capital, to finance new ventures and explore new markets. If a corporation's stock plunges in value, these dreams dissolve. If the plunge persists, corporations are forced to tighten their belts—to close plants, to fire or lay off workers, to cut other expenses and costs to the bone. These measures cost people their jobs through no fault of their own.

Another way that the effects of the crash were felt throughout the American economy was through the banking system. People deposit money in banks to keep it safe and to earn income—*interest*—from their savings deposits. Banks do not keep this money lying about. They invest it in stocks, bonds, and other enterprises to produce income; they pay out some of this income as interest to their depositors and keep the rest as their profit. Banks suffered losses due to the crash. More important, investors who were wiped out by the crash ran to their savings accounts for money to pay off their debts. So did workers and others who lost their jobs. When all of a bank's depositors converged on that bank at once, the bank could not meet all their demands to withdraw their deposits because they did not have the funds on hand (they were invested elsewhere). Banks failed throughout the nation, leaving millions of Americans without savings.

In this period of American history, people believed that you were on your own in the economy. It was not government's job to help people who lost their jobs or their life's savings or their homes. Secretary of the Treasury Andrew Mellon summed up this view: "Let the slump liquidate itself. Liquidate labor, liquidate stocks, liquidate the farmers. . . . People will work harder, live a more moral life. Values will be adjusted, and enterprising people will pick up the wrecks from less competent people." But the American people's expectations began to change in the years following the 1929 crash—years that are known as the *Great Depression.* Someone had to do something for the millions of jobless, homeless Americans thronging the roads and streets of the United States.

The Hoover Administration was unwilling to take massive action to combat the suffering caused by the Depression. The President and his advisers believed that the United States had no constitutional authority for such measures. Aid to the homeless and the unemployed were matters for state and local governments, if at all. Increasingly the Administration found itself out of step with the people.

In 1931, the Republicans lost control of the House of Representatives. The 1930 congressional elections had cut the Republican margin to one vote, and the deaths of several leading Republicans enabled the Democrats to become the majority party by scoring victories in the special elections to choose replacements. The Senate was also changed by the 1930 elections, with the Republican majority hanging on to control by one vote. For these reasons and because he preferred to deal with the Depression in his own way without the interference of Congress, President Hoover chose not to call a special session of Congress. Thus, Congress did not convene after the 1930 elections until December 1931.

The House chose a new Speaker, Democrat John Nance Garner of Texas, and under his leadership considered and passed emergency measures to deal with the Depression. The Norris-La Guardia Act of 1932, for example, protected labor unions from the most serious abuses of their rights by management. The Senate also proved willing to consider such measures, as conservatives were shouldered aside by their progressive colleagues, Democrats and Republicans alike.

The Senate used its power of investigation to examine the ways in which the nation's financial community, based in Wall Street in New York City (the home of the New York Stock Exchange), conducted business. Were there any connections between these business methods and the 1929 crash? Republican Peter Norbeck of Nebraska, a member of the progressive group of Republicans, chaired the Senate Banking Committee investigation of this subject. The committee's chief counsel, or lawyer, was Ferdinand Pecora. Under Pecora's able and brilliant direction, the committee laid bare the shortsighted and dangerous abuses in the stock market. The committee's findings eventually resulted in such major legislation as the Securities Act of 1933, the Securities Exchange Act of 1934, and the Banking Act of 1933.

These steps, and the publicity given by the Pecora investigations to the need for reforming the nation's financial system, were not enough to deal with the major crisis that the Depression posed for the American economy, and even for the continued survival of constitutional government. The American electorate demanded change, and in 1932 they got it. Not only was President Hoover turned out of office by Democratic nominee Franklin D. Roosevelt (and his running-mate, Speaker Garner), the Democrats scored overwhelming victories in the congressional elections as well, winning control of the Senate and solidifying their hold on the House.

Banks continued to fail throughout 1932 and the early months of 1933, and the entire nation lived under a cloud of hopelessness and despair. Rumors abounded of plots by the military to take over the government. President-elect Roosevelt narrowly escaped assassination in Miami, Florida, in February 1933. Instead of Hoover's predicted ultimate triumph over poverty, the United States seemed to have reached rock bottom.

# CHAPTER NINE

# DEPRESSION AND WAR

Inauguration Day, March 4, 1933, dawned cold and bleak. President Hoover and President-elect Roosevelt rode silently in a limousine to the Capitol building. Hoover was bitter; he had been turned out by the voters in a massive rejection of himself and his policies. He had sought Roosevelt's cooperation in the months between Election Day and Inauguration Day, but the President-elect rebuffed him. Roosevelt did not want his hands tied, nor did he want to be tainted by any alliance with the discredited Hoover Administration.

Roosevelt wasted no time. In his inaugural address, he pledged "action—and action now." He asserted that as President, he had the power and the duty to lead the nation in dealing with the crisis posed by the Depression. He promised to ask Congress for bold measures to combat the Depression's effects on the people. He was as good as his word.

Roosevelt's first step was to proclaim a bank holiday to provide a breathing space for those banks that had not closed their doors. Next, he called Congress into special session to consider emergency legislation. By invoking this power (under Article II, Section 3 of the Constitution), Roosevelt was further distancing himself from his predecessor, who had not seen fit to call a special session of any sort.

When the new Congress gathered in the House and Senate chambers on March 9, they found proposed legislation waiting for them. The first bill, an emergency banking measure, went through the House in thirty-eight minutes flat, with no printed copy of the bill for members to consult. In fact, most members voted for it with a whoop and a roar, not having bothered to read it. The Senate followed suit later in the day, and Roosevelt signed the bill into law that night.

This first bill was followed by many more. The one hundred days that this first session of Congress lasted stand as one of the great periods of cooperation between the President and Congress. In both houses of Congress, the leadership put together steering committees to ensure that laws were considered and passed as quickly as possible in order to give the President and the rest of the Executive Branch the authority and the tools to deal with the Depression. In some instances, the haste to act led to badly drafted and ill-considered laws. At the same time, some of the most lasting achievements of the Roosevelt Administration emerged from the Hundred Days: the Social Security Act, the National Labor Relations Act, and the laws establishing the Federal Deposit Insurance Corporation and the Tennessee Valley Authority. Many of these laws were the handiwork of leading progressive Senators such as George W. Norris and Robert F. Wagner (Democrat-New York).

Shell-shocked at first by the magnitude of their 1932 defeat, Republicans in the House and the Senate reacted to Roosevelt's tornado of legislation in several ways. Some, such as Senators Norris and Arthur Vandenberg of Michigan, worked with the Administration when they felt they could. Others, such as Republican Minority Leader Representative Bertrand Snell of New York and Representative Dewey Short of Missouri, did their best to hold the tide. Short at one point declared that the House was a "supine, subservient, soporific, superfluous, supercilious, pusillanimous body of nitwits." He and his beleaguered colleagues denounced Roosevelt as little short of a dictator, and they raged at their colleagues for following the White House's lead.

In some ways, Snell and Short had a point. During the first years of Roosevelt's Administration, Congress looked to the White House for guidance, direction, and leadership. The President reciprocated; he came more and more to expect that Congress would act on his direction and suggestion. In times of crisis throughout American history, vigorous, activist Presidents have seized the opportunity to place themselves at the focus of events and to lead the government and the nation in dealing with troubles facing the nation. In such times, Congress often follows suit. The question becomes when and how Congress will assert its independence and its right to a voice in the decision-making process.

Roosevelt was buoyed in 1934 by congressional elections that increased the Democrats' control of the House and Senate. And when he ran for a second term, in 1936, he scored one of the most decisive triumphs in the history of American politics, again carrying Congress with him. This extraordinary success had unfortunate consequences, however. The President began to believe that any opposition to his policies could be ignored due to his overwhelming popular mandate.

Alone of the institutions of government at the national level, the Supreme Court was not marching in step with what journalists and government officials alike dubbed the *New Deal*. The Court was dominated by a conservative group of Justices known as "the Four Horsemen of the Apocalypse." The three liberal Justices—Louis D. Brandeis, Benjamin N. Cardozo, and Harlan Fiske Stone—often sat by helplessly as the Four Horsemen carried one or both of the remaining Justices with them. Many of the New Deal measures came before the Court during Roosevelt's first term, and the Administration suffered a string of major setbacks in the Court. The worst was the Justices' unanimous rejection of the centerpiece of the New Deal, the National Industrial Recovery Act. This law had created an agency called the National Recovery Administration (NRA), which organized the American economy by industries. Industry councils would have the authority to write codes for their members; any company violating such a code would be prosecuted by the NRA. The Justices held that this law violated the Constitution. Only Congress has the power to make laws, the Justices declared; Congress may not *delegate*, or hand over, that power to an executive agency, and especially not when that agency then delegates that power to private individuals or corporations.

The President secretly was relieved by the death of the NRA in 1935, for the agency was not having the effect its creators had intended or hoped. But he was angered by the Court's consistent rejection of his New Deal measures. He consulted with his Attorney General and came up with what he thought was a brilliant plan to clip the Court's wings.

Roosevelt made a speech to the nation in which he declared that the "Nine Old Men" of the Court needed help, for they could not keep up with the Court's business. They could not retire, for there was no retirement or pension system for federal judges. Thus, Roosevelt proposed, Congress should enact a law permitting the President to appoint a new Justice for each Justice over seventy years of age who chose not to retire.

Congress received the legislation with doubt and concern. Its opponents charged that Roosevelt was out to "pack" the Court with Justices who would vote to uphold New Deal measures. Even some of the President's supporters were suspicious of the new bill. The Senate Majority Leader, Democrat Joseph Robinson of Arkansas, demanded Roosevelt's promise that he would be the first appointee to the Court if he worked to push the bill through the Senate.

The leadership of the House was dubious of the bill. Texas Representative Hatton W. Sumners, chairman of the House Judiciary Committee, drew on his favorite game of poker to explain his reaction: "Boys, here's where I cash in." The President was aware that the House would not look favorably on the measure, so he submitted it to the Senate first, relying on Senator Robinson's skills as Majority Leader. But some of Roosevelt's most loyal allies knew that Robinson had extorted a promise of a Court appointment in return for his support of the bill, and they objected to the idea that this conservative Southern Democrat might wind up on the Supreme Court. Also, many Senators found themselves buried by mail from constituents opposing the measure. The people saw the Court's independence as being part of the Constitution, which in 1937 was 150 years old. They believed that any attempt to damage or cut back the Court's independence would injure the Constitution.

In the midst of the fight over the Court-packing bill, Senator Robinson died. The loss of the chief sponsor of the Court bill doomed the proposal. The Senate sent it back to the Judiciary Committee, burying it forever. The defeat signaled that Congress was no longer willing to jump to the President's commands. It also was a reproof to Roosevelt, who had read too much into his 1936 landslide.

Conservative Southern Democrats joined ranks with Republicans in the Senate to forge a new coalition to oppose the President. In response, still believing that his mandate was a blank check to govern, the President campaigned in the 1938 elections to unseat key members of this coalition, even members of his own party. Roosevelt's efforts to turn the voters against Senators Millard Tydings of Maryland and Walter George of Georgia failed. These Democrats returned to the Senate, determined to wreak vengeance on the President who had trampled party loyalty in his efforts to turn them out of office.

The coalition held its ranks, and the President scored few victories on the domestic front thereafter.

Meanwhile, as the President watched developments in Europe and Asia with concern, a feeling of *isolationism* dominated the House and the Senate. *Isolationism* is a shorthand term for the belief that the affairs of Europe, Asia, and Africa are no concern of the United States. Just as the Monroe Doctrine vested primary concern for the affairs of the Western Hemisphere in the hands of the United States, isolationists argued, it meant that the affairs of the Eastern Hemisphere were their own business. They cited the heartbreaking experience of Woodrow Wilson during the negotiations of the Treaty of Versailles nearly two decades earlier. Look, they said, at what happens when we try to tell Europe how to behave.

Thus the isolationists ignored the warning signs in the 1930s: the growing ambitions of the Japanese in the Far East; the rise of dictators Adolf Hitler in Germany and Benito Mussolini in Italy; Mussolini's conquest of the African nation of Ethiopia; Hitler's annexation of Austria and, later, of Czechoslovakia. They suffered a major blow to their cause when Hitler and the Soviet Union invaded Poland on September 1, 1939, touching off the Second World War. As President Roosevelt told the nation, "This nation will remain a neutral nation, but I can not ask that every American remain neutral in thought as well." The United States began some preparations to shore up its military power. (In this campaign, the President had the support of Southern conservatives in the House and Senate—the same people who had opposed his domestic policies.) The first peacetime draft in the nation's history got under way in late 1940. In March 1941, Congress approved Roosevelt's inspired *Lend-Lease program*. The United States would supply the British with fifty over-age destroyers in return for ninety-nine-year leases of British military and naval bases in the Western Hemisphere. Isolationists charged that Roosevelt was scheming to drag the United States into war on the side of Britain and France against Germany, Italy, Japan, and the U.S.S.R., but they were ignored.

Still, the isolationists managed to resist the President's efforts to position the United States as a quiet, informal ally of Britain and France. In large part, they believed that European wars were irrelevant to American interests and needs, and they were confident that the United States was protected from involvement in war by the Atlantic and Pacific oceans. How, they asked, could any power strike a blow at American territory?

The Japanese surprise attack on the U.S. naval base at Pearl Harbor, Hawaii, on December 7, 1941, answered their question. The next day, the President appeared before a stunned Congress meeting in joint session. He read a six-minute address denouncing Japan and demanding a declaration of war. Congress responded with a thunderous ovation. Meeting separately, the House and the Senate swiftly answered his call. One leading isolationist, Republican Senator Arthur Vandenberg of Michigan, repented before his colleagues: "I have fought every trend which I thought would lead to needless war; but when war comes to us—and particularly when it comes like a thug in the night—I stand with my Commander in Chief for the swiftest and most invincible reply of which our total strength may be capable." In the Senate, the vote to declare war was unanimous. In the House, one lone Representative held out: pacifist Jeannette Rankin, a Montana Republican who had been returned to the House in the 1940 election. Miss Rankin had voted against American entry into the First World War as well; she was the only member of either house of Congress to oppose both wars. (As in 1918, she was defeated for reelection in 1942.) On December 10, Congress also declared war on Germany and Italy.

Both the House and the Senate supported the Administration's measures to prosecute the war, but conservatives were vigilant against any attempt by the Administration to continue the work of the New Deal under the guise of wartime measures. At the same time, Congress tried to monitor government spending on the mammoth war effort. A little-known Senator from Missouri, Democrat Harry S Truman, became chairman of the Senate's Special Committee to Investigate the National Defense Program. Truman was a loyal supporter of Roosevelt (he had even backed the President's ill-fated Court-packing bill in 1937), but he worked vigorously to expose and combat waste in wartime spending. His committee's investigations saved the nation millions of dollars and won the admiration of many Administration officials, including the President. Truman's sole rebuff came when he discovered and tried to investigate a secret government project, the Manhattan Project. High-ranking Administration officials explained to Truman, and to leading members of the House, that this project was vital to the war effort and that it was essential to preserve its secrecy. The Representatives and Senators accepted these explanations.

Truman's work against government wartime waste made him an attractive national candidate in 1944. Roosevelt had already broken the hallowed two-term tradition for Presidents in 1940; because "Cactus Jack" Garner wanted to retire (and because he resisted Roosevelt's bid for a third term), the President had chosen his Secretary of Agriculture, Henry A. Wallace, as his Vice Presidential running mate. But Vice President Wallace proved to be too controversial, especially in his starry-eyed admiration for the U.S.S.R., a new ally of the United States and Great Britain in the war against Hitler and Mussolini. Roosevelt and his aides agreed to "dump" Wallace and selected Truman as his replacement. Thus, in January 1945, Roosevelt's third Vice President moved from the floor of the Senate, where he had served for nearly ten years, to the presiding officer's chair. He sat there for eighty-three days, writing letters to his family as Senators droned on in debate. On April 12, 1945, as he was having a drink with his political cronies in Speaker Sam Rayburn's Capitol hideaway office, Truman received a telephone call from the White House. He rushed to the President's residence, where he learned that Roosevelt had died an hour earlier at his health retreat in Warm Springs, Georgia. From a job where the only interesting thing he could do was to write letters, the Missourian had been catapulted into the most powerful office in the United States.

The new President soon discovered the truth about the Manhattan Project from Secretary of War Henry L. Stimson. The government had been working secretly to develop and perfect a weapon using the energy of the atom. Work on this new "atomic bomb" was proceeding satisfactorily, stimulated by fears that Germany was also working to develop such a weapon. Truman discussed his news only with those House and Senate leaders who already had been briefed by the War Department. No leaks emerged from the White House or from Capitol Hill of work on the atomic bomb. Even the first successful test of the weapon—on July 16, 1945, at Trinity Site, Alamogordo, New Mexico—was kept secret. It was not until three months after the suicide of Adolf Hitler and the surrender of Germany (V-E Day) that the nation and the world learned of atomic weapons. The United States exploded their last two over the Japanese cities of Hiroshima and Nagasaki, in August 1945. The nuclear destruction of these two cities led to Japan's abrupt and unconditional surrender (V-J Day). President Truman and Congress celebrated the end of the war and tried to figure out how to deal with the postwar world.

# CHAPTER TEN

# POSTWAR CRISES
# AT HOME AND ABROAD

The events of Franklin D. Roosevelt's Presidency—the Great Depression and the New Deal, the Second World War, and the development of the atomic bomb—caused a major shift in the balance of power and authority between Congress and the President. This change manifested itself in several ways:

1. The paralysis of President Hoover and of Congress during the first years of the Great Depression caused the American people to welcome a strong, activist Presidency such as that of Franklin Roosevelt. They came to expect a President to lead, to provide direction, clarity, and foresight about the interests of the nation at home and abroad. The President became the national spokesman, the national civics teacher, and the national source of American policy. Congress more and more found itself reacting to Presidential initiative, providing leadership of its own only when the President could not or would not lead.

2. Although Congress in the past had deferred to the President in matters of foreign policy, it still had retained control over questions of war and peace. As a result of the Second World War, however, the technology of communication and transportation had revolutionized warfare. The President could receive more information and act on it

far more rapidly than Congress could. President Truman unwittingly encouraged this trend in 1947 when he approved the creation of the Central Intelligence Agency. This agency, and its counterpart, the National Security Agency, permitted Truman and his successors to justify foreign-policy decisions by citing access to secret information. Critics of White House policy were answered with the wistful claim "If you knew what we know . . ."

3. The successful development of the atomic bomb gave the President, as Commander-in-Chief of the armed forces, control of a weapon that transformed warfare into a threat to the continued existence of human life. Just as Theodore Roosevelt could boast in 1906 that "I took the [Panama] Canal and let Congress debate," a modern President could launch a nuclear war by himself, with no time for Congress to debate. As a result, Congress deferred to an official possessing the power to end life on the planet.

4. Finally, the sudden emergence of the Soviet Union as the principal rival of the United States and the "leader of world Communism" terrified Congress, just as much as it alarmed President Truman and the American people. The U.S.S.R. had allied itself with the United States during the Second World War only after the German invasion in June 1941. Most Americans conveniently forgot that the Soviet leader, Chairman Joseph Stalin, had allied the U.S.S.R. with Germany, Italy, and Japan in the opening years of the war. At the war's end, the U.S.S.R. refused to withdraw its forces from the nations of Eastern Europe, imposed Communist-dominated governments on most of those countries, and annexed others (such as Estonia, Latvia, and Lithuania) outright. Former British Prime Minister Winston S. Churchill, in a 1946 speech at Westminster College, in Fulton, Missouri, described the Soviet Union as having lowered "an iron curtain" across Europe. The U.S.S.R. had also developed atomic weapons—a development that representatives of the U.S. armed forces had assured the nation was impossible for decades. A few years later, the U.S.S.R. had surpassed the United States in the arms race by developing the hydrogen bomb, the first of a class of thermonuclear weapons far outstripping the power of atomic weapons. The United States and the U.S.S.R. faced each other in an atmosphere of mutual suspicion and hostility barely short of actual armed conflict. Journalists dubbed this tense rivalry the Cold War. The threat of the Soviet Union, whether real or exaggerated, dominated foreign policy for nearly fifty years and helped to shape Congressional action at home as well.

At first, the end of the Second World War left the United States in a commanding position on the stage of world affairs. President Truman shepherded into existence the United Nations, the late President Roosevelt's dream for an international peacekeeping organization with teeth. Unlike Woodrow Wilson's disastrous experience with the Senate nearly thirty years earlier, President Truman worked closely with Republican leaders in the Senate, such as Arthur Vandenberg, making partners in the creation of the United Nations and in determining the shape of the postwar world. Vandenberg also became the architect of another international alliance, the North Atlantic Treaty Organization. The Senate approved both the Truman Doctrine in 1947, which authorized postwar economic aid to Greece and Turkey, and the Marshall Plan in 1948, which did the same for war-ravaged Europe.

Truman had little success on the domestic front, however. American voters resented what they saw as the slowness of the nation's return to a peacetime footing. They wanted an end to price and wage controls, an end to shortages and rationing of such items as gasoline, paper, and rubber. In the congressional elections of 1946, the Republicans took back control of both houses of Congress. They systematically frustrated President Truman's attempts to build on the New Deal legacy of President Roosevelt.

The Republican-dominated Congress enacted over a Presidential veto the Taft-Hartley Act of 1947, a significant law governing labor-management relations. Management cheered the adoption of Taft-Hartley, which they thought evened the balance between management and labor that the National Labor Relations Act had tilted in labor's favor. Labor naturally resented the new law, which permitted many states (mostly in the South and Midwest) to adopt *right-to-work laws* forbidding management to make membership in a labor union a condition of employment. Senator Robert A. Taft of Ohio, the architect of the Taft-Hartley Act, became the leading candidate of conservative Republicans for the 1948 Presidential nomination.

The Democrats made it a priority to regain control of Congress in the 1948 elections, although many party leaders feared that the Democrats would face disaster unless they dumped President Truman. Truman refused to be dumped, however. He won nomination for a term of his own, but the Southern wing of his party walked out of the Democratic National Convention in anger over the party's adoption of a strong civil-rights plank in its platform. The "progressive" wing also walked out, declaring its opposition to the Truman Administration's Cold War policy of confrontation toward the Soviet Union.

The Senate Historical Office

*On June 1, 1950, Senator Margaret Chase Smith (1897—) (Republican-Maine) won national recognition for her eloquent "Declaration of Conscience" speech denouncing the anti-Communist hysteria that was sweeping the nation and Congress. In that speech, she defended "the right to criticize; the right to hold unpopular beliefs; the right to protest; the right of independent thought." She added, "As an American, I want to see our nation recapture the strength and unity it once had when we fought the enemy instead of ourselves."*

The President rallied the remaining Democrats at their listless convention. He tore into the "do-nothing Eightieth Congress" and announced that he was calling Congress back into session to deal with his domestic agenda. He spent the rest of the campaign traveling 31,700 miles around the nation by train, lambasting the "do-nothing" Congress at every whistlestop, making 356 speeches in all. At the same time, the Democratic strategists picked able, talented, and committed liberal candidates to lead their effort to retake Congress from the Republicans. Both campaigns worked. Truman surprised journalists, pollsters, and political experts throughout the country by scoring a narrow but decisive victory over Republican Governor Thomas E. Dewey of New York, and the Democratic "class of 1948" handed Congress back to the Democrats. The freshmen Democratic Senators who took office in 1949 included such later titans as Lyndon B. Johnson of Texas, Hubert H. Humphrey of Minnesota, Paul Douglas of Illinois, Russell Long of Louisiana, and Estes Kefauver of Tennessee.

Also a member of the "class of 1948," but a Republican, was Margaret Chase Smith of Maine, the first woman to be elected to the Senate without having first succeeded her husband. (Governors formerly appointed the widow of a deceased Senator to serve out his term.)

The Democrats' triumph was short-lived, however. The Republicans capitalized on American fears of the U.S.S.R. in the Cold War and mounted a series of sensational congressional investigations in the House and the Senate. The House Un-American Activities Committee, which had been launched in the late 1930s to investigate Nazi and Communist movements in the country, focused its attention on the American Communist Party and on other organizations affiliated with, supported by, or sometimes simply agreeing with the Communists. One member of the Committee was a young Republican from California, Richard M. Nixon. Nixon's shrewd understanding of the Communist issue and his gift for investigation led him to Whittaker Chambers, an editor of *Time* magazine, who disclosed that he had been a member of the Communist Party and that he had engaged in espionage for the Soviet Union during the 1930s and early 1940s with the help of a State Department official named Alger Hiss. Hiss, a highly respected member of the liberal "establishment," confronted Chambers at a well-publicized session of the Committee; he challenged Chambers's story and accused him of *perjury* (lying under oath). But Nixon and his aides believed Chambers and managed to uncover sufficient evidence to cast at least some doubt on Hiss's story. Thus, it was Hiss—not Chambers—who was indicted for perjury and eventually convicted and imprisoned. Nixon's sharp questioning of Hiss during the Committee session, and his relentless digging for evidence to rehabilitate Chambers, attracted national attention. He later built on the Hiss-Chambers case to score a surprise victory in his 1950 bid to represent California in the Senate.

One Republican Senator who learned from Nixon's success with the Communist issue was Joseph McCarthy of Wisconsin. McCarthy was floundering in his career in the late 1940s, seeking a headline-making issue to keep himself afloat. In several widely publicized speeches in 1950, McCarthy charged that anywhere from 81 to 205 members of the Truman Administration were known Communists and active agents of the Soviet Union. Democratic Senator Millard Tydings of Maryland convened a hearing of a special panel of the Senate Foreign Relations Committee to hear McCarthy's charges. The committee rejected McCarthy's claims as unfounded and condemned the Senator for foisting "a fraud and a hoax" on the American people. But McCarthy bounced back, denouncing Tydings as a dupe of the international Communist conspiracy. That autumn, Tydings, who had survived President Franklin D. Roosevelt's attempts to drive him from office in 1938, was defeated—in large part by anti-Communist hysteria fomented by McCarthy and his allies.

Tydings was not the only victim of McCarthy's venom. When Republican Senator William Benton of Connecticut introduced a resolution in 1951 calling for his fellow Republican McCarthy's expulsion from the Senate, McCarthy replied: "Benton has established himself as a hero of every Communist and crook in and out of government." Benton lost his seat in the 1952 Senate elections, an unusual case in an election in which the Republicans won back the Senate. McCarthy claimed credit for Benton's defeat.

Tydings and Benton were merely the most notable victims of the Senator from Wisconsin. McCarthy and his counterparts on the House Un-American Activities Committee (HUAC) also helped to destroy the lives and careers of dozens of men and women in all walks of life. Unsupported accusations, followed by subpoenas commanding them to testify before either McCarthy's Permanent Subcommittee on Investigations of the Senate Government Operations Committee or the HUAC, left witnesses squirming under newsreel and television cameras as hostile questioners berated them for refusing to disclose information about their past lives. Some witnesses declared that they had a right under the First Amendment's guarantee of freedom of association not to disclose their past associations with Communist organizations or other organizations on various "subversive" lists. The committees rejected these claims, and they were backed up by the courts. Other witnesses invoked their right not to say anything that might be used against them, a right protected by the Fifth Amendment—but this tactic led to the term *Fifth Amendment Communist* and the unjustifiable suspicion in the minds of Congress and the general public that anyone invoking the Fifth Amendment must have something to hide. A new and ugly word entered the American language—*McCarthyism*, the use of unsupported charges and smear tactics to destroy someone's reputation and career.

Many journalists gave up in frustration trying to pin Senator McCarthy down. The Senator would make a host of charges, like a squid squirting ink, and while the press tried to sort out the facts to find out if the charges had substance, he would jet off in another direction, shooting off more charges. The exasperation of some of McCarthy's colleagues grew to the breaking point. Three Democratic members of

Senator Joseph R. McCarthy (1908—1957) (Republican-Wisconsin), a symbol
of the abuse of Congress's power to investigate, conducted witch-hunts for
communists and "traitors" in government and public life from 1950 to 1954.
McCarthy gestures with a pointer during the 1954 Army-McCarthy hearings;
watching him, hand on head, is Joseph Welch (1890—1960), the Army's
counsel in those hearings. The confrontation between the Senator and the Army
severely damaged McCarthy's credibility and led to his censure by his
exasperated colleagues in December 1954.

his committee resigned in protest at his tactics. When he offered to
make some changes in his procedures, they returned, only to be offended again as McCarthy resumed his usual methods.

One reason for McCarthy's success was that his anti-Communist
campaign coincided with the beginning of American military involvement in Korea. In June 1950, North Korea had invaded South
Korea. The United Nations voted to condemn the action and to send
an international peacekeeping force to the beleaguered peninsula.
President Truman, invoking his authority as Commander-in-Chief,
committed American soldiers to ground combat in Korea as part of
the U.N. effort. Although he did not ask Congress for a declaration of
war, there was little if any resistance to Truman's decision. It was thus
hard to challenge McCarthy's campaigns against alleged Communist
conspiracies at home when American soldiers were being killed re-
sisting Communist aggression abroad.

Many observers believed that McCarthy's reign of terror was designed to propel the Republican Party into the Presidency. With the election of Dwight Eisenhower in 1952, they hoped, the Senator would cease and desist. But McCarthy only stepped up his attacks. President Eisenhower was disgusted but did not reprove McCarthy. In early 1954, McCarthy overreached himself: He took on the U.S. Army, launching investigations into Army decisions to promote servicemen with alleged Communist connections and sympathies. But the Army was not like McCarthy's earlier targets. Secretary of the Army Robert Stevens demanded a chance to confront the Senator and answer his charges. The Army appointed noted Boston attorney Joseph Welch as its counsel. McCarthy and Welch tangled repeatedly from April through June 1954, as the nation watched on television. The American people finally had an in-depth exposure to the Senator's tactics, and they were repelled by what they saw and heard. Joseph Welch became an instant American hero for his insistence on fairness and his unfailing courtesy and willingness to abide by the rules. McCarthy made a fatal misstep aimed straight at Welch: He charged that a lawyer on Welch's staff was a former Communist. Welch, aghast at McCarthy's breach of ground rules that he and McCarthy had helped to frame, demanded of the Senator, "At long last, have you no sense of decency, sir?" The question reverberated throughout the nation, and within six months the Senate answered.

In December 1954, the Senate voted, sixty-seven to twenty-two, to *censure*, or condemn, McCarthy. Vice President Nixon, who had supported McCarthy earlier, now worked with the Senate leadership to handle the McCarthy censure as fairly and smoothly as possible. With his censure, McCarthy faded from respectability. The Democrats succeeded in winning back control of the Senate in the 1954 elections, and as a result McCarthy lost his committee chairmanships. His drinking problem got the upper hand, and in May 1957 the junior Senator from Wisconsin died, alone and forgotten. (One of the members of the committee hearing the censure charges was a freshman Democrat from North Carolina, Samuel J. Ervin, Jr. Twenty years later, while chairing a Senate select committee of his own, Ervin would remember his exposure to McCarthy's tactics.)

The McCarthy affair left a bitter taste in the mouths of Senators and Representatives alike. Doubts grew about the usefulness and appropriateness of televised congressional investigations. Senator Estes Kefauver, a freshman Tennessee Democrat, also had catapulted himself into the headlines in 1950 and 1951 with a series of dramatic investigations into organized crime. Kefauver never made unsubstantiated charges, but many of his colleagues wondered whether grilling reluctant witnesses under harsh television lights was anything more than sensational theatre and a way to grab headlines. In 1952, Speaker of the House Sam Rayburn (Democrat-Texas) barred television, radio, and film coverage of all House committee hearings. After McCarthy's censure, both the House and the Senate adopted stricter rules and procedures governing the conduct of committee investigations and preserving the rights of witnesses. In the late 1950s, the Supreme Court also handed down several decisions on Congress's powers over witnesses in its investigations, building on, but refining, its decisions from the 1920s to take more account of individual rights.

In 1954, nearly a century after the last instance of bloodshed in Congress, the nation was stunned by a terrorist attack on the House of Representatives. As the House was conducting a vote in open session, four gunmen opened fire from the visitors' gallery. As members dove for cover and the Speaker declared the session adjourned, five Representatives fell wounded. A sixth dashed up the stairs to the gallery and overpowered one of the gunmen. The four terrorists were Puerto Rican nationalists. They demanded independence for Puerto Rico, which has been a commonwealth under U.S. authority and protection since the Spanish-American War of 1898. The injured Representatives recovered, and the gunmen were eventually sent to prison.

Republicans lost control of Congress in 1954. Two Democrats from Texas, one a veteran and the other a relative newcomer, thus moved into leadership positions in the House and the Senate.

The quiet, universally respected Sam Rayburn reclaimed the Speakership from Republican Joseph W. Martin of Massachusetts. Rayburn was a different kind of Speaker. He believed in persuasion and reason rather than the force and bluster of earlier Speakers such as "Czar" Reed and "Uncle Joe" Cannon. He held the Speakership more than twice as long as any of his predecessors (1940–1947, 1949–1951, 1955–1961).

No one respected and admired Rayburn more than Lyndon B. Johnson, who had begun his legislative career in the House as a protégé of "Mr. Sam." When Johnson moved over to the Senate in 1948, he kept up his close ties with the Speaker. In 1953, after the death of Republican Senator Robert A. Taft of Ohio gave Democrats a one-vote margin in the Senate, Johnson became the youngest man (at forty-six) ever to hold the office of Senate Majority Leader. Although

*The Democratic leadership of Congress in the late 1950s was a tough, well-organized, professional team of legislators: standing, left to right, Senator George Smathers (Florida) (1913—), Senator Lyndon B. Johnson (Texas) (1908—1973), Senator Hubert H. Humphrey (Minnesota) (1911—1978), Representative John W. McCormack (Massachusetts) (1891—1980), Representative Carl Albert (Oklahoma) (1908—); sitting, left to right, Speaker of the House Sam Rayburn (Texas) (1882—1961), Senator Mike Mansfield (Montana) (1903—).*

more forcefully persuasive than Rayburn—Johnson used hardball tactics and the sheer raw power of his personality to woo or intimidate his colleagues—the new Majority Leader refused to make use of the blatant strong-arm tactics of a bygone era. In addition, he endeared himself to other freshman Senators by revising the Senate's methods of assignment to committees so that new Senators had a better chance of assignment to important ones such as the Foreign Relations or Judiciary Committees rather than having to serve in limbo on such bodies as the Committee on the Post Office. Johnson held this post from 1953 to 1961, when he became Vice President.

Rayburn and Johnson deferred to President Eisenhower in the fields of foreign policy and defense, but in one case, in 1954, they resisted a Presidential initiative. The French were facing defeat in their efforts to suppress a Communist-led independence movement in Vietnam, part of the dwindling French colonial empire. The President was ready to send American airplanes to provide air cover for the French forces besieged in the city of Dienbienphu. Johnson and Rayburn declared their opposition to the proposed measure and managed to avert it. (Johnson's part in this incident is especially ironic in light of American involvement in the Vietnam quagmire during his Presidency a decade later.)

In 1957, the Soviet Union shocked the United States by launching Sputnik I, the first man-made satellite, into Earth orbit. A few months later, the American space program suffered two embarrassing failures to get its first satellite into space. Senator Johnson made space his issue. He challenged the Eisenhower Administration's mild reaction to the Soviet achievement and urged in Congress and in the news media that the United States mount a vigorous space program. Johnson succeeded in his aim. The incident is significant because it shows how Congress can assume initiative in a given area of national policy if—but only if—a President cannot or will not provide that leadership.

Johnson also assumed leadership of the move to enact a civil rights bill in 1957—an ironic role for a Southerner. Virtually every Southern Democratic Senator had opposed civil rights measures since President Truman had attempted to secure the first a decade earlier. The quest for federal protection for civil rights had helped to divide the Democratic Party in 1948, and Southern Senators grew skilled in their use of Senate rules and tactics, such as the filibuster, to block enactment of such measures. It took the wiliness and brilliant political instincts of Lyndon Johnson to ram the 1957 bill through a reluctant Senate. Johnson demonstrated that he had the skills and the commitment to effect policy in the national interest. He became a leading contender for the 1960 Democratic Presidential nomination.

The last two years of the Eisenhower Administration witnessed major changes in Congress. The Democrats solidified their majorities in the House and Senate, and Congress clashed repeatedly with an increasingly conservative President. Both parties were positioning themselves for the 1960 Presidential election.

In the narrowest Presidential election since 1916, the Democrats captured the White House. The victorious candidate was Senator John F. Kennedy of Massachusetts. Not only was Kennedy the youngest man elected to the Presidency, and the first Catholic President, he was the first Senator to win the Presidency since Warren G. Harding in 1920. He had defeated Johnson for the nomination but chose the Texan as his running mate to demonstrate that the party had national support and appeal. The Kennedy-Johnson ticket edged the Republicans' nominees, Vice President Nixon and Henry Cabot Lodge (the son of the Massachusetts Senator who had led opposition to the Treaty of Versailles in 1919).

With the transfer of power from the Eisenhower to the Kennedy Administration, the United States and Congress moved out of the postwar era. The next few years would complete the transition from a generation of politicians molded by the New Deal to a new generation of politicians more skeptical of tradition and deference and more willing to shake things up in order to get things done.

# CHAPTER ELEVEN

# FROM THE
# NEW FRONTIER
# TO WATERGATE

In 1961, the year in which President Kennedy's Administration took office under the slogan "The New Frontier," the character of Senate leadership changed once again. The Democratic majority elected the gentle, soft-spoken Mike Mansfield of Montana its new Majority Leader. Mansfield's scholarly, low-key style was an abrupt change from the expansiveness of Lyndon Johnson. Some Democrats criticized Mansfield as being too weak, too willing to let Senators go their own way. Mansfield retorted that the traditions of the Senate encouraged its members to be independent; he was not going to try to steamroll his colleagues. But under Mansfield's tenure as Majority Leader, the divisions of the Democratic majority into liberals, moderates, and Southern conservatives grew.

The House, too, witnessed its share of difficulties. In his last great battle, Speaker Rayburn challenged the House Rules Committee. The committee's chairman, Representative Howard "Judge" Smith of Virginia, had used the committee's power over the agenda of the House to bottle up legislation that he opposed. Liberals were exasperated by his tactics and in the late 1950s tried to challenge Smith or to break the power of the Rules Committee. Speaker Rayburn headed them off, promising that in the next Congress he would ensure that the committee would no longer act as an obstacle to the work of the House.

The lines were drawn in January 1961. A new Democratic President was relying on the old Speaker (Rayburn was nearly twice Kennedy's age). Rayburn and Smith dueled for weeks in a now-legendary battle over rules, committee size and membership, and votes. Rayburn's goal was to increase the size of the committee; Rayburn would appoint enough liberal Democrats to break the Southern conservatives' hold on the agenda of the House. Republicans cheered on the conservative Democratic chairman. One journalist reported that pressures on both sides were so high that one Representative changed his mind six times during the course of the contest. During the last roll-call vote, the House and the galleries held their collective breath waiting for the tally. By a vote of 217–212, Rayburn prevailed. His defeat of "Judge" Smith was his last major triumph; he died of cancer in November of that year. Rayburn's victory did not solve all of the Administration's problems, for Smith was still chairman of the committee, but his power had been weakened significantly.

The early 1960s were frustrating years for the Kennedy Administration because the President had little success in getting his domestic agenda through Congress. As a result, the President became more and more interested in foreign affairs, where Congress generally deferred to Presidential leadership. The Kennedy Administration never made effective use of its most able and experienced expert on Congress—Vice President Johnson, who languished in frustration and boredom, aching to be consulted. It is still not clear why Kennedy never called on the services of his Vice President, although many observers of the Kennedy-Johnson relationship have cited the mutual distrust between the Vice President and Attorney General Robert F. Kennedy, the President's brother and closest adviser.

During the 1960 campaign, John Kennedy had chided his predecessor, Dwight Eisenhower, for his failure to provide vigorous executive leadership. In 1962, a chastened and reflective President Kennedy met three network news correspondents for a televised conversation about his Presidency and mused that Congress looked different from his end of Pennsylvania Avenue from the way he had seen it when he was in the Senate in the late 1950s.

As the friendly, anti-Communist government of South Vietnam came under increasing pressure from the Communist government of North Vietnam and from a pro-Communist local resistance movement (the Vietcong), President Kennedy decided to continue to honor the Eisenhower Administration's commitment to South Vietnam and to expand American involvement in that conflict. Congress again backed up the President in a foreign-policy initiative. It was the beginning of a massive American commitment that would tear the nation apart before the end of the decade.

With Kennedy's assassination on November 22, 1963, Lyndon Johnson became President. The new Chief Executive appeared before a joint session of Congress and declared, "All I have I would gladly give not to be standing here today. . . . Let us continue." At last Johnson was in a position to use his unsurpassed political skills to push a legislative program through Congress. He repeatedly invoked the murdered Kennedy and reminded the gasping members of the House and Senate, "I'm the only President you've got." Within a year, he had rammed through a legislative agenda, including new and stronger civil rights bills, that Kennedy had tried without success to get enacted. Congress meekly followed the President's lead.

President Johnson confronted the growing American involvement in Vietnam in the summer of 1964. Reports of a clash in international waters off the coast of North Vietnam between an American destroyer and North Vietnamese patrol boats induced Congress to adopt the *Tonkin Gulf Resolution*. It permitted the President "to take all necessary measures to repel any armed attack against the forces of the United States and to prevent further aggression . . . [and] to take all necessary steps, including the use of armed force, to assist any member or protocol state of the Southeast Asia Collective Defense Treaty requesting assistance in defense of its freedom." The House adopted the resolution by a vote of 416–0; the Senate adopted it by a vote of 88–2. President Johnson repeatedly invoked this resolution as the equivalent of a declaration of war authorizing American military involvement in Vietnam.

Congressional opposition to the Vietnam conflict grew, however, as the 1960s dragged on with little sign that the war was accomplishing anything in support of democracy or defense of America's allies. Senators Wayne Morse (Republican-Oregon) and J. William Fulbright (Democrat-Arkansas) took the floor to speak out against the war, and Fulbright's Senate Foreign Relations Committee held televised hearings that cast doubt on the war's aims, legality, and eventual success. Two Democratic Senators—Eugene McCarthy (Minnesota) and Robert F. Kennedy (New York), the former Attorney General—each challenged Johnson for the 1968 Democratic Presidential nomination. When Johnson (realizing that he would lose his bid for renomination) withdrew from the campaign in March 1968, Vice President Hubert H. Humphrey of Minnesota became the Administration's candidate. In a bitter, divisive year that witnessed the assassination of Senator Kennedy on the night of his victory in the California primary and the murder in Memphis, Tennessee, of the Nobel Peace Prize-winning civil rights leader Reverend Martin Luther King, Jr., the Presidential election resulted in a narrow victory for former Vice President Richard M. Nixon, the Republican nominee. Nixon's victory did not manage to break the Democrats' control of either the House or the Senate, however.

Congress dealt in these years with outcroppings of corruption among its members. The former secretary to Lyndon Johnson when he was Majority Leader, Bobby Baker, was indicted and convicted for tax fraud and other violations of the federal corrupt practices laws. Democratic Senator Thomas F. Dodd of Connecticut was censured by his colleagues for conduct "which is contrary to accepted morals, derogates from the public trust expected of a Senator and tends to bring the Senate into disfavor and disrepute." In 1967, the same year as Dodd's censure, the House voted to oust Democratic Representative Adam Clayton Powell of New York for a variety of offenses. In a special election, Powell's constituents returned him to his seat, sympathizing with his claims that the House had acted against him because he was black. He filed suit in federal court challenging his ouster and again won re-election in 1968. In 1969, the Supreme Court ruled that the House had no power to take Powell's seat away from him; later that year, the House voted to fine him $25,000 and strip him of his *seniority*—the increased status and privileges that go with length of service in Congress. Powell was defeated in a 1970 Democratic primary in his district.

The year 1969 witnessed a rebellion against the power of the Speaker of the House. Frail, old Democrat John McCormack of Massachusetts had succeeded the late Sam Rayburn as Speaker in 1961. An insurgent movement among liberal Democratic members challenged McCormack's bid for re-election as Speaker; the rebels backed Democratic Representative Morris K. Udall of Arizona. Udall was defeated, but McCormack got the message and announced that he would retire from the House at the end of his term. (He was succeeded by Representative Carl Albert of Oklahoma.) Again, the traditions of the House, like those of the Senate, were under assault by new members who had different ideas about what Congress should be.

President Nixon was not generally popular and disdained working with Congress. As a result, he suffered significant defeats in key items on his agenda. In 1970, he was unable to get two Supreme Court nominees, Clement Haynsworth and then G. Harrold Carswell, confirmed by the Senate. The Carswell defeat, which was unprecedented in the history of the Senate or of the Court, was due largely to the clear contempt for the Senate that Nixon had demonstrated by picking so unqualified a nominee for the Supreme Court. Other legislative initiatives failed as well. In fact, in late 1970, Congress repealed the Tonkin Gulf Resolution. The Senate also adopted a resolution sponsored by Republican John Sherman Cooper of Kentucky and Democrat Frank Church of Idaho restricting the use of American combat forces in Cambodia, the next-door neighbor of South Vietnam. It was a direct response to the President's unilateral ordering of "incursions" into Cambodia in April 1970 to attack Vietcong bases there. Finally, in 1973, Congress passed the *War Powers Resolution*, an attempt to curb Presidential power over war that had grown beyond restraint since President Truman authorized American participation in the Korean Conflict in 1950. President Nixon vetoed the resolution, but Congress enacted it over his veto. The War Powers Resolution sets up a complex system of required reporting on American military involvement and voting by Congress to approve or reject such involvement; it has not successfully restrained later Presidents, however.

President Nixon's re-election in 1972 gave rise to what seemed at first a comic farce. Five employees of the Committee to Re-Elect the President (CREEP) were arrested in June 1972 during an attempted break-in at the Democratic National Committee headquarters at the Watergate apartment complex in Washington, D.C. The Watergate break-in had little effect on the November election, in which Nixon routed his Democratic opponent, Senator George McGovern of South Dakota, who had unsuccessfully pleaded with the news media to investigate the break-in. When journalists from the *Washington Post* and other news organizations finally dug into the story, Watergate took on larger dimensions and a sinister cast.

In early 1973, the Senate appointed a select committee to investigate the unraveling scandal. Chaired by Democratic Senator Samuel J. Ervin, Jr., of North Carolina, the Watergate committee conducted nationally televised hearings throughout the spring and summer of 1973. It uncovered an extraordinary story of "dirty tricks" designed to eliminate all but the weakest Democratic candidates from the 1972 campaign and, even worse, a conspiracy to obstruct justice in the investigation of the Watergate break-in, which involved the FBI, the CIA, and even the highest levels of government.

President Nixon was forced by early revelations, even before Senator Ervin's committee convened, to accept the resignations of his closest aides, Chief of Staff H. R. Haldeman and Domestic Affairs Adviser John R. Ehrlichman, and of his Attorney General, Richard H. Kleindienst. But these resignations did not end the scandal or the investigations. The discovery that the President had tape-recorded White House conversations, including discussions of the attempt to stage a cover-up of the break-in, provoked the major controversies of the Watergate affair. The President's new Attorney General, Elliot Richardson, had appointed a special prosecutor, Harvard Law School professor Archibald Cox, to conduct an investigation of the case. When Cox insisted on subpoenaing the White House's tape recordings of critical meetings, the President directed the Attorney General to fire him, which Richardson would not do. This demand led to the notorious "Saturday Night Massacre" in October 1973, which cost the two highest officials of the Justice Department their jobs and astonished the nation. The Watergate inquiry took on new momentum. The President was forced to retreat from his harsh stand. A new special prosecutor carried on where Cox had left off. The burgeoning disclosures and discoveries of the various investigations into Watergate led to another series of televised Congressional hearings in the spring and summer of 1974.

The Constitution provides for a process of *impeachment* by which high officials, including the President of the United States, can be tried and removed from office for "Treason, Bribery, or other high Crimes and Misdemeanors." In the modern Congress, the House Judiciary Committee is the place where charges of impeachment are first brought. In July 1974, the committee, led by its chairman, Democratic Representative Peter J. Rodino of New Jersey, conducted formal hearings and debates on the question of impeaching the President of the United States. Not for over a century had an impeachment movement against a President gone this far. Rodino presided over the hearings with dignity and fairness; the members of the committee, Democrats and Republicans, opponents and defenders of the President, generally matched Rodino's high standard. On July 24, 1974, the Supreme Court ruled, eight to zero, against the President's attempts to resist the special prosecutor's subpoena for the White House tape recordings. Three days later, the committee voted, twenty-seven to eleven, to recommend articles of impeachment to the full House.

*The House Judiciary Committee, under the chairmanship of Peter J. Rodino (1909—) (Democrat-New Jersey), debated the impeachment of President Richard M. Nixon in July 1974. The committee voted to send three articles of impeachment to the full House of Representatives; these charges focused on President Nixon's abuses of power and obstruction of justice in the Watergate scandal. Nixon resigned on August 8, after making public damning evidence of his guilt but before the full House could vote on the issue of impeachment. Chairman Rodino is the gray-haired man with glasses in the top row, just under the American flag.*

The special prosecutor turned over further evidence to the House Judiciary Committee as he received it. Within a week, the eleven dissenters had changed their minds and agreed to support the first resolution, charging the President with obstruction of justice in the Watergate case. On August 8, 1974, Richard Nixon bowed to the inevitable and resigned from the Presidency.

The Watergate hearings conducted by the House and the Senate presented substantial evidence of Presidential wrong-doing before the American people. They were a valuable lesson in the ways that the Constitution and the system of government it authorizes are supposed to work. They also restored the dignity and credibility of Congress and diminished the previously unshakable authority of the Presidency.

In the fall of 1973, Vice President Spiro T. Agnew had resigned his office due to charges of alleged wrongdoing having nothing to do with Watergate. President Nixon had named and Congress had confirmed a replacement under the Twenty-fifth Amendment to the Constitution, House Minority Leader Gerald R. Ford of Michigan. When Nixon resigned in August 1974, Vice President Ford became President. His pledge to the nation—"Our long national nightmare is over"—reassured the American people. At last, they hoped, politics would return to normal.

# CHAPTER TWELVE

# THE MODERN CONGRESS

Since the resignation of Richard Nixon, the federal government has continued to experience great stresses and strains, testing the durability of the system of government created by the Constitution. Those who hoped for a resumption of normal politics after Watergate were destined to be disappointed.

The aftereffects of Watergate included select committee investigations by both the House and the Senate of the conduct and abuses of power of American intelligence agencies. But Congress soon found itself challenged to live up to the higher ethical standards resulting from the Watergate scandal:

• Two powerful Democratic chairmen of House committees, Wilbur Mills of Arkansas (chairman of the Ways and Means Committee) and Wayne Hays of Ohio (chairman of the Administration Committee), were toppled from power after revelations of their scandalous private lives.

• The worst case was the FBI's so-called ABSCAM operation. Agents posing as Arab sheiks seeking favorable treatment from members of Congress on immigration matters in exchange for bribes managed to catch six Representatives and one Senator. All seven fell from power soon after the FBI unveiled ABSCAM; they faced criminal charges based on the operation.

• Finally, the House was forced to investigate itself concerning charges arising out of the "Koreagate" scandal, in which South Korean financier Tongsun Park allegedly had bribed several Representatives to vote favorably on aid for South Korea. The investigation ended inconclusively.

These and other scandals involving Congress undid much of the prestige that Congress had acquired for its handling of the Watergate scandal. In the meantime, President Ford had pardoned former President Nixon for his involvement in the Watergate affair. Ford suffered considerable political damage for this gesture. Taken together, these incidents injured the reputation of government and of politicians across the board.

Congress sought to improve its methods of doing business and its image by reforming its systems of assigning members to committees, by revamping the structure and number of committees, and by opening its proceedings to television coverage. The House and then the Senate permitted gavel-to-gavel coverage of their sessions.

Congress's relations with President Ford were not as stormy as they

Collections of the Library of Congress

*Speaker Thomas P. "Tip" O'Neill (1912—) (Democrat-Massachusetts) was one of the last "old-time" national politicians. O'Neill was famous for his candor, his folksy style, his gift for story-telling, and his two laws of politics: "First, all politics is local. Second, it's always nice to be asked."*

had been with President Nixon, but the two branches of government did not work comfortably together. Nor did conditions improve under Ford's successor, Democrat Jimmy Carter of Georgia. Carter had defeated his rivals for the 1976 Democratic Presidential nomination and then the Republican nominee, President Ford, by portraying himself as an outsider, not tainted by the "mess in Washington." But his status as an "outsider" prevented him from working well with Congress, and some of his advisers, the so-called "Georgia Mafia," openly disdained Congress. In response, the new Speaker of the House, Thomas P. "Tip" O'Neill of Massachusetts, sought to defend Congress and to guide the Carter Administration in the proper ways to deal with the national legislature. O'Neill was one of the more effective Speakers of the century, a master of the "old politics" who was uncomfortable with the impatient, scrappy practitioners of the "new politics" who thronged into the House in the late 1970s. O'Neill emulated Sam Rayburn's methods, favoring moderation and persuasion rather than arm-twisting and pressure. O'Neill's counterpart in the Senate was Democratic Majority Leader Robert C. Byrd of West Virginia, another traditional politician who respected the traditions and heritage of the Senate and tried to defend those traditions against younger colleagues of both parties.

President Carter managed to secure Senate ratification of a treaty restoring ultimate control over the Panama Canal to Panama. Its supporters hailed the treaty as a long-overdue redress of a great wrong the United States had committed against Panama; its opponents denounced it as a giveaway of a vital American possession. The President was not so fortunate in his attempts to ratify a strategic arms limitation treaty (SALT) he had negotiated with the Soviet Union. The SALT II treaty built on an earlier accord, the handiwork of President Nixon. But conservative Senators blocked the treaty, hoping for a favorable result in the 1980 Presidential election. They got their wish: President Carter was defeated for re-election by the Republican nominee, former Governor Ronald W. Reagan of California.

Reagan, at sixty-nine the oldest man ever elected to the Presidency, ran as an outsider, as Carter had, but did so far more effectively. He promised to reduce the size of the government, to cut federal spending, to cut taxes, to increase defense spending, and to balance the budget. He was so popular that, for the first time in a generation, the Republicans won control of the Senate.

Reagan's landslide gave him a remarkable political mandate—a mandate given a new lease on life by John W. Hinckley's attempt to assassinate him two months after the inauguration. During his first term in office, the President rammed nearly all of his agenda through a reeling Congress. Only the House, led by Speaker O'Neill, put up resistance to "the Reagan Revolution." But the President's policies did not have the effect that he promised. The budget deficit did not go away; instead, it increased dramatically. The economic recovery caused by the tax cut did not produce the increased revenues that the President had hoped for. And his efforts to cut the federal budget ran into difficulty in both houses of Congress as Representatives and Senators alike balked at cutting popular "entitlement" programs such as Social Security.

The President asserted broad executive authority over foreign policy and defense issues. In October 1983, he ordered American forces into combat on the tiny Caribbean island of Grenada in the West Indies. The President claimed that American citizens (medical students attending a medical school on the island) were in danger from a Marxist coup. When angered members of Congress charged that the President had disregarded the War Powers Resolution of 1973, the President responded by expressing grave doubts about the constitutionality of the measure.

President Reagan easily won a second term in 1984, defeating Democratic nominee (and President Carter's Vice President) Walter F. Mondale. But his second term was more difficult and less successful than his first:

• The 1986 Congressional elections resulted in the return of a Democrat-controlled Senate determined to resist proposals by the Reagan Administration.

• An emboldened Congress overturned the President's vetoes of several key pieces of legislation. His most crushing defeat was Congress's 1988 override (73–24 in the Senate and 292–133 in the House) of the Civil Rights Restoration Act.

• The Senate rejected his nomination of Judge Robert H. Bork to the Supreme Court by the largest margin ever recorded for a vote against a Court nominee. Reagan's next choice, Judge Douglas H. Ginsburg, withdrew his name after allegations surfaced concerning his use of marijuana while he was a professor at Harvard Law School. Not until his third try did the President succeed. Judge Anthony Kennedy of California was unanimously confirmed by the Senate in early 1988.

• Finally, the President's long campaign to support the anti-Communist Nicaraguan rebels, the *contras*, against the Marxist Sandinista government of that country caused him his most serious problems.

Congress refused to fund the *contras* and passed a measure, known as the Boland Amendment, forbidding the government to aid the *contras* with federal funds. Within President Reagan's National Security Council, an operation developed to raise funds for the *contras* from other sources, including arms deals with the hostile nation of Iran. When this scandal broke in late 1986, several congressional committees leaped into the fray. The scattered and disorganized investigations continued into early 1987, when the leadership of Congress agreed to appoint two select committees to hold joint hearings on the matter. The Iran-*contra* investigation continued through the summer and fall of 1987, coinciding with the Bork confirmation controversy and the two-hundredth anniversary of the Constitution. Those hoping for an investigation of the quality of the Watergate hearings of the 1970s were disappointed. (The Iran-*contra* matter is still unresolved at this writing.)

When Speaker O'Neill retired in 1987, he was succeeded by the House Majority Leader, Jim Wright (Democrat-Texas). Wright, a protege of Sam Rayburn and Lyndon B. Johnson, practiced a hard-nosed, vigorous method of leadership. Ambitious and determined, he became a key figure in foreign affairs; he was instrumental in brokering a peace agreement between the government of El Salvador and the country's leftist insurgents, and he forced the Administrations of Ronald Reagan and George Bush to abandon their support of the *contra* rebel movement in Nicaragua. House-watchers suggested that Wright could become one of the great Speakers in congressional history.

But House Republicans fiercely attacked the Speaker, charging that his partisanship made a mockery of House traditions. They maintained that nearly thirty years of unbroken Democratic control of the House caused leading Democrats to treat the Republican minority as an inconvenience to be brushed aside rather than as a group of colleagues.

Majority Leader Thomas Foley (Democrat-Washington), collegial and low-key, was held in high regard by members of both parties. His second-in-command, Tony Coelho (Democrat-California), chaired the House Democratic Campaign Committee (DCCC). Coelho was a talented legislator and a skilled fund-raiser; he had a special knack for tapping the resources of political action committees (PACs), a contrivance by which hundreds of special-interest groups evaded legal limits on campaign contributions.

New leaders also took command in the Senate. In December 1988, Robert C. Byrd of West Virginia became Senate President *pro tempore*, and George J. Mitchell (Democrat-Maine) succeeded Byrd as Majority Leader. A thoughtful former federal judge, Mitchell had stood up to Oliver North during the Iran-*contra* hearings, defending the ideals of the rule of law and civilian supremacy over the military.

In 1989, however, Congress was rocked by a series of scandals that brought down some of its leaders and all but destroyed public confidence in the institution. Speaker Wright's career was shattered by evidence that he had abused his office for personal gain. The allegations seemed trivial—he had taken gifts from a longtime business associate with business before the government and had made a lucrative royalty deal on his book that got around House limits on outside income. But these petty abuses formed a pattern of arrogance and greed.

Wright's conduct became a partisan issue in Republican hands, but many Democrats, some of whom resented the Speaker's hard-driving methods, failed to rally behind him. In June 1989, Wright resigned from the Speakership and the House; he was the first Speaker to resign due to ethical problems.

Wright's departure was only the first injury that Congress suffered during the One Hundred First Congress (1989–1991). Issues that had been festering for years finally exploded into public view; the most serious of these was the savings and loan crisis.

In the 1970s and 1980s, many critics of the federal government promoted *deregulation*—the doctrine that too many laws and rules strangled the economy and prevented prosperity. As part of the push for deregulation, Congress—and the Carter and Reagan Administrations—crafted a series of bills deregulating the savings and loan industry.

Savings and loan institutions (also known as "thrifts" or "S&Ls") started in the early twentieth century as cooperative businesses. They would lend depositors' money to borrowers who wanted to buy or build new homes; these loans would generate profits for the S&L, new houses for the borrowers, and jobs for the construction industry. After the Great Depression, the federal government enacted deposit insurance laws protecting depositors in commercial banks and S&Ls; depositors could recover their money, up to a set limit, even if the bank or S&L went bankrupt.

But the late 1970s were a tough time for thrifts, and economists argued that the S&L regulations would destroy the thrift industry unless relaxed. There was truth in these arguments, but the deregulation measures became law mostly because of political pressure by lobbyists who contributed tens of thousands of dollars to the campaign funds of incumbent Senators and Representatives. Tony Coelho, head of the DCCC, was an integral part of the flow of campaign money, though he was personally honest. Several of his colleagues were not—most notably Fernand St Germain (Democrat-Rhode Island), then-chair of the House Banking Committee and the principal sponsor of the key deregulation measure, who was instrumental in deflecting public and government attention from the growing problems of the thrift industry. (In 1988, as the S&L crisis exploded in the news media, St Germain lost his House seat.)

Congress abolished many requirements that S&Ls formerly had to meet, made it easier to start an S&L, and more than tripled (to $100,000) the insurance limit on S&L accounts. Congress and the Reagan Administration also cut the resources of the federal agencies responsible for regulating the industry, the Home Loan Bank Board and the Federal Savings and Loan Insurance Corporation (FSLIC). FSLIC had fewer bank examiners to watch over ever more S&Ls.

The thrift industry went wild in the 1980s. Some thrifts became bloated financial behemoths; many made huge loans to shaky real estate projects and investments in corporate takeover battles far exceeding their ability to cover the potential losses. Officials of some of the largest thrifts spent S&L funds lavishly on themselves and their friends—including their friends in the House and the Senate. Even if the S&Ls got into financial trouble, they reasoned, FSLIC would pick up the tab.

In 1988, financial journalists began to notice a pattern of spectacular S&L failures. They dug into the story, and uncovered a complex web of shaky deals, imprudent loans, bad investments, and huge campaign contributions. They also discovered that FSLIC could not keep up with the mounting S&L losses, and that some government regulators continued to deny that a problem even existed.

These reports, which politicians at first dismissed as alarmist, turned out to be understatements. By 1989, it had become clear that S&L deregulation had not given rise to prosperity or saved the thrift industry; rather, deregulation had become a blank check that speculators and financial pirates had used to create a financial catastrophe. The nation's taxpayers would have to assume the cost.

The scandal grew, implicating several Senators and Representatives. Because of the sudden departure of Jim Wright, and Thomas Foley's promotion to the Speakership, public attention focused on Tony Coelho, who was the front-runner to succeed Foley as Majority

Leader but was tainted by his connections with S&L owners who gave lavishly to Democratic congressional campaigns. Even though Coelho had tried to take the lead in drafting laws to reform congressional campaign finance, he found that he could not survive the public firestorm of criticism directed at Congressional "fat cats." In June 1989, he resigned from the House. Richard J. Gephardt (Democrat-Missouri), who had unsuccessfully sought the 1988 Democratic Presidential nomination, became the new Majority Leader.

The S&L crisis refused to go away. Estimates of the cost of the S&L scandal exceeded $100-billion. That awesome figure combined with media exposures of free-wheeling, big-spending S&L magnates to create the spectacle of a runaway Congress. The most famous case that damaged public confidence in Congress revolved around Charles Keating, chairman of the Lincoln Savings & Loan of Irvine, California, and the nation's foremost S&L speculator. Five Senators—dubbed the "Keating Five" by the news media—had hob-nobbed with, received campaign contributions from, and done favors for Keating—including intervening with federal investigators on his behalf. The Senate's investigation exonerated Senator John McCain (Republican-Arizona) and slapped the wrists of John Glenn (Democrat-Ohio), Dennis DeConcini (Democrat-Arizona), Donald Riegle (Democrat-Michigan), and Alan Cranston (Democrat-California). Glenn, DeConcini, and Riegle weathered the storm of public criticism; Cranston retired from the Senate in 1992.

Even without the fallout from the S&L scandal, the American people had reason to be dissatisfied with "the mess in Washington." "Gridlock"—the popular term for the repeated deadlocks between an executive branch dominated by the Republicans and a legislative branch controlled by the Democrats—seemed to elevate partisan politics above the needs of the nation. Presidents Reagan and Bush regularly used their vetoes to block proposed domestic legislation, and Congress retaliated by burying bills proposed by the Reagan and Bush Administrations. The budget deadlocks of the 1980s persisted into the 1990s, and deficits continued to spiral upward. As politicians pointed fingers at one another, the public grew tired of them all.

In late 1991, as the Senate Judiciary Committee held hearings on the nomination of Judge Clarence Thomas to the U.S. Supreme Court, many citizens were stunned by the spectacle of a group of middle-aged white men trying to sort out the truth of the sexual-harassment charges brought by a black woman, Professor Anita Hill, against a black man, Justice-designate Thomas. Many women were

*Many televised congressional hearings have attracted national attention, but few were so controversial as the fall 1991 Senate Judiciary Committee hearings on the testimony of Professor Anita Hill (1956—) of the University of Oklahoma Law School against the nomination of Judge Clarence Thomas (1948—) to the United States Supreme Court. This photograph shows Professor Hill testifying in the committee's second round of hearings.*

incensed that, although they made up more than fifty percent of the population, they had only two percent of the seats in the Senate; they grew even angrier as they realized that the Senators "just didn't get it."

In early 1992, public discontent with Congress exploded yet again when a mini-scandal exposed the sloppy management of the "bank" maintained by the House of Representatives for its members. Over two hundred Representatives had "bounced" checks drawn on the House credit union. Some had blundered only a few times for small amounts, due to the inefficiency of the bank's administrators. But others had bounced hundreds of checks equaling or exceeding their annual salaries. The scandal touched off a spasm of public anger at "the people's branch." Several of the major offenders in the House of Representatives were defeated for re-election. Others recognized the handwriting on the wall and announced their retirement.

The House bank scandal caused citizens to take a new, hard look at the politicians whom they had elected and re-elected. As Senators and Representatives racked up careers of two, three, or even four decades, the people they were supposed to represent began to wonder whether the nation's lawmakers were too removed from the folks back home, too comfortable and secure, and too cozy with the capital's teeming corps of lobbyists and influence-peddlers.

Talk surfaced of amending the Constitution to impose limits on the number of years that someone could serve in Congress. Some journalists predicted that the House bank scandal would spur the movement to adopt a term-limit amendment. President Bush pointed out that it seemed unfair to impose an eight-year term limit on Presidents (codified in the Twenty-second Amendment) when Representatives and Senators could serve for thirty, forty, or even fifty years. Voters in fourteen states approved proposed term-limit measures in 1992; these proposals would impose term limits as matters of state election law. But many scholars argue that nothing short of a constitutional amendment can impose valid term limits on members of Congress.

Opponents of term-limit measures point out that these proposals seduce voters into evading their responsibilities. The surest cure for an incumbent staying in office too long, they maintain, is for the voters to throw him or her out. In a complex system which takes years to understand, they ask, what point is there in forcing a legislator to retire just as he or she has mastered the job? Even if the problem is that professional politicians are out of touch with their constituents, it is no solution to exchange one crew of professionals for another.

One other event in 1992 showed how frustrated the American voters were with Congress, the institution that is supposed to represent them. One of the twelve constitutional amendments proposed by Congress in 1789 barred any measure changing congressional pay from taking effect until after the next congressional election. Ten of the twelve proposals were ratified and became the Bill of Rights, but the salary proposal sat neglected for eighty-four years. In 1873, Congress passed the "salary grab" act, which gave all Representatives and Senators a fifty-percent pay increase (from $5,000 to $7,500 per year) and made the increase retroactive to 1871, giving each Senator and Representative a $5,000 windfall. Public anger forced Congress to repeal the salary grab act. The Ohio legislature ratified the 1789 amendment as a key part of its protest against the salary grab. Over a century later, in 1978, another Congressional pay increase spurred the Wyoming legislature to ratify the 1789 amendment.

In 1982, a college student at the University of Texas, Gregory

*Carol Moseley Braun (1947— ) (Democrat-Illinois) was Recorder of Cook*
*County at the time of the Thomas-Hill hearings. Outraged by the Senate's*
*treatment of Anita Hill and the vote to confirm Thomas, Braun ran against*
*incumbent Senator Alan Dixon for the Democratic Senatorial nomination. Her*
*upset victory made her a hero to millions of American women. On October 20,*
*1992, Braun appeared at a campaign rally in Chicago with Democratic*
*Presidential nominee Governor Bill Clinton (1946— ) (left) and his running-*
*mate, Senator Al Gore (1948— ). On November 3, Braun became the first*
*African-American woman ever to be elected to the United States Senate.*

Watson, wrote a term paper about the 1789 amendment. He argued
that it was still validly before the states and urged that it be adopted.
(He got a C on his paper, because his instructor told him that the
amendment never would be revived.) Watson began a lonely quest to
persuade state legislators to act on the amendment. By May 1992, ten
years after he wrote his paper, thirty-seven of the states had voted to
ratify the amendment. On May 7, Michigan ratified the amendment,
making it the Twenty-seventh Amendment to the Constitution; New
Jersey, Illinois, and California followed suit. Nervous members of
Congress realized that the success of the Amendment was yet another
sign of public fury.

The 1992 elections sent a mixed message to Congress. Voters
elected 110 new Representatives (the greatest number since the 118
elected in 1948) and 13 new Senators, but few Congressional incum-

bents were defeated, despite analysts' predictions of unprecedented voter anger against "politics as usual." The One Hundred Third Congress (1993–1995) numbered in its ranks nearly double the number of women, African-American, and Hispanic lawmakers present in the One Hundred Second Congress (1991–1993).

Of ten women running for Senate seats, only four (all Democrats) prevailed—Dianne Feinstein and Barbara Boxer in California, Patty Murray in Washington, and Carol Moseley Braun in Illinois. Braun, the first African-American woman to be elected to the Senate and the first African-American Senator since Edward Brooke (Republican-Massachusetts) lost a re-election bid in 1978, had defeated Democratic incumbent Alan Dixon in a primary campaign focused on Dixon's vote to confirm Clarence Thomas. Braun, Boxer, Feinstein, and Murray raised the total number of women in the Senate from two to six.

The One Hundred Second Congress passed into history nicknamed the "Gridlock Congress" by The New York Times. The leaders of the One Hundred Third Congress vowed that they were aware that the electorate, and the new Clinton Administration, would not tolerate continued stalemate between the executive and legislative branches. The question remained: Could Congress forge a consensus behind vital measures, or would Congress continue to be held hostage by a combination of special-interest pressure and the desperate need to raise campaign funds?

# CONCLUSION:

# WHAT TO DO
# ABOUT CONGRESS?

As the form of government authorized by the Constitution completed its first two hundred years, several proposals circulated for restructuring the government of the United States.

Some call for the adoption of a *parliamentary* system of government, like that of Great Britain or Canada. Under this system, the national legislature would be the central institution of government. Political parties would compete to win a majority of seats in the national legislature, and the leaders of the majority party would become the Prime Minister and other Ministers of the government. If the government is put to the test in the legislature—what is called a *vote of confidence*—and loses, the leaders then resign their executive offices, and a new election is held. A separately elected executive, such as a President, would serve the same function as the monarch does in Great Britain: to perform ceremonial tasks and responsibilities, to accept the resignation of a toppled Prime Minister, and to call upon the leader of the victorious party in a parliamentary election to form a new administration. This proposal is popular with many political scientists who favor ways to make the political parties stronger in our system of government. Most Americans, however, are not ready for such a sweeping measure.

Less extreme proposals include amendments to:

• Permit former Presidents and Cabinet members to sit as nonvoting Senators and to take part in debate so that the nation can still profit from their knowledge and experience;

• Permit Cabinet members to sit in either the House or the Senate so that they are able and required to engage with Congress in debate of Administration policy;

• Extend the term of Representatives from two to four years and schedule House elections to coincide with Presidential elections, strengthening the parties in the constitutional system.

None of these three proposals has won significant support outside the scholarly community so far.

Of the three branches of government created by the Constitution, Congress has the lowest reputation and the most uncertain future. Although buffeted by passionate criticism of some of its decisions, the Supreme Court enjoys the respect of most Americans. And, despite charges growing out of the Iran-*contra* affair, the Presidency has managed to regain much of the prestige it lost as a result of the Watergate scandals. Congress, on the other hand, still suffers from public scorn —when, indeed, the public consents to think about Congress at all.

What are the causes of the low public opinion of Congress? As we suggested at the beginning of this part, one reason may be the public's growing impatience with and lack of understanding of politics—the bargaining and horse-trading and compromising out of which public policies and legislation emerge. Of the three branches of our government, Congress is the most clearly and unavoidably political. The Supreme Court is a legal institution; most people do not think of it as political. And it has long been a favorite tactic of Presidents to claim that they are speaking for the general interest, the common good, and not being political. Congress has no choice in the matter.

Congress could recover its lost authority—if the American people learn once again to accept that the Constitution divides the powers and responsibilities of government among three branches: the legislative, the executive, and the judiciary. Congress is a key part of that delicately-balanced structure.

Congress does not have a monopoly on the shaping of government policy; that became clear in the first decade of its existence. But Congress is the only institution of our government where representatives of different states, different sections of the country, different economic and cultural and ethnic and racial interests can come together and discuss what policies would be best for the nation as a whole. Congress is the only part of our government that permits— even demands—wide-ranging debate over how government policies are to be framed and how they are to be carried out.

Many people express impatience with the slowness of Congress, with its members' obsession with politics and their inability to get things done. But public policy is not made instantly. It is not like fast food or television commercials, which do their job quickly and leave no trace behind. Public policy is made slowly, often with great care. The compromises and uncertainties of what Congress does are necessary, in part, to make certain that it does its job well.

Today *politics* is a dirty word for most Americans. But politics is the only successful way that human beings have found to make sure that government performs its role without endangering the rights of individuals. It may be slow, it may be boring, it may sometimes even be ugly or depressing—but politics is central to the way that Americans govern themselves.

Perhaps the only way that Congress will become an institution as deserving of respect as the Presidency and the Supreme Court is for the American people to rediscover the need for—and the virtues of— politics.

# THE PRESIDENCY

The executive Power shall be vested in a President of the United States of America.

—Constitution of the United States
Article II, Section 1

*The Presidency*

For Kathleen Spencer and Nathan Spencer . . . future leaders of the rising generation.

R.B.B.

*The White House, the home of Presidents of the United States since 1800, is a symbol of national power and authority. This 1947 photograph by Hirst Milhollen shows the building's South Front. The balcony was added during the Truman Administration's renovations of the structure.*

# CHAPTER ONE

# IN THE SHADOW
# OF TWO GEORGES:
# THE BIRTH
# OF THE PRESIDENCY

For more than two hundred years, Presidents of the United States have sworn the oath of office set forth in the Constitution—the same oath that George Washington took when he became the first President in 1789.

Americans take the Presidency for granted. One political scientist wrote in the 1950s that most children know only two persons in government—the police officer on the corner and the President of the United States. Even when we grow up, we think of the President as the living symbol of our government, the central figure in our public life.

People think of the President as the most powerful person in the United States, and even in the world. They put their faith in the President and are slow to withdraw that faith even when the President is not up to the job. Some scholars even suggest that Americans expect more of the Presidency than any person or institution can deliver.

It was not always this way. In fact, two hundred years ago, the American people debated whether we needed a President at all. To understand the Presidency, we have to go back to the beginnings of the office to see what ideas, fears, hopes, and doubts shaped it.

Collections of the Library of Congress

*The Pennsylvania State House (known affectionately as Independence Hall) appears here in one of the famous series of engravings of Philadelphia made in 1799–1800 by William Russell Birch and his son, Thomas Birch. In 1787, the Federal Convention drafted the Constitution here; one of the principal features of the new plan of government was an independent chief executive, the President of the United States.*

The Presidency was invented in the Assembly Room of the Pennsylvania State House—the building we now call Independence Hall —in Philadelphia in the spring and summer of 1787. Its inventors were a few dozen men from twelve of the thirteen original states, the delegates to the Federal Convention. (Rhode Island did not send delegates to the Convention.) These men thought long and hard about the troubles facing the new nation. Their job was to frame a document creating a new form of government for the United States of America. As they argued and scribbled and pondered, the delegates worried most about *executive power*. (An *executive* is a person in an organization, such as a government, who has the authority to make sure that things get done.) Every form of government that the delegates to the Convention knew of had one person or a group of persons who exercised this executive power. What kind of executive was right for the United States?

The delegates knew their history. Several of them had spent another difficult spring and summer in that same room eleven years earlier, in 1776. They had been among the delegates to the Second Continental Congress, the group that had declared America's independence from Great Britain—a key step in the American Revolution. Many of the reasons for the American Revolution had to do with executive power and with abuses of that power. The delegates remembered that when their states were British colonies, the royal governors (chief executives appointed by the King far away in London) for no good reason had rejected, or vetoed, laws passed by the colonial legislatures. They also remembered that, when Parliament declared that it had the right to tax the colonists even though they were not represented in Parliament, King George III and his advisers had not supported the colonists. George III had ignored every one of their appeals to him to defend their rights. When Thomas Jefferson drafted the Declaration of Independence, he made George III the villain—and the Continental Congress agreed with him. The shadow of George III hung over the Federal Convention.

The delegates also knew about the new states' experiments in government. Generally, the new state constitutions adopted between 1776 and 1780 had cut back on executive power. One state, Pennsylvania, had even done away with an independent, one-person executive; its constitution set up a Supreme Executive Council under the thumb of the state's legislature. Most of the other states had a single executive, called a governor, but the governors were usually chosen by the legislatures and could be fired by the legislatures if they became too independent. As did the Second Continental Congress, the states' constitution-makers thought of George III as the villain.

Some Americans disagreed with this fear of executive power. John Adams of Massachusetts, a great lawyer and student of government, argued that a single executive was a necessary part of a government—if the government had built into it a system of separation of powers and checks and balances to make sure that the executive did not become a tyrant. When Adams wrote the first draft of the Massachusetts constitution of 1780, he put these ideas into practice. The state's governor would be elected by the people. He would have the power to veto laws passed by the legislature. He would command the armed forces of the state. He would have the power to appoint other state government officials, such as department heads and judges. A few other states, such as New York, adopted similar constitutions. The delegates to the Federal Convention knew about Adams's ideas and made use of them. (Adams himself was three thousand miles away, serving in London as the first American Minister to Great Britain.)

Adams's ideas had not shaped the new nation's first charter of government, the Articles of Confederation. Written in 1777 and adopted by the thirteenth and last state, Maryland, in 1781, the Articles of Confederation created only one institution of government, the Confederation Congress. This body had a president, but he was nothing like the President of the United States we know today, for he had almost no power.

The Articles of Confederation were too weak to work as a system of government. After years of frustration, the Confederation Congress and the state legislatures agreed that something had to be done. George Washington of Virginia, the retired Commander-in-Chief of the Continental Army and the most revered man in the nation, put it best in a private letter: "We are fast verging to anarchy and confusion!" And so the Confederation Congress authorized a convention to think about how to revise the Articles, and the legislatures of twelve states chose delegates to go to Philadelphia in the late spring of 1787.

One of the first things that the delegates decided was that revising the Articles would not be enough. They would have to start from the beginning; a whole new charter of government was needed. This new form of government should be responsible to the People of the United States. It should have the power to deal with national problems and to protect national interests. It should have all three elements of a fully-organized system of government: a legislature, to make laws; an executive, to enforce the laws; and a judiciary, or court system, to settle disputes under the laws and interpret the laws.

The delegates decided these general issues quickly and with little argument. They spent most of their time and energy figuring out how each part of the system should work. They worried most of all about the executive. Their blueprint, the Virginia Plan drafted by James Madison, was silent on how the executive might be chosen or how many persons should make up the executive. When James Wilson of Pennsylvania suggested that there should be one chief executive, some delegates charged that Wilson was planting a seed that could grow into a monarchy. Other delegates disagreed, pointing out that the state governors had not become kings or tyrants. They reminded their colleagues that the Confederation could not pull itself together and speak with one voice for American interests. Surely the answer to this problem would be a one-man chief executive. Finally, the delegates voted in favor of a one-man chief executive, and they never looked back.

During the debate on the executive, the Convention's president, George Washington, looked on silently. Washington was one of seven Virginia delegates to the Convention, but Americans everywhere thought that he was their greatest man. He was honorable, honest, and able. He had led the Continental Army with dignity and resolve through the darkest days of the Revolution to victory and independence. He had rejected many attempts to make him king of America. At the war's end, in December 1783, he had retired from public life to Mount Vernon, his beloved plantation on the Potomac River. He had gone to Philadelphia and put at risk his "harvest of glory" only because he believed that the problems facing the new nation were so great that they might destroy the success of the Revolution. He owed a duty to his country. His fellow delegates unanimously had elected him the Convention's president, and he justified their faith in him.

Washington must have known that the other delegates were looking at him while they discussed the chief executive—which they decided to call the President of the United States. He must have known that he almost certainly would be the first man to fill that office if the charter the delegates were drafting won the support of the people. And he must have known that, because the delegates trusted him, they were willing to take a gamble or two as they shaped the Presidency.

By September 17, 1787, the Constitution was finished, and thirty-nine of the forty-two delegates present signed it, led by George Washington. As Washington pored over the Constitution, he may well have read Article II with special care. Article II created the Presidency.

The President would be chosen for a term of four years by specially-selected officials called *presidential electors*. The states would pick the electors (some states used their legislatures; others, such as Connecticut, relied on the people). The electors would vote for two men, at least one of whom could not be from their home state. A joint session of the House and the Senate would meet to count these *electoral votes*. The candidate with the most votes would become President, and the candidate with the second-highest number of votes would become Vice President. The Vice President would preside over the Senate and would take over for the President if the President should die, resign, or be removed from office.

The President's powers were not clearly defined. He would be pitted against the other two branches of government. He did have the power to appoint officers of government and federal judges—but the Senate had to approve his appointments. He could veto bills passed by Congress—but Congress could overturn his veto by a two-thirds vote of both the House of Representatives and the Senate. If he committed "treason, bribery, or other High Crimes and Misdemeanors," the House could vote to *impeach* him (file formal charges against him); the Senate would try him on those charges and remove him from office by a two-thirds vote if they found him guilty. Still, the office of President of the United States had the potential to be what the holder of the office made of it. This potential was the result of the shadow of George Washington.

The delegates had managed to find a middle road between the two Georges: They were willing, by and large, to trust the President, but they made sure that there were ways to limit his power and stop him in his tracks if he abused that power.

After the Federal Convention adjourned, a special messenger carried the Constitution by stagecoach to New York City, where the Confederation Congress was meeting. The Convention had adopted a special procedure for adopting the proposed new charter of government: Each state would hold elections for a special convention. These conventions would then vote whether to *ratify*, or adopt, the Constitution. If nine states' conventions ratified it, it would replace the Articles of Confederation.

After nearly a year of politicking and controversy, eleven states' conventions had adopted the Constitution. (The last two, North Carolina and Rhode Island, voted to ratify it in 1789 and 1790, respectively, after the charter had gone into effect.) During the ratification controversy, the Constitution's opponents, the Anti-Federalists, had charged that the President might become a tyrant like George III. The Constitution's supporters, the Federalists, answered that George Washington supported the Constitution and hinted that he would be the first President. They also argued that Congress and the judiciary would keep the President in line. The President, they said, was a necessary part of the active and vigorous national government the United States needed to stay free and independent.

By April 6, 1789, the Constitution was beginning its work as the new charter of government of the United States. The people had elected members of the House of Representatives. The state legislatures had chosen Senators and Presidential electors. Now, in their first joint session, the House and the Senate waited as the electoral votes were counted. To nobody's surprise, George Washington was the unanimous first choice for President, with all sixty-nine electoral votes. John Adams had only thirty-four of sixty-nine votes, but as the clear second-place candidate, he was the first Vice President. Congress sent messengers to Virginia and Massachusetts, respectively, to inform Washington and Adams of their election.

Washington was not pleased by the news. He knew that his election had been certain——even though in this first Presidential "contest" there were no official candidates and no active campaigns for office. He wrote, "My feelings upon assuming this office are not unlike those of a culprit going to the place of execution." He knew that he was about to assume a crushing burden. Everything he did or did not do—every statement, every act, every failure to act—would set a precedent for everyone who filled the office of President after him. He was about to lead his country into unexplored territory.

Washington was one of the richest men in the United States, but he had so little cash on hand that he had to borrow money to finance his trip to the inauguration in New York City, the nation's first capital. He was greeted by cheering crowds every step of his journey north. His arrival in New York City on April 23, 1789, was marked by a thunderous demonstration of the love, trust, and support of the American people. (John Adams had arrived more quietly a few days before and on April 21 had been sworn in as the Vice President.) A week of ceremonies and preparations led up to the first Presidential inauguration, on April 30, 1789.

Chancellor Robert R. Livingston of New York, one of that state's highest judges, swore in the new President. (There were no federal judges yet because Congress had not yet written the law setting up the federal courts.) The ceremony took place on the balcony of Federal Hall, the new capitol of the United States. A huge crowd of people watched, expectant and proud, at the corner of Wall Street and Broad Street. Washington took pains to give the right impression in his first public appearance as President. He refused to wear his army uniform, choosing instead a suit of brown American-made broadcloth to show his support for American industry. At the last moment, the officials on the balcony of Federal Hall realized that there was no Bible on hand for the ceremony. A messenger hurried around the corner to a Masonic lodge to borrow its Bible. After the grave and composed

Washington took the oath, every church bell in New York City pealed forth. Chancellor Livingston shouted: "God save George Washington, President of the United States!" The people cheered and threw their hats and bouquets of flowers into the air.

Inside Federal Hall, Washington delivered his Inaugural Address to a joint session of the House and the Senate. But, to the surprise of the new First Congress, the man who had braved cannon fire and battle in a long and distinguished military career read his speech in a trembling voice and with shaking hands. One Pennsylvania Senator, William Maclay, wrote in his diary that he was crushed that his hero "was not first in everything."

The glorious display of fireworks that evening, the finest ever seen in America, dispelled the Senators' and Representatives' surprise at Washington's nervousness. Everyone felt pride that the great American experiment of self-government was under way.

# CHAPTER TWO

# PARTY POLITICS AND IMPARTIAL PRESIDENTS: FROM GEORGE WASHINGTON TO JOHN QUINCY ADAMS

Professor Ralph Ketcham, a leading expert on the first four decades of the Presidency, has shown that our first six Presidents believed that a President should be President of all the people. He should not be associated with any special group, political party, or interest. He should try to govern the country in the national interest and for the general good.

George Washington took great care to act as an impartial, nonpartisan President. He was careful to defer to Congress. He did not propose legislation—that was the job of Congress. Once Congress passed laws creating the departments of government (State, Treasury, and War), the President's aides worked with Congress to make policy. Washington merely kept an eye on the process. His job, as he saw it, was to carry out the will of Congress, to enforce the laws, to oversee the running of the government, to act as the symbol of the nation, and to uphold the values of the Constitution. Washington took great pains to carry out these tasks with care and good judgment.

The President knew that he was not a brilliant man, but he knew who the brilliant men were, and he brought them into the government. He worked closely with Representative James Madison of Virginia. He relied on his longtime friend and wartime aide Secretary of the Treasury Alexander Hamilton of New York, Secretary of War Henry Knox of Massachusetts, and two more of his fellow Virginians —Thomas Jefferson, the Secretary of State, and Edmund Randolph, the young, able, but erratic Attorney General. These four men made up the President's *Cabinet*—a term borrowed from British politics of the period to mean the President's leading advisers. Washington also named his old friend John Jay of New York to be the first Chief Justice of the United States and took great pains in naming the other federal judges as well.

In choosing federal officials, from the highest post to the lowest, the President used three rules of thumb: He wanted the best-qualified candidates; he wanted supporters of the Constitution in the ratification controversy; and he wanted geographical balance so that no one could say that any state or region dominated the new government.

Washington pondered issues of policy, requested reports and opinions from his principal advisers, and gathered advice from as many sources as possible before making up his mind. Jefferson declared, long after Washington's death in 1799, that the President's judgment "was slow in operation, but none was ever sounder."

All these men, not just President Washington, were operating "in a wilderness without a path to guide us," as James Madison complained. There were times when they simply did not know what to do. At one point in his first months as Chief Executive, Washington appeared in person before the Senate to lay a treaty before them and seek their advice and consent. The embarrassed Senators sat silently for a while, then asked the President if they could consider the matter and send him their answer. Washington stalked from the chamber, furious and humiliated, and told his secretary, Tobias Lear, that he would never go back there again.

Similarly, in 1793, Washington and Jefferson tried to get advice from the Justices of the Supreme Court about whether certain measures to protect American neutrality during a brewing European war would be constitutional, but Chief Justice Jay and his colleagues respectfully refused. They explained that the Constitution permitted the federal courts only to give opinions on actual disputes, not to give advice. In this way, feeling things out step by step and making an occasional mistake, the Washington Administration reshaped American politics to fit within the framework of the Constitution.

One thing that nobody expected—not Washington nor any of his advisers nor anyone else in American politics—was the development of institutions that we now take for granted as an essential part of our system of government: political parties. Most politicians in this period believed that they should discuss issues of policy together to achieve what was best for the nation as a whole. They believed that political parties were selfish groups of people who wanted to advance themselves and not the common good. But different groups had different ideas of what the common good was, and as a result the nation's first political parties came into being.

Two issues shaped the first political parties under the Constitution. The first was the dispute over the economic policies advocated by Treasury Secretary Hamilton. Hamilton was trying to solve the problem of the huge federal and state debts left over from the Revolution. His complex and daring proposals were designed to give the new nation a stable currency, to systematize the various debts crushing the economy, and to give a badly needed boost to American commercial and manufacturing interests. But his critics, led by Madison and Jefferson, charged that Hamilton was favoring the wealthy Eastern interests at the expense of the rest of the nation. They said that he was bending the Constitution out of shape in order to make the national government more powerful. In addition, they claimed, manufacturing and commerce were fine for Europe, but farming was the only fit way of life for Americans who wanted to preserve their freedoms.

The other catalyst of parties was foreign policy—specifically, American reactions to the French Revolution that had begun in 1789 and toppled King Louis XVI. The crowned heads of Europe soon led their nations into war against the revolutionary French government. Many Americans believed that the overthrow of the French monarchy and nobility was only the first outbreak of a worldwide revolutionary movement that would result in government by the people in every nation on earth. Jefferson, Madison, and their allies welcomed this possibility. They argued that the United States should support the French, in part because of the 1778 treaty between the United States and France that had resulted in decisive French military aid to the American revolution. Hamilton, John Adams, John Jay, and those who agreed with them feared that revolutionary zeal might overthrow good governments as well as bad. They believed that Great Britain, which had been the new nation's foe during the Revolution, was leading the forces of civilization against disorder. And President Washington worried that the United States was still too weak to risk getting pulled into what was becoming a world war. For this reason, in 1793 the President proclaimed that the United States would be neutral as to the war raging in Europe.

The battle lines were drawn. If you opposed the French Revolution or favored neutrality, supported Hamilton, and favored a strong national government, you were a Federalist. (These Federalists were different from the Federalists of 1787–1788, who had supported the Constitution during the ratification controversy.) If you supported the French Revolution, opposed Hamilton, and favored limiting the powers of the national government, you were a Republican.

Parties were becoming central to American politics, and President Washington was disheartened by this development. In the spring of 1792, as the government was settling into its quarters in Philadelphia and the nation's second Presidential election approached, he determined to retire. Divided on most other issues, Jefferson and Hamilton agreed that it was vital for the President to continue in office. Washington reluctantly gave in to their pleas. The Electoral College once again elected him unanimously, but he took no joy in winning another four years of holding the nation together.

On the home front, Washington and Hamilton were confronted with a direct challenge to the power of the United States. Farmers in western Pennsylvania refused to pay the federal tax on whiskey adopted as part of Hamilton's financial policies. They depended on distilling whiskey from their surplus grain to make ends meet and resented a tax that would cut back on their profits. Now they were taking up their guns to resist federal agents who had been sent into Pennsylvania to collect the whiskey tax. Hamilton was outraged by the farmers' defiance of federal authority. He persuaded the President that drastic measures were called for. A 13,000-man army composed of militia from four states was called together on Presidential authority, and President Washington donned his uniform and in his constitutional role of Commander-in-Chief took the field to command this army to crush the "Whiskey Rebellion." The show of force worked, and the "rebels" melted away. But Republicans were alarmed, fearing that this army would be used to suppress them as well. Although the army quickly disbanded after the rebellion's end, Republicans remembered and resented the President's resort to force.

By 1796, Washington was in his mid-sixties and so tired and disgusted with politics that he was adamant about stepping down from the Presidency. Both Jefferson and Hamilton had retired during his second term, and the President felt abandoned. Washington also began to take the Republican party's pro-French and anti-Administration stand personally. He believed that the Republicans were undercutting his authority, questioning his honesty and patriotism, and

Collections of the Library of Congress

*George Washington (1732—1799; term, 1789—1797) was the first of only two Presidents to take the field as Commander-in-Chief. (Abraham Lincoln was the other.) In 1794, he reviewed militiamen on their way to force angry farmers in western Pennsylvania to pay federal taxes on home-distilled spirits. The suppression of the Whiskey Rebellion vindicated the authority of the national government.*

endangering the Constitution. "The spirit of party" was fostering geographic schisms and foreign intrigues. He had had enough.

Washington asked Hamilton to prepare a farewell address and discussed what it should say with the brilliant New Yorker. The President then took Hamilton's draft and completely reworked it so that it expressed his ideas in his own words. The Farewell Address first appeared in the center two pages in a leading Philadelphia newspaper, David Claypoole's *American Daily Advertiser*, on September 19, 1796. In it, he expressed his hope that the nation would continue on a virtuous path, leading the rest of the world to liberty. It was Washington's most important statement of his views as a political thinker and has had lasting influence. Today, Americans value Washington's advice about foreign policy, good government, and national union, but in 1796 the Republicans resented the President's charges that they were threatening the stability of the nation. Washington did not care what they thought. He was going home, relieved to be rid of the cares and frustrations of office.

Washington did something else important by stepping down from the Presidency. His decision that two terms were enough established a rule for his successors that lasted for nearly 150 years: the "two-term tradition."

With Washington's retirement, the nation faced its first Presidential election in which political parties chose candidates to compete for the job. Informal meetings of leading Federalists and Republicans chose each party's candidates. The Federalists rallied behind Vice President John Adams; the Republicans backed former Secretary of State Thomas Jefferson. The Electoral College chose Adams to be the second President. Jefferson was the runner-up—and thus became the new Vice President.

Adams and Jefferson had been close friends for two decades, but now they were political rivals, their friendship in ruins. Similarly, Alexander Hamilton and James Madison had been friends and allies in the task of framing and adopting the Constitution, but they parted ways under the pressure of party strife. The years from 1797 to 1801 were difficult for all these men, and for the nation.

On March 4, 1797, as John Adams was taking the Presidential oath of office, he noticed Washington's gaze fixed upon him. The outgoing President seemed to be saying, "Aye, I am fairly out and you are fairly in. We will see which of us is happier." The pessimistic Adams worried about the burdens he would face. He had already spent eight years as understudy to the most revered man in the United States—a daunting task for even the strongest personality. Adams was usually a stubborn, independent man, not afraid to speak his mind no matter what the result. He also believed that he was smarter than Washington. But the new President was nervous about doing anything that might be taken as criticism of Washington. Thus, he kept on Washington's advisers as his own. This turned out to be a major mistake, for in his second term Washington had picked his Cabinet based on the advice of Alexander Hamilton. The Federalist Party was split between Hamilton men and Adams men. The Cabinet was filled with friends and supporters of the former Treasury Secretary, and Hamilton still "pulled the strings." Meanwhile, President Adams, not realizing who was *really* running his government, spent months at a time at his home in Massachusetts.

The Adams Administration's most serious problems had to do with foreign policy. War was raging across the Atlantic between the French Revolutionary government and the European powers led by Great Britain. The United States was neutral in this war, following President Washington's 1793 proclamation, but French ships had begun to harass and even to capture American ships sailing to and from British ports.

President Adams decided to send a delegation to France to try to stop French plunder of American shipping. He appointed two Federalists, Charles C. Pinckney of South Carolina and John Marshall of Virginia, and one Republican, Elbridge Gerry of Massachusetts. Pinckney, Marshall, and Gerry cooled their heels in frustration as French Foreign Minister Talleyrand kept them waiting. Finally, the three Americans were approached by three middle-level French officials, who hinted that the Americans would have to bribe them to ensure progress in the American-French negotiations. Pinckney, Marshall, and Gerry were outraged. Pinckney declared: "No, no, not a sixpence!" John Marshall sailed back to Philadelphia home with the delegates' report on the bribe offer by the French agents, code named X, Y, and Z in the report.

Marshall was given a hero's welcome. The President released Marshall's report to Congress, and the "XYZ Affair" infuriated the American people. The Republicans, who had supported the French Revolutionary cause, were disgusted with the French blunder. The Federalists, who believed that Great Britain and the other allies were fighting for the cause of civilization against the French menace, were delighted. They adopted as their slogan the phrase "Millions for defense; not one cent for tribute!"

Calls for war went up throughout the nation, but Adams adopted a more moderate course. He got authorization from Congress to direct the American Navy to take action against French ships that menaced American shipping. This was America's first *undeclared* war—that is, the first military conflict that Congress did not begin by declaring war as provided by the Constitution.

The Federalists in Congress rammed through two bills, quickly signed into law by President Adams, that were intended to protect American security at home. The Alien Act made it more difficult for people from foreign countries to become American citizens and gave the federal government the power to *deport*, or throw out, foreign subjects residing in the United States. The Sedition Act made it a crime to criticize the President or other officers of the government. The Federalists used the Sedition Act to prosecute and jail critics of President Adams and the war.

The Republicans struck back at the Alien and Sedition Acts. The legislatures of Virginia and Kentucky passed resolutions claiming that these laws were unconstitutional. The Kentucky Resolutions, secretly written by Vice President Jefferson, declared as well that these acts were null and void within the state of Kentucky. The Virginia Resolutions, secretly the work of former Representative Madison, declared that Virginia would resist federal attempts to enforce these laws until the other states helped to settle the issue whether they were constitutional. No other state supported the Virginia and Kentucky legislatures, but the Republicans skillfully linked the Federalist Party, and President Adams, with the hated Alien and Sedition Acts.

Adams also called for the assembling of an army in case the French should actually invade the United States. He called George Washington out of retirement to lead this army. But the former President set a condition for his service that made the President cringe—Washington demanded that Hamilton be named his second-in-command. Adams gave in, but this army never saw action.

In late 1799 and early 1800, the President discovered that Hamilton secretly had been running his Cabinet and thus the government. In a towering rage, Adams confronted his Cabinet and forced all of them to resign. He surrounded himself with advisers who were loyal to him. He also sent Chief Justice Oliver Ellsworth, William Vans Murray, and William R. Davie to France to negotiate an end to the undeclared naval war. Adams thus saved the nation from a full-scale war, the goal of the Hamiltonian Federalists. But the President had destroyed his political career, for the vindictive "High" Federalists were now sworn to cost him the Presidency in the election of 1800.

The 1800 Presidential election once again pitted John Adams against his Vice President, Thomas Jefferson. But the harshest attacks against the President came from Alexander Hamilton, who recklessly wrote and published a furious pamphlet against Adams. This pamphlet played into the hands of Jefferson's supporters.

By now, both political parties had learned to designate Presidential and Vice Presidential candidates. Until 1824, political parties picked their candidates by gatherings of party leaders (caucuses) in Congress. Adams's running-mate was Major General Charles C. Pinckney of South Carolina; Jefferson's was Senator Aaron Burr of New York. Hamilton and his allies worked to ensure that Adams would not win a second term. They hoped to elect Pinckney, whom they could influence. But their strategy backfired. Both Adams and Pinckney were soundly beaten by the Republican ticket.

But the Republican victory was flawed. Somehow, nobody had made certain that the Republican electors would give Jefferson more votes than Burr. Thus, each man received seventy-three electoral votes—a tie for the Presidency. Under the Constitution, the House of Representatives, with each state voting as a unit, had the task of picking the new President if there were a tie in the electoral votes or if no one candidate received a clear majority. Ballot after ballot failed to break the deadlock.

The Federalist Representatives held themselves aloof from the voting, trying to figure out which man to support. Watching from the sidelines, Hamilton thought long and hard about the advice that he should give his Federalist colleagues. He decided to tell them to vote for Jefferson. Jefferson was an honest man, even though the Federalists disliked his politics; by contrast, Hamilton distrusted Burr's ideas *and* doubted his honor. The Federalist Representatives, still angry with Hamilton, resisted his advice until they realized that they had no choice; Jefferson was finally elected in mid-February 1801, after thirty-six ballots, by a vote of ten states to four, with two not voting.

During all this, President Adams sulked, sad and bitter, in the Executive Mansion in Washington, D.C. He had averted a disastrous war with France, only to be betrayed—as he saw it—by his own party. He feared for the future of the country. But there were still several weeks left before Adams and the old Congress had to leave office. They now worked together to create dozens of federal judgeships and to appoint deserving Federalists to those posts. At least the Federalists would keep control of one branch of the government. President Adams stayed up till long after midnight on his last day in office, signing and sealing the commissions of the last batch of judicial appointees. (Republicans angrily nicknamed these men the "midnight judges.") On the morning of March 4, 1801, Inauguration Day, President Adams left Washington, D.C., choosing not to attend Jefferson's swearing-in. Adams, the first President to live in the new capital city, was glad to know that he would never have to return.

Thomas Jefferson awakened on Inauguration Day in his boarding house, dressed, and walked along Pennsylvania Avenue—a mud-lined dirt track in those days—to the unfinished Capitol building. There, his distant cousin and political enemy, Chief Justice John Marshall, administered the Presidential oath of office. Jefferson delivered an eloquent Inaugural Address but, because he was a poor orator who hated and feared public speaking, he could not be heard beyond the first few rows of the audience. Once the ceremony was over, Jefferson shook hands with friends and supporters and walked back to his rooming house, where he had to wait to be seated for lunch. Government was simple and primitive in the first years of the nineteenth century.

*Shown here in an 1801 engraving by Cornelius Tiebout after a portrait by Charles Willson Peale, Thomas Jefferson (1743—1826; term, 1801—1809) (Republican-Virginia) was one of the half-dozen greatest Presidents in American history. His achievements in office included the acquiring of the Louisiana Territory in 1803, the sending of the Lewis and Clark expedition to explore that vast new possession, and the building of the first Republican Party. He also founded the "Virginia Dynasty" that held the Presidency until 1825.*

Jefferson was determined to make this simplicity the theme of his Administration.

Jefferson was proud of his victory over Adams and the Federalists. He called it a revolution, and in a way it was. It was the first time under the Constitution that power had shifted from one political party to another. But much of the credit for this achievement rests, in the end, with the Federalists. Although they had controlled the machinery of government, they did not try to prevent the lawful transfer of power to the Republicans.

Jefferson's "Revolution of 1800" did not change the direction of public policy, as he had hoped. Hamilton's economic system, now more than a decade old, could not be abolished or replaced. Jefferson mourned that the national debt could be paid off in ten years, "but we can never get rid of his system." The President also found that he could not stick to his view that the Constitution gave the federal government only specific, limited powers. Here, too, Hamilton's ideas prevailed.

The most famous instance when President Jefferson was obliged to go beyond the words of the Constitution was the Louisiana Purchase. In 1802, Spain transferred to France ownership of the city of New Orleans and the land on both sides of the lower Mississippi River. For nearly twenty years, Americans had tried to buy New Orleans for the new nation to ensure access to the river and the Gulf of Mexico for western settlers who depended on the Mississippi to ship their goods and crops. But Spain had resisted. Now Jefferson thought that France might be willing to deal. He sent two diplomats, James Monroe of Virginia and Robert R. Livingston of New York, to Paris to negotiate with Emperor Napoleon I and the durable Count Talleyrand. It turned out that Napoleon had no desire for vast American possessions. He needed money to finance his European wars. He thus offered to sell New Orleans *and* the whole Louisiana Territory to the United States for $15 million—about two-and-one-half cents per acre. (It was an area larger than the combined areas of France, Germany, Italy, Spain, and Portugal.) Monroe and Livingston were delighted but uncertain. They sent word of Napoleon's proposal back to Jefferson, who also was unsure. Nothing in the Constitution specifically authorized the federal government to enter into a treaty to purchase land. Jefferson even drafted a proposed constitutional amendment to authorize the treaty. But in the end Jefferson and his Secretary of State, James Madison, decided that the deal was constitutional because the Constitution's words did not *forbid* treaties of this kind.

The treaty, ratified by the Senate in 1803, more than doubled the size of the United States. (Because of the huge outlay for the Louisiana Purchase, the President felt that the United States did not have the money to buy Cuba, also for sale.) To find out what benefits the Louisiana Territory held for the United States, the President, under a $2,500 grant authorized by Congress, sent out his private secretary, Captain Meriwether Lewis, and Lieutenant William Clark to explore the region, where no white man had gone before, and to discover a water passage to the Pacific—the age-long search for the Northwest Passage. The Lewis and Clark Expedition discovered 24 Indian tribes, 178 plants, and 122 animals previously unknown to the Western world, established the U.S. claim to the Oregon territory, and sailed the Snake and Columbia rivers to the Pacific Ocean—a 4,000-mile round trip with the loss of only one man (due to a ruptured appendix). Jefferson's decision to send out this scientific expedition further expanded the powers of the federal government and the Presidency, and expanded the nation's destiny westward.

In dealing with the Barbary Pirates, the President also found himself forced to exercise powers not specifically prohibited by the Constitution. These pirates, based in North Africa, sailed the Mediterranean, seizing ships and hostages from nations that refused to pay them *tribute*, or protection money. They held these ships and hostages for ransom. Other nations had bought off the Barbary Pirates, but for nearly thirty years the United States had refused to do so—both out of principle and for the practical reason that the new nation could not afford tribute or ransom. Finally, President Jefferson sent a naval expedition, commanded by Lieutenant Stephen Decatur, who led a detachment of U.S. Marines across the desert and surprised the pirates at their headquarters in Tripoli. The Americans broke the power of the Barbary Pirates.

The Presidential election of 1804, in which Thomas Jefferson was triumphantly re-elected for a second term, was the first governed by the new Twelfth Amendment to the Constitution. This amendment, ratified just before the election, was designed to prevent a replay of the Jefferson-Burr tie four years earlier. It required the members of the Electoral College to vote separately for President and Vice President.

Jefferson had a new Vice President for his second term, George Clinton of New York, who had been the state's governor for all but six years between 1777 and 1804. The Republicans had silently agreed to "dump" Vice President Burr. Nobody in the party or in Jefferson's Administration trusted Burr after the drawn-out election of

1800. The New Yorker decided to switch parties in 1802 and ran against Clinton as the Federalist candidate for governor of New York, but Hamilton engineered Burr's defeat.

Burr and Hamilton had much in common. Both were short and brilliant men in their late forties, both were polished speakers and able lawyers, and both were popular with the ladies. The two men grew to loathe each other. Hamilton's son Philip was killed in a duel with a Burr supporter in 1801, and the heartbroken Hamilton felt responsible for his son's death. In 1804, Hamilton recklessly denounced Burr as a politician and attacked his private character as well. Angered, Burr demanded an explanation, which Hamilton refused to give. Burr finally "demanded satisfaction"—a standard phrase of that time for a challenge to a duel—and Hamilton agreed to meet Burr on the "field of honor." On July 11, 1804, the two men faced each other, pistols in hand, across a dueling field on a narrow tree-bowered ledge of Weehawken Heights, New Jersey, on the banks of the Hudson River. Hamilton's shot went wild. Burr's shot mortally wounded Hamilton, who died in agony the next day.

Dueling was illegal in New York, and a New York grand jury indicted Burr for defying the law. A New Jersey grand jury indicted Burr for murder, though the dueling laws were not enforced in that state. The Vice President found refuge in Philadelphia and then fled to the South, where he was welcomed as a hero in a region that considered dueling to be an honorable custom among gentlemen. But Federalists and Republicans joined forces in denouncing Burr, whose political career crumbled into ruins. (Eventually, the grand jury indictments faded away and were forgotten.) Hamilton was briefly honored as a martyr and then largely forgotten.

In his last days as Vice President, Burr helped to strangle one of President Jefferson's most important projects. The President was bitter about the Federalists' takeover of the federal courts. He and Secretary of State James Madison had refused to deliver judicial commissions to some of the "midnight judges" appointed by President Adams, but the scheme backfired. In a landmark 1803 case, *Marbury v. Madison*, Chief Justice John Marshall had asserted that the Supreme Court had the power to decide whether federal laws violated the Constitution. Jefferson and his allies in Congress decided to use the constitutional power of impeachment to clear Federalists out of the judiciary. They argued that impeachment was simply a process to determine whether someone holding a federal office should be replaced—not a way to punish a federal office-holder for violating the law or abusing his power. The Jeffersonians in Congress managed to oust old, senile, drunken Judge John Pickering of the federal district court in New Hampshire, but their effort to remove Supreme Court Justice Samuel Chase failed in the Senate. Vice President Burr presided over the Senate's trial of Justice Chase. He conducted it with strict fairness, and the Senators voted to acquit the Justice. Jefferson was furious but could do nothing.

Jefferson's second term was more difficult than his first. As another round of wars engulfed Europe, the President was determined to keep the United States neutral and at peace. He declared an *embargo*, or ban on trade, with all the warring European powers. He hoped that the loss of American trade would force the Europeans to bring the war to an end. But French and British warships raided American ships trading with neutral nations, and American merchants suffered terribly.

Aaron Burr was still causing trouble for the President as well. Federal authorities arrested Burr in Alabama in the western territories. Jefferson believed that Burr had been plotting to lead an armed conquest of the Louisiana Territory, the western states, and Mexico in order to create a new empire with himself as emperor. Attorney General George Hay followed Jefferson's orders and prosecuted Burr for treason and conspiracy in the U.S. Circuit Court in Virginia. Chief Justice John Marshall presided over the trial. Marshall and Jefferson got into another tangle when Burr's lawyers issued a formal order, or *subpoena*, demanding that the President be called as a witness and that he produce government documents. Jefferson refused to testify, but he turned over most of the documents that Burr had requested and that Marshall had ordered produced. Historians are still unsure what Burr's real hopes or plans were, and it is likely that Burr had no idea himself. In any event, to Jefferson's alarm and fury, Burr was acquitted on the charge of treason. The former Vice President sailed for Europe, a crushed man; he lived thirty more years but never again had influence in American politics.

In 1808, Jefferson decided that he would not seek a third term. He was tired of public life, and he agreed with Washington that no President should serve more than two terms in office. Secretary of State James Madison became the Republican Presidential candidate and handily defeated Federalist Charles C. Pinckney.

The new President was short, quiet, and reserved, and in some ways a more realistic politician than Jefferson had been. He lifted Jefferson's embargo on trading with warring countries, delighting merchants along the Eastern coast. But the European war continued, and American shipping still suffered at the hands of British warships. When British officers seized, or *impressed*, American sailors to replace British sailors who had been killed in battle, died on the high seas, or jumped ship, Madison and the Republicans in Congress believed that going to war with Great Britain was the only way to preserve American independence. In 1812, the President sent a message to Congress asking for a declaration of war because of British interference with American shipping. Congress answered Madison's call before word arrived that the British had repealed the "orders in council" authorizing these attacks.

Some pro-war Americans enthusiastically called the new three-year war "the Second War for Independence," but most later historians simply call it the War of 1812. Radical members of the House of Representatives, such as Henry Clay of Kentucky and John C. Calhoun of South Carolina, demanded that the American army conquer Canada to add it to the Union and to deny the British a valuable base for military operations in the Western Hemisphere. But the American military expeditions to Canada ended in disaster for the United States. Other American military operations had mixed results. After a few brilliant victories, the American Navy was bottled up by a British blockade. British armies trounced American forces in most of their battles. The low point for the United States came in 1814 when a British force captured and burned Washington, D.C., in revenge for the Americans' burning of the Parliament building in Toronto. Madison was forced to flee for his life; he watched from the Virginia hills as the capital burned. His wife, Dolley Madison, remained at the Executive Mansion long enough to save several priceless objects from destruction, including Gilbert Stuart's official portrait of George Washington.

The War of 1812 ended as inconclusively as it had begun. American and British diplomats meeting in the city of Ghent, Belgium, agreed on a treaty that left things pretty much as they had been when the war started. Two weeks after the treaty was signed, but long before that news reached the United States, a British army besieged New Orleans. The American commander, General Andrew Jackson, aided by the French pirate Jean Lafitte, directed the American defense. The tiny American force inflicted a shattering defeat on the British, and Jackson became a national hero. President Madison also basked in the glory of the Battle of New Orleans—though it had been a useless battle, a fitting end to a largely useless war.

Madison's greatest domestic problem during the War of 1812 was connected to the war. In the first days of "war fever," he easily won a second term in the Presidential election of 1812. But the New England states, the last stronghold of the disintegrating Federalist Party, soon became grim and discontented about the war. The New England Federalists hated the war because it was choking their trade and profits, and they felt a natural sympathy for Great Britain. The five New England states resisted the government's calls for soldiers and supplies. Some New England politicians even suggested that their states leave the Union, or *secede*, to form their own country or to return to the British Empire. They called a convention to meet at Hartford, Connecticut, but the Hartford Convention broke up in disarray when news of the Treaty of Ghent and the Battle of New Orleans arrived.

President Madison announced his retirement after two terms, reinforcing the "no third term" tradition of Washington and Jefferson. His Secretary of State, James Monroe of Virginia, won a landslide victory in 1816 over the last Federalist Presidential candidate, Rufus King of Massachusetts. Monroe was the fifth President, the fourth to come from Virginia. During his first term, the Federalist party finally dissolved. In 1820, Monroe ran unopposed for a second term. One Presidential elector (William Plumer of New Hampshire) cast his vote for Secretary of State John Quincy Adams, however, arguing that only George Washington deserved the honor of being elected to the Presidency unanimously.

Monroe's most famous achievement, known today as the Monroe Doctrine, was actually the work of Secretary of State John Quincy Adams. Monroe and Adams were responding to the breakup of the Spanish Empire in the Western Hemisphere. Spain's colonies, inspired by the American and French Revolutions, threw off the rule of their mother country and established themselves as republics. Spain was determined to reconquer its former colonies, but Great Britain opposed Spain's plans. The British suggested that they and the United States issue a joint guarantee of the independence of the new Latin American republics. But President Monroe and Secretary Adams resisted these British efforts to direct the affairs of Latin America. In December 1823, Monroe sent his sixth annual message to Congress. He warned all European powers not to interfere in the affairs of the Western Hemisphere. If any nation would guarantee the independence of the nations of the region, it would be the United States. This was the Monroe Doctrine.

By 1824, the "no third term" rule laid down by George Washington had become a tradition. Monroe gladly retired to private life. His eight years in office had become known as the "Era of Good Feeling" because of his popularity. But the Republican Party was badly divided, and in the 1824 Presidential election it broke apart. Four candidates battled to become the sixth President: Secretary of State Adams, the candidate of the National Republicans; General Andrew Jackson, backed by the newly formed Democrats; Treasury Secretary William Crawford, the choice of Republicans in Congress; and Henry Clay.

When the electoral votes were counted, no candidate had a majority. Jackson led with ninety-nine electoral votes; Adams had eighty-four; Crawford had forty-one; and Clay had thirty-seven. (Crawford actually was out of the running; he had suffered several crippling strokes.) The House of Representatives once again would have to choose the next President. There is still controversy over what happened in the House, but Clay endorsed Adams. Thus, Adams was able to defeat Jackson. He then named Clay his Secretary of State. Jackson's infuriated supporters charged that a "corrupt bargain" had taken place. They planned to punish Adams and Clay in the next election, in 1828.

John Quincy Adams was one of the most able men ever to become President. He had been one of the greatest Secretaries of State the United States has ever had. Adams was an imaginative man with wide-ranging interests and talents. If he had had a chance, he would have been one of America's greatest Presidents. But, like his father, John Adams, he was stubborn, independent, and at times out of touch with the American people. For example, when an Englishman named James Smithson died and left his fortune to the United States to be used "for the increase and diffusion of knowledge among men," President Adams proposed the creation of what we now call the Smithsonian Institution—despite the demands of Senators and Representatives that the money be used to found an agricultural college or even be put straight into the U.S. Treasury. Years passed before Adams's views prevailed. History proved him right, but in this and many other controversies he could not win popular support for his views.

By 1828, the use of the Congressional caucus as a way to select Presidential and Vice Presidential candidates had ended. Instead, political parties held conventions at which party leaders and delegates from state party organizations picked the candidates.

The year 1828 also marked the end of the American Presidency as a nonpartisan office that would identify and serve the common good. In the dawn of a new era of politics, President Adams lost his bid for a second term. Andrew Jackson ran as the common man's candidate and triumphed.

# CHAPTER THREE

# FROM JACKSON TO BUCHANAN

Andrew Jackson was a gaunt, ill-tempered man. His opponents thought that he was a barbarian or a savage. He had fought duels, and he had hanged men. In 1828, he was racked by illnesses that left him weighing only 127 pounds though he was six feet tall. But his iron will kept him going even when most physicians wondered that he was still alive. This force of will enabled him to dominate American politics for eight years.

Andrew Jackson went to his inauguration in 1829 wearing black, for he still mourned the death several months earlier of his beloved wife, Rachel. When Andrew and Rachel Jackson wed, both believed that Rachel had been divorced from her first husband. But Rachel's husband had not carried out the legal formalities. When he disclosed this fact, the heartbroken Rachel Jackson took to her bed and died. Jackson, anguished and bitter, blamed her death on his political enemies. He was in an unforgiving mood as he assumed the Presidency.

Inauguration Day, 1829, was a triumph for the common man that quickly got out of hand. Jackson had invited his supporters to the Executive Mansion, and they came in droves, stomping muddy footprints all over the carpeting and furniture, breaking windows, and passing out drunk in the East Room. Friends helped the President escape from the crush through an open window.

In an election as in a war, Jackson argued, "to the victors belong the spoils." In this case, the "spoils" were government jobs. Jackson named loyal supporters to those jobs regardless of the men's abilities. His opponents were outraged but helpless. Jackson thus solidified the *spoils system* that lasted for more than half a century, until passage of the Federal Service Act in 1883.

President Jackson also acted from constitutional principle. In his first term, the most important issue was an old standby in American politics: Did Congress have the power under the Constitution to establish a national bank? The means to create a bank was to issue a document called a *charter*. Congress had voted to renew the charter of the Second Bank of the United States, based in Philadelphia. But Jackson believed that the Bank was a bastion of wealth and privilege

Collections of the Library of Congress

*Andrew Jackson, the seventh President (1767—1845; term, 1829—1837), plunged the Presidency into the thick of party politics. The hero of the Battle of New Orleans (1815) was the target in 1835 of the first known attempt to assassinate a President. Richard Lawrence's pistols misfired at point-blank range. Jackson was not injured and had to be restrained from beating the crazed house painter to death.*

oppressing ordinary Americans. He also believed that, because the Constitution did not specifically authorize Congress to charter a bank, Congress did not have this power. For these reasons, which he set forth in a biting message to Congress, Jackson vetoed the Bank bill. The Bank's head, Nicholas Biddle, was a wealthy, well-educated, aristocratic Philadelphia lawyer who represented everything Jackson loathed. Biddle tried to get Congress to override Jackson's veto, but the President prevailed. Biddle managed to get the state of Pennsylvania to recharter the Bank as a private corporation.

Jackson ordered his Secretary of the Treasury to withdraw federal funds deposited with the Bank. The Secretary refused because he disagreed with Jackson's veto, and the President fired him. Jackson appointed a new Secretary of the Treasury, but the new man defied him, too, and Jackson fired him. Finally, Jackson named Roger B. Taney of Maryland as his third Secretary of the Treasury, and Taney did the President's bidding. The Bank could not survive this blow and closed its doors. The economy was also battered by Jackson's "Bank War." Meanwhile, Jackson rewarded Taney several times over for his loyalty, ultimately naming him to succeed the late John Marshall in 1835 as the nation's fifth Chief Justice.

President Jackson considered Indians to be his personal enemies. When the state of Georgia and greedy land speculators conspired to seize the lands of the Cherokee, the most "civilized" tribe by white standards, the law-abiding Cherokee invoked the protection of treaties and federal law. Chief Justice John Marshall spoke for the Supreme Court, ruling in their favor. But the President ignored the decision, and the state of Georgia ousted the Cherokee from their ancestral lands. Eventually, the Indians were forced by the Army to march under armed guard 1,000 miles west to the Oklahoma territory —a journey the Cherokee called the "Trail of Tears."

President Jackson was committed to enforcing the authority of the United States against state challenges. The tariff crisis of 1832—1833 that bridged his first and second terms provided an opportunity for him to enforce federal power. The federal government had adopted a tax on imported goods, or *tariff*, which outraged the people of South Carolina, who relied on inexpensive imported goods. The state's legislature declared the tariff to be null and void (without legal force) within the state's borders.

South Carolina's action revived an issue as old as the Constitution itself—the relationship between federal power and state *sovereignty*. Advocates of state sovereignty argued that the Constitution was the creation of the several states and that the federal government was the creature of those states. Federal policy could not outweigh a state's right and duty to protect its vital interests. Thomas Jefferson and John C. Calhoun were the principal advocates of this view. But other politicians disagreed. Men such as George Washington, Alexander Hamilton, John Marshall, and Daniel Webster argued that the Constitution had been created by the people of the United States. The federal government was supreme over the states, and no state could resist the authority of the federal government.

President Jackson was ready to resist any attempt by South Carolina to defy federal authority. His first Vice President, John C. Calhoun, had resigned to go back to his native state; he returned to Washington, D.C., as a Senator from South Carolina to lead the cause of state sovereignty against the "Tariff of Abominations."

Jackson issued a fire-breathing message to the Union and the people of South Carolina. The state legislature rejected this warning. Jackson was prepared to send the federal army to enforce the tariff in South Carolina. Finally, Senator Henry Clay of Kentucky came forward with a compromise. If the tariff were amended to take account of the needs of South Carolina, then the state would give up its opposition. Both sides accepted the compromise with relief. But the shadow of the tariff crisis would not go away. Someday a state might carry out a threat to secede from the Union, and this possibility hung over the land.

Andrew Jackson always behaved as if his will alone would determine what was law and what was government policy. He did not abide by the pattern of cooperative, nonpartisan leadership established by the first six Presidents. He challenged whatever authority tried to stand in his way. He used his veto power to reject bills that he disagreed with, departing from his predecessors' use of the veto only to reject bills they believed to be unconstitutional. Deciding to retire at the end of his second term, in late 1836, he handpicked his successor, Martin Van Buren, his second Vice President. Van Buren, leading the Democrats, defeated the new opposition party, the Whigs.

Van Buren, a New Yorker, was the first President to be born after the Declaration of Independence. He tried to continue Jackson's policies but immediately ran into trouble. The problem was a legacy from his predecessor. Jackson had issued an executive order that federal lands could be paid for only in hard cash (gold and silver) rather than in bank notes (paper money) issued by state-chartered banks. Jackson intended his "Specie Circular" to curb free-wheeling banks that behaved as though they had an unlimited license to print money. But this gusher of paper money fueled real-estate speculation throughout the nation. The Specie Circular thus set off the Panic of 1837, the worst economic slump the country had ever faced. President Van Buren was blamed for the Panic. His opponents turned Jacksonian ideas of equality against him, charging that Van Buren dined in the Executive Mansion with silver knives and forks from plates of gold.

The Whig Party took its name from the eighteenth-century British political party that had supported the Americans during the Revolution. In 1840, it had a Presidential candidate in the tradition of Andrew Jackson—General William Henry Harrison. In 1811 Harrison had defeated the Shawnee River Indian leader Tecumseh at the Battle of Tippecanoe in Indiana. He was backed by a well-organized political machine with voters joining Tippecanoe clubs, and there were slogans and even a media event: The Whigs built a gigantic ball of paper and rolled it across the nation as a symbol of Harrison's momentum. Their slogans "Keep the ball rolling" and "Tippecanoe and Tyler too" (John Tyler of Virginia, Harrison's running-mate) entered the American language.

A Democratic editor snidely denounced Harrison, claiming that the general would be content with a jug of hard cider that he could drink on the front porch of his log cabin. The Whigs instantly seized on both symbols, hammering home the contrast between the "aristocrat" Van Buren and the unpretentious Harrison. In fact, Harrison was a Virginia aristocrat who had resettled in Ohio, in those days a western state. His handsome mansion was hardly a log cabin. But facts were scarce in the 1840 campaign, as were ideas. In fact, Whig political strategists kept Harrison at home, in the first "front porch" campaign. In addition, they rarely let Harrison make policy statements; instead, they formed a committee to draft vague, reassuring letters answering questions from voters for him to sign. Nobody was really sure what Harrison stood for, but it did not matter very much. He was elected triumphantly.

The sixty-eight-year-old Harrison was just as stubborn in his own way as Andrew Jackson had been. He insisted on delivering his ninety-minute inaugural address, on March 4, 1841, despite the cold and rainy weather; then, bare-headed, he led the Inaugural Parade on horseback. He also insisted on doing his own shopping. Within two weeks of his inauguration, he had caught a cold; within four weeks, he was dead of pneumonia, the first President to die in office.

Suddenly the all-but-forgotten Vice President, John Tyler, was ensconced in the White House. Tyler set the precedent that when the President dies or resigns, the Vice President becomes President. The matter was not settled by the text of the Constitution; some authorities argued that only the powers and duties of the office, not the office itself, went to the Vice President when a President died or otherwise left office. In 1967, the Twenty-fifth Amendment wrote Tyler's view into the Constitution.

Tyler was a stubborn man, and he disagreed with his own party's domestic policy, which favored federal power to build roads and canals and other "internal improvements." He used his veto power with zest, and the Whigs decided to dump him in 1844.

The Whigs' 1844 Presidential candidate, Henry Clay, lost to the Democratic nominee, James K. Polk of Tennessee, who had the unexpected support of John Tyler. Polk had been an unexpected nominee —the first *dark horse*. Polk's Presidency was dominated by the first major American war in thirty years.

In the 1820s, Americans had begun to settle in Texas, which was part of Mexico. In 1836, they revolted against Mexican rule, creating the Republic of Texas under the leadership of Sam Houston, a former governor of Tennessee and a commander of the Texas army. In 1845, the Texan Republic ended nine years of independence by joining the union as the twenty-eighth state. Texans and other Americans in the South and the West had designs on more Mexican territory. In early 1846, President Polk informed Congress that a detachment of American soldiers had been attacked by Mexican soldiers on American soil. Congress declared war, but some Whig Senators and Representatives had questions about the incident. Representative Abraham Lincoln of Illinois demanded that Polk point out the exact spot on American soil where Mexican soldiers had shed American blood.

The Mexican War was a slugfest in which Mexico found itself hopelessly outclassed. The Whigs denounced the war as a land grab designed to distract the nation from more pressing problems. Opponents of slavery charged that the war was intended to win more territory to create more slave states. In early 1848, Presidential envoy Nicholas Trist, who had studied law with Thomas Jefferson, had negotiated the Treaty of Guadalupe Hidalgo. Mexico was forced to give up about half its territory to the United States in exchange for $15 million. This territory included the present-day states of California, New Mexico, Arizona, Colorado, Utah, and Nevada. President Polk had repudiated Trist but could not quarrel with the treaty he had negotiated, and Congress quickly adopted it. Polk had promised not to run for a second term and indeed stepped down. He stunned the nation by dying in July 1849, four months after his retirement.

Although the Whigs had opposed the Mexican War, they were willing to profit by it. They picked a hero of that war, General Zachary Taylor, as their 1848 Presidential candidate, to run against Democrat Lewis Cass. Taylor was elected, but in July 1850, less than halfway through his term, the old general succumbed to a stroke four days after laying the cornerstone of the Washington Monument. His successor, Vice President Millard Fillmore of New York, was another little-known politician who had been picked to balance the ticket. Fillmore helped to avert a major crisis between North and South by working with Senator Clay to put together a compromise package governing where slavery would be permitted or prohibited in the new territories. He also sent a naval expedition under Commodore Matthew C. Perry to "open" Japan to American trade and diplomatic relations. But Fillmore had little support in the Whig Party and was not nominated in 1852 for a term of his own.

The 1852 election resulted in another Democratic victory. Franklin Pierce of New Hampshire defeated another Whig Mexican War hero, General Winfield Scott. Pierce was a weak President who worked hand-in-glove with proslavery Southern Democrats. By this point, antislavery sentiment was beginning to organize for political action. In 1848, the antislavery Free Soil Party had nominated former President Martin Van Buren, and he had done surprisingly well in the race with General Taylor and Lewis Cass. The party did not do so well in 1852, but its members joined with survivors of the disintegrating Whig Party and other groups to forge a new political organization.

The Republican Party was born in 1856, taking its name from the party founded over sixty years earlier by Thomas Jefferson and James Madison. The Republicans opposed the expansion of slavery beyond those states where it was already strong. Radical members of the party wanted to do away with slavery altogether but did not press the issue. The Republicans' first Presidential candidate was the flamboyant, erratic General John C. Frémont, a noted explorer (the "Pathfinder") and military hero; he had captured Los Angeles during the Mexican War. Frémont lost to the Democratic candidate, James Buchanan of Pennsylvania, but Frémont's campaign showed that the Republicans would be a permanent force in American politics.

The new President was, at least on paper, one of the most experienced men ever elected to the office. He had been a diplomat (Minister to Great Britain) and a long-time legislator in Washington and

President Polk's Secretary of State. He was also bumbling, indecisive, and given to telling everyone what they wanted to hear. Like President Pierce, he was a "doughface"—a Northern Democrat allied with proslavery Southern Democrats. He did nothing to try to heal the splits in his party between Northern and Southern Democrats and wrung his hands as tensions between North and South increased.

In 1857, as Buchanan took office, he announced that the Supreme Court was about to settle the issues of slavery once and for all and urged all Americans to abide by the Court's decision. Chief Justice Roger B. Taney had leaked to Buchanan the substance of the Court's impending decision in *Dred Scott v. Sandford*. In that case, Chief Justice Taney ruled that slavery was protected by the Constitution and that any attempt to reach a compromise to control its spread was a violation of the Constitution. Opponents of slavery were furious. They denounced the Court and the President. Buchanan's authority and prestige faded away.

In the election of 1860, the Democrats shattered into three factions. Moderates, led by the "Little Giant," Senator Stephen A. Douglas of Illinois, stood for the principle that the people of each state should be able to vote for or against slavery. At the same time, they urged all Americans to obey the Supreme Court's decision in the *Dred Scott* case, though these two ideas were inconsistent. Proslavery Democrats endorsed Senator John C. Breckinridge of Kentucky. Those Democrats who thought it still might be possible to cobble together a compromise between North and South founded the short-lived Constitutional Union Party and put up John Bell of Tennessee.

The Republicans chose former Representative Abraham Lincoln of Illinois as their candidate. Lincoln had garnered a national reputation two years earlier when he unsuccessfully challenged Stephen Douglas in a Senate election in Illinois. The two men had debated the issues of slavery throughout the state, and the encounters received national publicity. Lincoln was a prosperous corporation and railroad lawyer, and he had argued cases before the U.S. Supreme Court; he owned one of the finest houses in Springfield, Illinois. But his supporters depicted him as a humble "rail-splitter," dubbing him "Honest Abe" (though he hated the nickname). The three-way Democratic split all but guaranteed that Lincoln would become the sixteenth President. On Election Day 1860, Lincoln indeed prevailed—with only forty percent of the popular vote.

Lincoln's victory shocked the South. Angry politicians claimed that Lincoln was the enemy of the South. His election made it impossible for the Southern states to remain in the Union. As Lincoln's inauguration approached, South Carolina, Mississippi, Florida, Alabama, Georgia, Louisiana, and Texas adopted formal declarations that they were leaving the Union. Four more states—Virginia, Arkansas, Tennessee, and North Carolina—warned that they would use force to oppose federal efforts to block any state's attempt to secede.

Buchanan declared lamely that secession would violate the Constitution—but that the United States lacked the constitutional power to prevent a state from leaving the Union. Most Americans turned away from Buchanan in disgust and waited to see what the new President would do.

# CHAPTER FOUR

# ABRAHAM LINCOLN

The tall, thin man from Illinois who traveled east to assume the Presidency in early 1861 was an unknown quantity to most Americans. But everyone knew that he faced the most difficult task confronting any President since George Washington. Secession, so long the "doomsday machine" of American constitutionalism, had become a reality. President Buchanan was powerless and, in fact, was predicting that he would be the last President of the United States. Most of the nation's leading military officers had resigned their commands in the U.S. Army to return home to stand with the South.

Lincoln did not believe that the Southern states would carry out their threat to leave the Union. The federal government had to stand firm. In his Inaugural Address, he made it clear that he would not disturb slavery where it existed but that he was unalterably opposed to its expansion. He warned the South against secession: "In *your* hands, my dissatisfied fellow-countrymen, and not in *mine*, is the momentous issue of civil war. The Government will not assail *you*. You can have no conflict without being yourselves the aggressors. *You* have no oath registered in heaven to destroy the Government, while *I* shall have the most solemn one to 'preserve, protect, and defend it.' "

The Southern states ignored the President. Virginia, Tennessee,

North Carolina, and Arkansas joined the seven states that had already seceded. The eleven states held a convention in Montgomery, Alabama, and declared themselves "the Confederate States of America." They adopted a constitution modeled on the U.S. Constitution and elected Jefferson Davis of Mississippi, a former Senator and Secretary of War, as their President. The Confederates then issued demands to Lincoln: The United States must evacuate federal military posts throughout the South. Lincoln refused.

In April 1861, Northerners and Southerners alike focused on Fort Sumter, in the harbor of Charleston, South Carolina. Lincoln vowed to resupply the federal garrison there. On the morning of April 12, Virginia-born Edmund Ruffin, a fierce, fire-eating partisan of slavery and secession, was given the honor (as he called it) of firing the first shot of the Civil War. The federal soldiers surrendered only after Confederate cannon had spent nearly a day pulverizing the fort's walls.

Lincoln issued a call for federal volunteers and ordered Congress to convene on July 4, 1861. He declared that the Confederates were a conspiracy to commit treason against the United States and refused to recognize them as a lawful government. To the President, and to most other Northerners, the conflict was "the War of the Rebellion." Southerners called it "the War Between the States" or the "Second War for Independence." Historians call it the Civil War.

Neither side expected the Civil War to last long. They reasoned that after one good battle, the losing side would quickly sue for peace. Instead, the war lasted for four years and cost more than 600,000 American lives, North and South—more than in any other war in American history.

The war did not start out as a war over slavery. It was a struggle between two different views of the Constitution and the Union. President Lincoln was the latest of a long line of politicians and theorists going back to George Washington and Alexander Hamilton who had argued that the Constitution and the Union were created by the American people and were thus supreme over the states. Jefferson Davis was the latest spokesman of the "state compact" or "state sovereignty" theory of the Constitution most often associated with Thomas Jefferson and John C. Calhoun. Reason and argument and compromise had not decided the issue—now it would be resolved by force of arms.

The war forced Lincoln to change the way that the Presidency fit into the constitutional system. Because the United States was at war to preserve the Constitution and the Union, the President could no longer just carry out policies decided by Congress. He had to make policy as well, as part of his responsibility as Commander-in-Chief under the Constitution. President Lincoln seized the opportunity to resolve the crisis of the Union through the authority of the Presidency.

Some critics of Lincoln and his Administration charged that the President was setting himself up as a dictator. One of his measures provoked particular alarm. An important cornerstone of the American legal system is that the government cannot arrest and detain anyone it wants to. It must have reasons, and those reasons must be authorized by law. Any person held by a government official may apply to a court for a special document called a *writ of habeas corpus*. This writ compels the government official to bring the prisoner before the court and explain the valid reasons for holding the prisoner in custody. If the court rejects these reasons, the prisoner must go free. The Constitution permits the government to suspend the writ in extreme circumstances. Lincoln issued an order suspending the writ, even though critics argued—with some reason—that only Congress could take that action; later, Congress passed a law ratifying Lincoln's order.

Lincoln recognized that the effort to preserve the Union was endangering individuals' civil liberties. He justified his measures by saying that, even if he had violated the letter of the Constitution, he had done so to save the Constitution. Should he let the entire Constitution fall because he might violate a part of it? To Lincoln, the answer was clear. Jefferson Davis and his colleagues took similar steps in the South.

Throughout the war, Lincoln was a vigorous Commander-in-Chief, frequently urging particular strategies and tactics on his generals. He appointed and supported the best generals he could find, and fired and replaced them when he believed that they were not effective or determined enough to achieve victory. In 1862, at the Battle of Norfolk, Virginia, the President was so exasperated by one general's failure to move against Confederate forces that he actually took the field himself and directed Union soldiers to victory. Many generals who had spent their lives in uniform resented this civilian who had been only a volunteer captain in the Illinois militia in skirmishes against the Indians thirty years earlier.

The Civil War reached into Lincoln's family. Several relatives of his wife, Mary Todd Lincoln, fought for the South. At one point,

President Lincoln appeared before a secret session of a Congressional committee investigating his wife's loyalty to assure them that his wife was not a rebel agent. The problems of the Lincolns and the Todds were examples of conflicts afflicting many other families throughout the United States.

At one point during the Civil War, the United States was nearly plunged into a war with Great Britain. A Union ship seized two Confederate envoys bound for Great Britain on a British ship. After Queen Victoria's husband, Prince Albert, and President Lincoln intervened, the envoys were released, and war between Great Britain and the United States was averted. The Confederate envoys failed in their attempt to forge an alliance with the British, and the Confederacy never managed to find a foreign ally to support their struggle.

At first, the strategy of the war was dictated by assumptions that had been adopted fifty years earlier, during the European Napoleonic Wars. The object of each side was to capture the enemy capital. Thus, Lincoln sought a general who could capture Richmond, Virginia, the Confederate capital, and Robert E. Lee, the leading Confederate general, tried time and time again to encircle and conquer Washington, D.C. But Lincoln eventually realized that the Civil War was the first example of a new kind of war—one of populations and resources and technology. The old, chess-like strategies of war were no longer relevant. The Civil War was the first total war.

As the war dragged on, Lincoln was more and more willing to revise the war's aims. He knew that declaring that the war's goals were to crush slavery as well as to preserve the Union would win the Union cause increased popularity in the North, and in Europe as well. In the summer of 1862, he drafted a proclamation freeing the slaves in the Confederate states, but his Cabinet persuaded him to wait for an appropriate time to release it. A Union victory on the battlefield would be best, they cautioned. And so the President waited until the Union triumph in the Battle of Antietam in Maryland. In one of the bloodiest contests of the whole war, the Confederate forces under General Lee were forced back across the Potomac River. This was enough of a victory for Lincoln. The date was September 17, 1862, the seventy-fifth anniversary of the signing of the U.S. Constitution.

The Emancipation Proclamation was carefully crafted not to offend slaveholders in states remaining loyal to the Union. It freed all slaves in areas *still in rebellion* against the United States, a clause that exempted areas already under federal military control. It offered slaveholding rebels a choice: Submit to the Union and your slaves may not

Collections of the Library of Congress

*Abraham Lincoln, the sixteenth President (1809—1865; term, 1861—1865), ranks with George Washington as one of the two greatest Presidents. His aim during the Civil War was to preserve the Union and the Constitution at all costs. Once it became clear that the United States would win, he also declared the war to be a war against slavery. He was the first of four Presidents who have been assassinated.*

be freed, or persist in your rebellion at the risk that, if you lose, you will lose everything. The Proclamation had great symbolic value, and when Union armies conquered Southern territory, they freed the slaves they found there.

Lincoln and Congress wrestled over the conduct of the war. Congress established the Joint Committee on the Conduct of the War, which aided Lincoln by exposing corruption and mismanagement but also tried to dictate strategy and policies to be pursued in the defeated Confederacy. In matters pertaining to the war, Lincoln insisted on his constitutional authority as Commander-in-Chief. In other matters, Lincoln deferred to Congress or cooperated with Congressional leaders.

Lincoln's Cabinet was a mixed blessing. It included men of unquestioned ability, such as his former rival Secretary of State William Seward, and corrupt hacks, such as Secretary of War Simon Cameron. Lincoln was saddled with Cameron, who had been the Republican "boss" of Pennsylvania, as the result of a political deal at the 1860 Republican convention. Thanks to the investigations of the Joint Committee on the Conduct of the War, Lincoln was able to transfer Cameron to the harmless job of American Minister to Russia. He replaced him with a tough-minded War Democrat, Edwin M. Stanton, who cured the Department's corruption, improved its efficiency, and placed it squarely behind the war effort. When Lincoln finally settled on General Ulysses S. Grant as the Union commander in the field, the President, Stanton, and Grant functioned as a smoothly working, winning team.

The Presidential election of 1864 was the most unusual in American history, as it was carried on while the nation was torn apart by war. Lincoln believed that it was vital to demonstrate to the American people and the rest of the world that the orderly processes of government continued despite the rebellion. Republicans and War Democrats joined forces for this election as the National Union Party; their candidates were President Lincoln and Andrew Johnson of Tennessee, the only Southern Senator not to walk out of Congress. The Democratic Party nominated General George B. McClellan, formerly commander of the Union Army of the Potomac. McClellan had championed intensive military buildups but was overly cautious about using these forces against the Confederates; he was denied any field command after failing to pursue General Lee's retreating Confederates from Antietam. He ran as a peace candidate, hoping that his popularity among Union soldiers might bring him enough votes for victory. The Democrats also hoped that their choice of a war hero idolized by the rank-and-file soldiers of the Union would dispel public doubts about their patriotism.

Lincoln feared that he might not be re-elected. To lay the groundwork for a peaceful transfer of power, he had his Cabinet sign a folded piece of paper without telling them what he had written on it. It was a mass letter of resignation, which Lincoln would accept as the first step for preparing the transition to a McClellan administration. It proved unnecessary. Lincoln defeated McClellan by a margin large enough to give him a mandate for his war policy.

Photographs of Lincoln made as he began his second term show a worn, exhausted man carrying on his conscience every death, Union and Confederate, caused by the war. The early months of 1865 brought news that the war was finally coming to an end. General Grant was hemming in the remnants of Lee's Army of Northern Virginia; General William T. Sherman's campaign of fire and devastation in Georgia and South Carolina was pulverizing Southern resistance. The President's Second Inaugural Address, delivered on March 4, sketched his hopes for the society that would emerge from the war:

> With malice toward none, with charity for all, with firmness in the right as God gives us to see the right, let us strive to finish the work we are in, to bind up the nation's wounds, to care for him who shall have borne the battle and for his widow and his orphan, to do all which may achieve a just and lasting peace among ourselves and with all nations.

Grant's strategy of wearing Lee down had paid off. Within four weeks of Lincoln's inauguration, Richmond, the Confederate capital, had fallen. On April 9, 1865, General Grant accepted General Lee's surrender at Appomattox Courthouse, Virginia. (The white flags of truce, actually a towel and a pair of underdrawers, were accepted by Major General George A. Custer, who would enter the history books again at the Battle of Little Bighorn, in 1876.) The Confederate States of America was dead; the Union was secure. When he heard the news of the fall of the Confederacy, old Edmund Ruffin, who had fired the first shot of the war and had enlisted with rebel forces as a symbolic gesture, committed suicide by placing the barrel of a silver-mounted rifle in his mouth and pulling the trigger.

President Lincoln had only five days to savor the Union's victory and the adulation of his countrymen. After four years of vilification and criticism, the President was now the most popular man in the Union. On Good Friday, April 14, he chose to relax by attending a popular British comedy, *Our American Cousin*, at Ford's Theatre in Washington, D.C. As Lincoln and his party sat in the Presidential box laughing at the play, a twenty-six-year-old actor named John Wilkes Booth slipped past a negligent security guard, crept up behind the President, and fired a bullet into his brain. Lincoln never regained consciousness; he died the next day. Secretary Stanton said at the moment of Lincoln's death, "Now he belongs to the ages." It was the first murder of a President in American history.

Booth was a rabid Southern sympathizer. He had continued his acting career in Northern theaters during the war but burned to do something for the rebel cause. In early 1865, he had spun a mad plot to kidnap the President and hold him hostage for the Confederacy's independence. He changed his mind, however, and assembled a gang of third-rate thugs, criminals, and hangers-on to murder every high official of the Administration. Booth would deal with Lincoln himself. Another conspirator, assigned to murder Vice President Johnson, lost his nerve. Still another stabbed Secretary of State Seward, but Seward survived the attack.

Secretary of War Stanton took charge in the hours after Lincoln's murder. Union soldiers cornered Booth in a barn a few miles from the capital. A deranged private, Boston Corbett, shot Booth dead, acting (he claimed) on orders from God. The other conspirators were swiftly arrested, tried, convicted, and hanged.

Lincoln's funeral was the occasion for a national outpouring of grief. Even former rebels expressed sorrow. They were also fearful. They were not sure what fate the vengeful Johnson Administration would mete out to the defeated South.

Lincoln had hoped for a peaceful retirement in Springfield, where he might practice law and write his memoirs. Fate denied that wish, but his memory lives. He ranks with Washington as one of the two greatest Presidents, and many would agree that he is the nation's most beloved historical figure.

# CHAPTER FIVE

# FROM FORD'S THEATRE
# TO EXPOSITION HALL

In 1865, President Abraham Lincoln was shot dead. In 1901, President William McKinley was mortally wounded by the gunfire of another assassin. These two gunshots, both at point-blank range, marked the beginning and the end of an era in the history of the Presidency. In this thirty-six-year period, most Americans believed that the Presidency should subside into its "normal" role of carrying out the will of Congress. In his classic work *The American Commonwealth*, which first appeared in 1888, the Scottish historian and diplomat James Bryce devoted a chapter to the question "Why Great Men Are Not Chosen President." Trying to explain why such ciphers as William Henry Harrison, Franklin Pierce, and James Buchanan had become President while such great men as Henry Clay, John C. Calhoun, and Daniel Webster had not, Bryce suggested that the office provided no room for great men to do great things.

Lincoln's successor, Andrew Johnson, helped to bring about the situation that Bryce described, for he nearly brought the Presidency to disaster. At first, Johnson shared the desire of "Radical" Republicans in Congress to punish the Southern states for their rebellion, for Lincoln's murder, and for the pain and suffering left by the Civil War. But Johnson did not have a strong commitment to racial equality and to helping the freed slaves, as Lincoln and the Republicans had. He was willing to restore the conditions of Southern political life to what they had been before the war—with the whites safely in charge. But the Republicans who controlled Congress believed that it would be too dangerous for the nation to allow the politicians who had ruled the South in the years before the war to resume their power.

Congress framed a policy to govern the defeated Southern states as conquered territories and to protect the civil rights of freed slaves and other black Americans. This policy was called *Reconstruction*. President Johnson bitterly opposed Reconstruction and used his veto power to prevent Reconstruction bills from becoming law. Congress overrode Johnson's vetoes, but the President stubbornly refused to carry out the laws. This contest over Reconstruction policy escalated into a showdown between the President and the Congress.

The flashpoint came when Congress, fearing that the President would fire Cabinet members who agreed with Reconstruction, enacted over Johnson's veto a law known as the Tenure of Office Act: If the President wanted to fire any official whose appointment had required the consent of the Senate, he had to get Senate authorization to fire the official. Johnson tried to fire Secretary of War Edwin Stanton, but when the Senate refused its permission, the President defied the Senate and fired Stanton anyway. The Secretary of War barricaded himself in his office at the War Department and sent word to Congress.

Congress saw a chance to get rid of Johnson once and for all. The angry House of Representatives declared that the President had committed "high Crimes and Misdemeanors" justifying his removal from office through the constitutional process of impeachment. The Representatives did not care that Johnson had only a year left in his term of office. With remarkable speed, the House voted to impeach Johnson for violating the Tenure of Office Act. They framed eleven articles of impeachment and sent these formal charges to the Senate for trial.

The spring of 1868 was dominated by the first Presidential impeachment in American history. The President's defenders claimed that he could not be removed from office unless the House and Senate could show that he had committed specific violations of law, such as murder or fraud, for which a person could be indicted by a grand jury. Johnson's accusers replied that an impeachable offense was something more than a violation of criminal law. It could be whatever a majority of the House and two-thirds of the Senate thought it to be—or, at the least, a severe political offense against the Constitution and laws.

As required by the Constitution, the Chief Justice of the United States, Salmon P. Chase, presided over the Senate's trial of the President on the charges brought by the House. Chase worked hard to make certain that the Senate's trial would be fair and impartial. He did not want the process to degenerate into a political lynching.

Due to the Chief Justice's efforts, the supporters of impeachment began to worry that their campaign to oust the President might fail. They calculated that one-third of the Senators would vote to acquit the President. One more vote would save him, for the Constitution requires a two-thirds vote by the Senate for conviction and removal from office. As the roll call proceeded, Senator Edmund G. Ross of Kansas quietly waited for his name to be called. He was a Radical Republican who favored Congressional Reconstruction and often had voted against Johnson's vetoes, but he had his doubts about the impeachment effort. The pro-impeachment forces had counted him among their ranks, but when the clerk of the Senate called Ross's name, the Senator answered firmly: "Not Guilty." He had saved Johnson and the Presidency—and destroyed his own political career.

Historians agree that if Johnson had been convicted, the independence of the Presidency would have been destroyed. Congress would have had the power to oust a President simply for disagreeing with it rather than for the serious reasons that an impeachment requires. Nonetheless, the impeachment effort left a deep scar on the Presidency. For the rest of the century, Johnson's successors had to defend the office from the encroachments of Congress.

Johnson's successor, General Ulysses S. Grant, made peace with Congress—but on Congress's terms. The victorious Union general was a national hero, and the Republicans believed that he would be their ideal candidate in the 1868 election. Grant indeed triumphed in 1868, and won re-election in 1872, as the symbol of the common man. Unfortunately, in office he turned out to be all too common. Congress quickly let him know who was really running the government, and Grant gave in. All that can be said in favor of Grant's Presidency is that he was the first President since Andrew Jackson, four decades earlier, to serve two full terms of office. Grant went along with Congressional Reconstruction but did little to protect the rights of freed slaves. His Administration was notable mainly for its epidemic of corruption at almost every level of government. When he left office in 1876, the nation breathed a collective sigh of relief.

Americans wanted to remember Grant as the military leader who had triumphed over the Confederate armies, not as the symbol of American political corruption.

The 1876 Presidential election was a paradox: It was the dirtiest campaign, and yet it featured two of the cleanest Presidential candidates, in American history. Republican Rutherford B. Hayes, the Governor of Ohio and a former Union general, squared off against Democrat Samuel J. Tilden, the Governor of New York. At first, it seemed that Tilden, with fifty-one percent of the popular vote, had been elected. Hayes even conceded defeat to a reporter. But Republicans swiftly charged that vote fraud in three Southern states—Louisiana, Florida, and South Carolina—had cost Hayes the election. As the Constitution provides, the disputed election went into the House of Representatives, but Congress decided instead to name a special investigating commission to weigh the claims of each candidate to the disputed electoral votes. Tilden needed only one of these electoral votes to win the election, but Hayes needed all nineteen of them. After a still-mysterious series of deals and trades, the commission awarded the Republican Hayes all the electoral votes of the disputed states. In return, Republicans in Congress pledged to end Reconstruction and withdraw the federal soldiers who occupied the Southern states.

President Hayes was an honest man who was the prisoner of the Republican Party organization; all he could do was close his eyes to the wheeling and dealing that had put him into the Executive Mansion. He complied with the pledges made by the Republicans in Congress, ordering the withdrawal of the occupying army from the former Confederate states. North and South tried to pretend that the Civil War was behind them.

Hayes's great cause was civil service reform. He fought for laws to establish qualifications for government jobs and a system of merit selection to make sure that only the best qualified persons could win office. His integrity was widely respected, but the Republican Party organization was not willing to renominate him in 1880.

Both the Republicans and the Democrats now resorted to nominating Civil War generals for the Presidency. The Democrats chose Winfield Scott Hancock, nicknamed "Superb" for his valiant stands in battle. The Republicans resisted the blandishments of former President Grant, seeking a chance for an unprecedented third term at the urging of Senator Roscoe Conkling of New York. They settled on a compromise ticket. Their candidate was Representative James A.

Garfield of Ohio (a former general of the Union's Army of the Cumberland). The Republicans were split into two great factions, the Stalwarts (party loyalists who resisted such reforms as civil service) and the Mugwumps (who accepted these reforms). Garfield was a Mugwump, and his running mate, Chester A. Arthur of New York, was a Stalwart and a Conkling protege. The Republicans narrowly defeated the Democrats in a dull campaign.

Garfield was a polished orator, but he was a weak man who bent to the pressure of the party bosses. He found no joy in the Presidency, but he did not last long. In the summer of 1881, after only four months in office, he was walking with Secretary of State James G. Blaine through the waiting room of the Baltimore and Potomac railroad station in Washington, D.C., when thirty-nine-year-old Charles J. Guiteau shot him twice in the back at point-blank range. Crying out, "My God, what is this?," Garfield fell to the floor as bystanders disarmed Guiteau. The assassin surrendered without a fight. "I am a Stalwart, and Arthur is President!" he shouted confidently. The mentally unstable Guiteau had made a nuisance of himself demanding a government job for having supported Garfield, who had ignored his requests. But Guiteau was not given the political reward he expected. Instead, he was arrested and jailed. His lawyers tried to persuade the court that Guiteau was insane, but he refused to permit the tactic. He told the court that God had ordered him to kill the President. He was convicted, sentenced to death, and—singing "I am going to the Lord, I am so glad"—hanged. President Garfield lingered in agony for more than two months before dying on September 19.

Speculation swirled around the elegant, easy-going Chester A. Arthur. In the 1870s, he had been Collector of Customs at the Port of New York, a job he owed to Senator Conkling, and in that post had turned a blind eye to the rampant corruption flourishing there. Once he became President, however, Arthur amazed all who had known him: He became an even more ardent opponent of corruption and champion of civil service than Hayes had been. Arthur was not considered for nomination in 1884. As it happened, Arthur was suffering from Bright's disease, a fatal kidney ailment, and he died less than two years after leaving office.

The 1884 Presidential election was another lively—and dirty—campaign. The Democratic candidate, Governor Grover Cleveland of New York, seemed incorruptible—until a young woman came forward and accused him of being the father of her illegitimate son. The unmarried Cleveland admitted that her charges were plausible and promised to assume responsibility for the child. His opponent, the handsome and articulate James G. Blaine of Maine, was nicknamed the "Plumed Knight" by his adoring supporters. But Blaine turned out to have been mired in several of the worst scandals of the Grant era.

One anonymous editor suggested that Cleveland's public career was honorable but that his private life was stained; Blaine's private life was above reproach, but his public record was open to question. Therefore, the voters should choose Cleveland for the Presidency and retire Blaine to private life. The voters did prefer Cleveland, but the Democrat's victory was due mostly to a joke made by a Republican clergyman who denounced the Democrats as "the party of Rum, Romanism, and Rebellion!" Democratic strategists made sure that every Roman Catholic voter heard about the slur in time for the election.

Cleveland was the most vigorous defender of the Presidency in this period. He became known as the "veto President" because of his 301 vetoes in his first term (and 584 in his two terms). Most of these vetoes rejected "private pension bills" to benefit veterans of the Civil War; Cleveland showed, in veto messages dripping with sarcasm, that the vetoed claims for pensions were completely unjustified. His first four years in office resulted in a budget surplus of $100 million.

Cleveland is the only President to be married in the Executive Mansion. The forty-nine-year-old President married his twenty-one-year-old ward in a wedding that was the social event of the year. John Philip Sousa and the Marine Band provided the music. Frances Cleveland won the hearts of the nation—and boosted her husband's popularity.

The Democrats cheerfully renominated the President in 1888. Against him, the Republicans pitted yet another Civil War general, Benjamin Harrison of Indiana, a hero in the Atlanta campaign. Harrison was the grandson of the ninth President, William Henry Harrison, and the Republicans made much of the family relationship (though "Tippecanoe" had served only one month). The principal issue of the election was whether, as the Republicans argued, the nation should adopt tariffs to protect American industries from foreign competition or whether it should continue its policy of *free trade*, allowing the forces of the market to determine prices and requiring American manufacturers to compete with European manufacturers. Cleveland edged Harrison in the popular vote—but Harrison carried states with a majority of electoral votes and became President.

The Harrison Administration dissipated the surplus that the Cleveland Administration had amassed in the federal treasury. Congress abandoned free trade, but the tariffs injured American trade with Europe and led to an economic downturn. Scenting victory, the Democrats in 1892 called Cleveland out of political retirement and won back the Presidency. (Cleveland is the only President to have served non-consecutive terms.)

The economic slump under President Harrison grew into the Depression of 1893, which cast a pall over Cleveland's second term. Other economic problems plagued the nation as well. The most serious was the Pullman strike of 1894. The Pullman Palace Car Company, a manufacturer of railroad sleeping cars, had founded what it considered to be a "model town" for its workers and had sharply reduced employee wages. Pullman workers hated Pullman, Illinois, claiming that it was little better than a prison. They struck the company, demanding better wages and the right to be paid in cash, which they could spend anywhere, rather than in "scrip" good only at the "company stores" in Pullman. The employers called for government help to quell the strike, which spread to other railroads and crippled rail traffic between Chicago and the West Coast. U.S. Attorney General Richard Olney, himself a railroad director, persuaded the President to send in federal soldiers to break the strike to get the U.S. mail moving. In the bloody violence that followed, the workers suffered heavy casualties.

Cleveland had troubles in foreign policy as well. He defended the Monroe Doctrine so vigorously in a boundary dispute between Venezuela and the British colony of British Guiana that the United States nearly went to war with Great Britain. The dispute eventually was peacefully resolved in favor of British Guiana.

The President suffered a grave illness in his second term and underwent an operation for cancer. Half of his upper jaw was removed and replaced with a rubber prosthetic. The operation, carried out aboard a yacht on the East River in New York City, was performed in secret; not even Vice President Adlai Stevenson was informed. Not until twenty-four years later, ten years after Cleveland's death, was the operation disclosed to the public.

The farmers of the West were hit hard by the 1893 Depression and blamed their plight on Eastern bankers and politicians who kept a tight rein on the nation's money supply. The farmers claimed that the monetary system thus prevented them from being able to pay their debts. They demanded that the government issue silver money at the inflated rate of sixteen silver dollars for every gold dollar in circulation; "free silver," they thought, would make it easier for them to repay their debts. President Cleveland opposed this policy because he feared its effects on the stability of American money.

At the Democratic Convention in 1896, a thirty-six-year-old Nebraska lawyer and delegate, William Jennings Bryan, brought the delegates to their feet with an eloquent, impassioned plea for free silver. At the end of his speech, he cried, "You shall not crucify mankind upon this cross of gold!" The "Cross of Gold" speech won Bryan the Democratic Presidential nomination, though most of the delegates had never heard of him before the convention.

Bryan was the youngest man ever nominated for the Presidency by a major political party. He energetically campaigned across the nation by train, preaching the glories of free silver and denouncing the heartless Eastern financial community. By contrast, the Republican nominee, William McKinley, stayed home on his front porch in Ohio, receiving visiting delegations and making vague speeches for the newspapers. Governor McKinley, an experienced politician, was the last Presidential candidate to have served in the Civil War. He defeated Bryan and won the Presidency back for the Republicans.

Within a year of his inauguration in 1897, McKinley became a reluctant war President. The Americans had long distrusted Spain and resented the few remaining Spanish colonies in the Western Hemisphere and the Pacific islands, such as Cuba, Puerto Rico, and the Philippines. They listened eagerly to exaggerated reports of Spanish atrocities and mistreatment of Cubans, Puerto Ricans, Filipinos, and foreign nationals in these colonies. In February 1898, the battleship U.S.S. Maine, lying at anchor in the harbor of Havana, Cuba, suddenly and mysteriously exploded and sank, killing 260 American sailors. Infuriated Americans blamed Spain. The Spanish government insisted that it had not been responsible and offered all help needed to investigate the tragedy. But the American press and the American people had made up their minds, and Congress and the President soon fell into step. McKinley explained that, after much prayer, he had decided that the United States had to go to war to free and civilize "our little brown brothers."

The Spanish-American War was a disgrace. Mark Twain denounced it as the international equivalent of bullying. In battles on land and sea, American forces easily overcame the Spanish army and navy. The United States wrested Cuba, Puerto Rico, the Philippines, and other colonies in the Pacific from the Spanish. In an unrelated incident, American settlers in the independent kingdom of Hawaii overthrew the centuries-old monarchy there and persuaded the United States to annex the islands, which are more than 2,000 miles southwest of California. (The President told reporters, "God told me to take the Philippines"—but he admitted that he had no idea where they were.)

Bryan won the Democratic nomination again in 1900, this time denouncing the Spanish-American War and American "imperialism." He charged that the Republicans had conned the American people into grabbing an empire for the United States as greedily as the British, French, Germans, Belgians, and other Europeans were doing in Africa and Asia. The Republicans renominated President McKinley and chose as his new running-mate Theodore Roosevelt of New York. Roosevelt had been Assistant Secretary of the Navy in 1898, and had ordered the mobilization of the Navy immediately after the destruction of the *Maine*. He had then resigned to organize a volunteer cavalry unit, the "Rough Riders." Colonel Roosevelt became the hero of the Battle of San Juan Hill in Cuba and returned home to win the Governorship of New York. Terrified by TR's campaign for reform and efficiency in government, the New York Republican political machine successfully begged McKinley to "kick Roosevelt upstairs," to get him out of the state and into a job where he could do no damage. The President's mentor and campaign manager, Ohio industrialist Mark Hanna, despised Roosevelt, calling him a "damn cowboy." On being nominated, Roosevelt traveled by rail across the nation as energetically as Bryan, making hundreds of speeches while McKinley once again conducted a "front porch" campaign. Running on the theme of the "full dinner pail," which emphasized American prosperity, the Republicans kept the Presidency.

McKinley had no real enemies. He was popular with, even beloved by, the American people. In September 1901, he traveled to Buffalo, New York, to open the Pan-American Exposition taking place there. As he shook hands in a receiving line in the Exposition's Temple of Music, McKinley noticed that one guest had his right hand wrapped in a bandage. The President reached out to shake the man's hand.

Suddenly, two shots rang out from a pistol concealed under the bandage and McKinley collapsed, mortally wounded. His assassin was a twenty-eight-year-old unemployed mill worker named Leon Czolgosz, who declared that he had nothing against the President. His crime was an act of principle, Czolgosz explained in broken English; he was an *anarchist*, someone who wanted to abolish all governments. The President died after eight days, and the nation went into mourning. But Mark Hanna, who had built McKinley's political career, had special reason to mourn his friend's death and to worry about the future. "Good Lord!" he cried. "Now that Goddamn cowboy is President of the United States!"

# CHAPTER SIX

# THE PROGRESSIVE PRESIDENTS: THEODORE ROOSEVELT, TAFT, WILSON

Theodore Roosevelt was the first President to have an understanding of the office that Americans would recognize today. He was the first President to use the office to take the lead in identifying national problems and proposing solutions to them. He was the first President to believe that the President has the power and the responsibility to set the national agenda. He declared that the Presidency was a "bully pulpit"—and he made the most of it. He knew how to get his message to the people through the press. He knew how to capture the popular imagination.

No one could be neutral about Theodore Roosevelt. His youth and vigor delighted and amazed the nation. His active, rambunctious children interrupted diplomatic negotiations and formal receptions, driving wagons through the halls of the White House (a name that Roosevelt gave official status) and engaging their father in wrestling matches before astonished dignitaries. One observer declared: "At every wedding, Theodore wants to be the bride. At every funeral, he wants to be the corpse."

On the domestic front, Roosevelt fought to conserve America's natural resources and such natural wonders as Yosemite National Park, on the west slope of the Sierra Nevada in California. His environmental mentor was Gifford Pinchot, whom Roosevelt named to head the new National Park Service. The President also sought to control the giant corporations, the monopolies and trusts and holding companies that controlled the wealth and economic life of the nation. He became known as the "trust buster."

On the world stage, the President pursued a strong, even aggressive foreign policy. He sent the American "Great White Fleet" around the world to show off American might. When Congress had resisted the idea, refusing to appropriate money to pay for the odyssey, Roosevelt ordered the expedition anyway. The fleet had only enough fuel to go halfway around the globe; Congress was forced to appropriate funds to pay for more fuel to bring the ships home—the outcome that the President had in mind all along.

When Colombia would not permit the United States to build a canal through its narrow strip of Central American land known as Panama, Roosevelt connived with American settlers and local revolutionaries. The result was a revolution in Panama. The President bolstered the Panamanian bid for independence by parking an American gunboat offshore to protect American citizens (who were helping to

*Theodore Roosevelt (1858—1919; term, 1901—1909) loved being President so much that he ran for a third term in 1912 (but lost). The "Rough Rider" brought boundless energy to the Presidency, making it the focus of modern American government.*

lead the revolution). When Colombia was forced to recognize Panama's independence, Roosevelt negotiated a treaty with the Panamanian government that granted the United States a perpetual lease of a ten-mile-wide strip across Panama. The United States thus got to dig the "great ditch," the Panama Canal, linking the Atlantic and Pacific oceans and eliminating the interminable ship passage around South America—the greatest engineering project of the age. Roosevelt later boasted: "I took the Canal—and let Congress debate." As the canal was being built, the President was so impatient to see the result of his maneuvering that he sailed to Panama to take a look for himself, becoming the first President to leave the continental United States while in office.

In 1904, Roosevelt ran for a term of his own. He won by a landslide, the first since President Lincoln had defeated General McClellan in 1864. His Democratic opponent was a conservative judge, Alton B. Parker of New York. Roosevelt's slogan, borrowed from the game of poker, was "Stand Pat." (Parker's running mate, Henry G. Davis of West Virginia, was, at eighty-one, the oldest major-party candidate ever nominated for national office.)

Roosevelt's second term was even more successful than his first in some ways, and his greatest achievement won international praise. In 1905, the President decided to try to end the destructive and useless war between Russia and Japan. He offered his services as mediator, and the two nations sent delegations to Portsmouth, New Hampshire, where Roosevelt bullied, charmed, and reasoned them into an agreement. For his role in negotiating the Treaty of Portsmouth, Roosevelt became the first American to receive the Nobel Peace Prize.

Roosevelt announced that he would not seek another term of office. He brushed aside questions about what an energetic fifty-year-old ex-President would find to occupy himself. He endorsed as his successor his friend and Secretary of War, William Howard Taft, who easily defeated William Jennings Bryan's third, and last, bid for the Presidency. Roosevelt went off to Africa to hunt big game.

Taft was the heaviest man ever to become President. The 350-pound Ohioan had been a distinguished lawyer and judge and Governor-General of the Philippines after the Spanish-American War. His lifelong dream was to become Chief Justice, but the opportunity never presented itself. Ironically, in 1910, he appointed another man to the office he craved for himself.

Taft pursued many of the policies that Roosevelt had launched. He actually was a more vigorous trust buster than Roosevelt had been.

His conservation policy differed from Roosevelt's, however. Secretary of the Interior Richard Ballinger tangled repeatedly with Gifford Pinchot in a bruising dispute over conservation. Roosevelt was outraged. He charged that Taft had betrayed his legacy. Rumors flew that Roosevelt was thinking of challenging Taft for the Presidency in 1912.

The Republican convention that year confirmed the rumors, but Taft beat back the Roosevelt forces. If the Republicans and the nation expected Roosevelt to take his defeat lying down, however, they were mistaken. The ex-President called for a new convention—a convention of "Progressives."

Historians identify Roosevelt as the first Progressive President. The Progressives were a wide and diverse movement of political, social, and economic reformers including Republicans and Democrats. Taft, too, was a Progressive, though not as consistent as Roosevelt. The break between the two men resulted in Taft's ouster from the Progressive movement.

The Progressive convention was a rag-tag collection of reformers and Rough Riders—and some political cranks. They organized themselves as a new political party, the Progressive Party, and nominated Roosevelt by acclamation. Roosevelt accepted the nomination, declaring, "My hat is in the ring" and "I feel as fit as a bull moose!" This defiant statement earned the Progressive Party the nickname of the Bull Moose Party. Roosevelt rallied his supporters to support the policies he dubbed "the New Nationalism," proclaiming: "We stand at Armageddon and we battle for the Lord!"

Meanwhile, the Democrats had chosen their nominee—another product of the Progressive movement, Governor Woodrow Wilson of New Jersey. Born in Virginia, Wilson was the first Southern-born candidate for the White House since Kentucky-born Abraham Lincoln in 1860. Wilson had been a lawyer, a scholar, and the president of Princeton University before the Democratic machine politicians of New Jersey picked him as a figurehead candidate for Governor. Anyone looking at Wilson's stubborn jaw should have known better. He was his own man, and he soon became known as one of the most liberal and forward-looking members of the Democratic Party.

Wilson differed from Roosevelt and Taft. They believed that not all concentrations of wealth and economic power were always bad. They maintained that government should break up such concentrations of wealth and power only when they clearly threatened the public interest. Otherwise, government should work cooperatively with business

Collections of the Library of Congress

*Woodrow Wilson (1856—1924; term, 1913—1921) (Democrat-New Jersey) was the first scholar-President since Thomas Jefferson and a leading advocate of the Progressive movement. Building on Theodore Roosevelt's model of the energetic Presidency, Wilson was the first President to address Congress in person since Jefferson gave up the practice over a century earlier. He led the nation into the First World War, but Senate opposition to the Treaty of Versailles shattered his cherished hopes for founding an international peacekeeping organization. He left office in 1921, broken in health and bitter in spirit, and died three years later.*

and labor. Governor Wilson agreed with his friend and ally the Boston lawyer and social critic Louis D. Brandeis that one of the greatest threats faced by the American people was the "curse of bigness." Wilson coined the phrase "New Freedom" to describe his policies.

The 1912 campaign was notable for the first attempt to assassinate a Presidential candidate. As Roosevelt was about to enter a hall in Milwaukee, Wisconsin, to make a speech, he was shot by John N. Schrank, a thirty-six-year-old German immigrant bartender who acted under the delusion that the ghost of President McKinley had ordered him to execute Roosevelt for McKinley's murder. Roosevelt was carrying a thick manuscript of his speech folded up in his breast pocket. The manuscript and the ex-President's metal eyeglass case absorbed the impact of the .32 calibre bullet, saving Roosevelt's life. Though the bullet fractured a rib, TR insisted on delivering the hour-long speech, and afterward was rushed to a hospital. (The bullet was never removed.)

In the election of 1912, the split between Taft and Roosevelt resulted in a popular vote of only 42 percent for Wilson, but he racked up a landslide (435 votes) in the Electoral College. Roosevelt outpolled Taft in both the popular and the electoral votes—the only time that a third-party candidate has outstripped a major party's nominee, and the incumbent at that.

To some extent, Roosevelt's defeat was his own fault. He had tried to defy the venerable two-term tradition. Although he argued that he had had only one full term of his own, this justification of his candidacy did not convince the voters. He returned to private life, to journalism, and to the frustration of being out of the arena. Taft retired to Yale Law School to teach and write.

President Wilson's stubbornness soon got him into trouble with Congress, and he was not consistently successful in getting what he wanted from it. But he scored a major coup. He became the first President since John Adams to appear before Congress to deliver his message on the "state of the Union" rather than to send it in writing. This step confirmed the President's role in setting the agenda of national politics.

Wilson supported a stronger antitrust law to break up large businesses. He won creation of a new government agency, the Federal Reserve Board, to regulate American currency and to help stabilize the economy.

The President's first wife had died in August 1914, but in December 1915 the nation buzzed with the news that the President had fallen in love again. The new Mrs. Wilson, a widow, Edith Bolling Galt, was extremely popular with the country and the press, which gushed over the "White House romance" and made the Presidential wedding front-page news.

In 1916, the President sought a second term. His Republican opponent was Charles Evans Hughes of New York, who had stepped down from a Supreme Court Justiceship. His reformist credentials satisfied even Theodore Roosevelt (though the former President grumbled that Hughes reminded him of the bearded lady at the circus). Hughes had been a capable governor of New York and a first-rate Justice. By accepting the Republican Presidential nomination, he united the Taft and Roosevelt wings of the party. The contest was close—so close that Hughes and Wilson both believed that Hughes had won. But Hughes had made a major mistake during the campaign. He had offended Republican Governor Hiram Johnson of California, who refused to lift a finger to help Hughes's campaign. As a result, California went for Wilson by a hair—giving the President a second term.

Wilson had campaigned on the slogan "He Kept Us Out of War." In 1914, war had erupted in Europe in the wake of the assassination of Archduke Franz Ferdinand of Austria-Hungary by a Serbian nationalist. The catastrophic struggle that we now call the First World War appalled Americans. Germany had invented a deadly, "invisible" weapon, the torpedo-firing submarine (or "U-boat"), and the German Navy followed a policy of unrestricted U-boat warfare against shipping destined for the British and French. Any shipping, not just enemy vessels, was fair game for the Germans. American warnings had persuaded them to give up this policy for a short time, but in early 1917 the Germans announced the resumption of unrestricted submarine warfare. On April 2, the President appeared before a joint session of Congress. Wilson asked for a declaration of war, and, four days later, Congress followed through.

The United States entered the war in opposition to Germany and Austria-Hungary (the Central Powers) and in alliance with Great Britain, France, Italy, and Japan (the Allies). Russia, which had entered the war on the side of the Allies, had been forced out of the war in 1917 by the internal Bolshevik "October Revolution." President Wilson declared that the United States had no ambitions for territory or conquest; it only wanted "to make the world safe for democracy." Wilson outlined American war aims in his famous "Fourteen Points" speech in early 1918. He called for an end to imperialism and colonialism and urged that all nations of the world be given the right to control their own lives (what he called "self-determination"). He also advocated free trade and the establishment of an international peacekeeping organization, the League of Nations.

Despite Wilson's idealism, many Americans believed that the war against Germany, the principal enemy, was a war for civilization against the "Huns." Reprisals in the United States against people of German descent were commonplace. German culture was shunned. German music, including the works of Bach and Beethoven, vanished from the concert halls. U.S. culture was purged of German influence. Sauerkraut became "liberty cabbage."

American manpower and supplies turned the tide of the war in favor of the Allies. Both sides were exhausted by the time the United States entered the war. Although the American Expeditionary Force did not see combat until June 1918 and fought independent of Allied control, they soon made the difference. Germany could no longer fight, and it sued for peace. On November 11, 1918, a peace agreement, or *armistice*, was signed. The people of the world erupted in joyful celebration.

The final treaty of peace was to be negotiated at the French palace of Versailles in the spring of 1919. Wilson chose to lead the American peace delegation himself against the advice of his aides, who begged him not to risk his prestige. Wilson believed that he and he alone could get the Allies to adopt his Fourteen Points as the basis of the treaty. He refused to follow his aides' advice that he appoint a bipartisan peace delegation to ensure that the Republicans in the Senate would be willing to ratify the treaty. He sowed the seeds of the treaty's destruction with these decisions.

The President's triumphant arrival in Paris convinced him that the people of the world supported his goals. He was sadly mistaken. The leaders of Britain, France, and Italy were eager to dismantle Germany's empire and share the pieces among themselves. They were prepared to redraw the map of Europe to their own advantage; they did not encourage self-determination. They were willing to grant the U.S. President only the League of Nations, and the battered Wilson seized on this "concession" as the one redeeming feature of an otherwise harsh and vindictive treaty.

President Wilson sailed home, hoping that the extraordinary popularity he had enjoyed among the citizens of Europe had swayed American public opinion in favor of the treaty. But the Senate was not convinced. As Senators examined the treaty, many did not like what they read. Some focused on the President's failure to restrain the greed and anger of the European allies. Many disliked the proposed League of Nations, believing that it would damage American independence. Republican Henry Cabot Lodge of Massachusetts, the chairman of the Senate Foreign Relations Committee, proposed a set of "reservations" to the treaty focusing on the League.

Wilson reacted with stubborn anger. He insisted that the treaty was not simply the best he could get—it was a great treaty that the peoples of the world wanted and deserved. American refusal to ratify would destroy the world's hopes for an end to war. The war had been a war to end all wars. The Senate must not stand in the way of that great dream.

The President decided to go over the heads of the Senate to the American people. He campaigned across the nation, giving dozens of speeches in twenty-nine cities in three weeks from coast to coast urging adoption of the treaty. In Pueblo, Colorado, the President suffered a physical breakdown. He was rushed back to Washington, where he soon suffered a severe stroke. The President was crippled and bedridden, a virtual recluse in the White House. Mrs. Wilson took charge; some critics said that she was the acting President. Vice President Thomas R. Marshall was kept in the dark.

Despite his illness, Wilson refused to give in to pressures to accept the Lodge Reservations. But the Senate finally defeated the treaty. Wilson suggested to close friends that he should run for a third term, making the League of Nations the focus of the campaign, but he was persuaded to drop the idea; he could walk only haltingly, and with a cane. The 1920 Democratic nominee, Governor James M. Cox of Ohio, endorsed both the treaty and the League. His running-mate was Franklin D. Roosevelt, the young and handsome Assistant Secretary of the Navy. (Many voters mistakenly thought that he was Theodore Roosevelt's son.) Wilson watched from the sidelines, taking some comfort from having been awarded the 1920 Nobel Peace Prize.

The Republicans scented victory, but they were bitterly divided. In late 1918, they had been prepared to unite behind former President Roosevelt, but he had died suddenly in January 1919. Several candidates claimed to be Roosevelt's legitimate political heir. But the Republicans looked elsewhere. They found a "safe" candidate—an obscure Ohio Senator named Warren G. Harding. The handsome but vague former newspaper publisher had no obvious drawbacks, and he seemed tailor-made to capture the bloc of women voters enfranchised by the newly ratified Nineteenth Amendment. As his running-mate, the convention picked dour, silent Governor Calvin Coolidge of

Massachusetts. The Vermont-born Coolidge had won national fame for his swift and brutal suppression of the Boston police strike of 1919.

Harding and Coolidge buried Cox and Roosevelt. Wilson despaired of the nation's judgment; he thought that his successor was an uncultured fool. But the nation was tired of war, tired of reform. The American people wanted to relax, and Harding and Coolidge promised "not nostrums, but normalcy."

# CHAPTER SEVEN

# THE REPUBLICAN REIGN

Warren Gamaliel Harding was in many ways a throwback to the days of McKinley. He had run a front-porch campaign, avoiding specifics about issues such as the Treaty of Versailles and the League of Nations. (A leading Republican boss, Boies Penrose, had sent word to Harding's managers from his deathbed: "Keep Warren home. Don't let him make any speeches. If he does, someone's bound to ask questions, and Warren's just the sort of fool to try to answer them!") Harding planned to run a largely passive Presidency.

Harding's time in the Oval Office included a few notable achievements. The Washington Disarmament Conference of 1921, orchestrated by Secretary of State Charles Evans Hughes, resulted in an agreement by the United States, Britain, France, Italy, and Japan to limit the size of their navies. Harding made the first Presidential civil rights speech in the Deep South. He had several able advisers, among them Secretary of State Hughes and Secretary of Commerce Herbert Hoover.

But Harding's Administration was more famous for its scandals than its accomplishments. For every Hughes and Hoover, Harding named two dunces, such as Secretary of the Navy Edwin Denby, and several outright crooks, such as Secretary of the Interior Albert B. Fall and Attorney General Harry Daugherty.

Harding knew his limits. He admitted that he was completely unqualified for the Presidency. He had suffered a nervous breakdown as a young man and had fragile nerves throughout his life. "My God!" he once exclaimed about the White House. "What is there in this job that a man should ever want to get into it?" His iron-willed wife, Florence, was more ambitious than Harding. She had been the driving force behind his quest for the 1920 Republican Presidential nomination, and she enjoyed being First Lady far more then he enjoyed being President. Harding preferred to play poker with his cronies.

The Constitution had been amended in 1919 to prohibit the sale or manufacture of alcoholic beverages. *Prohibition,* the short term for the Eighteenth Amendment and the laws enacted to enforce it, was unpopular, but few politicians could afford to offend women's organizations, religious groups, and the Anti-Saloon League by opposing it. Still, the American people generally wanted a drink. The United States became a nation of law-breakers, from President Harding on down.

This free-and-easy attitude toward the law swept through the Harding Administration. The Attorney General could not be bothered to enforce the laws—he was too busy collecting payoffs for his refusal to crack down on bootleggers. The head of the Veterans' Bureau milked his agency dry at the expense of thousands of veterans.

The worst scandal involved Secretaries Fall and Denby and two tracts of land called oil reserves belonging to the Navy: Teapot Dome, Wyoming, and Elk Hills, Nevada. These oil fields were held in reserve in case of another war, when they would provide American warships with guaranteed fuel supplies. Secretary Fall persuaded the amiable Secretary Denby to transfer control of the oil reserves from the Navy Department to the Interior Department. Denby asked no questions. Fall made a killing for himself as oil company executives deluged him with bribes for permission to drill in the reserves. When necessary, Fall gave a tangled and dishonest explanation about how such drilling was actually for the benefit of maintaining the oil reserves. It sounded convincing if one did not look too closely.

The President was only dimly aware of the sleazy deals being struck all around him. He was honest in his public life. His private life was something else again. He tried to forget his cares by gambling and drinking with friends in a small Washington townhouse nicknamed "the little house on K Street." He had given up one long-time mistress, the handsome wife of a dry-goods merchant in his home town of Marion, Ohio, but he carried on an affair in a closet in the White House with a second mistress, a stenographer named Nan Britton, with whom he had a daughter.

Harding was sick, he was tired, and he was fed up. In 1921, he had appointed former President Taft to be Chief Justice—and Taft repaid Harding's granting of his lifelong dream by bullying him to appoint conservative federal judges. Harding had named his friends to important jobs—and they had repaid him by stealing the country blind. As the President began to realize just how corrupt some of his appointees were, he became enraged. One visitor to the White House reported seeing Harding administering a terrible beating to Charles Forbes, the corrupt head of the Veterans' Bureau. Harding complained to the eminent journalist William Allen White, "I don't worry about my enemies—I can take care of them all right. It's my friends that keep me walking the floors at night!"

In the summer of 1923, the President made a cross-country Voyage of Understanding (in reality, a vacation) along the Pacific Coast. He visited the territory of Alaska, the first President to do so, and several cities in the Northwest. During a rest stop in San Francisco, as he listened to his wife read aloud a flattering magazine article about him, President Harding suddenly died.

Vice President Coolidge got the news of the President's death during a family visit at his father's home in Plymouth Notch, Vermont. The senior Coolidge, a justice of the peace and a notary public, administered the Presidential oath of office to his son by the light of a kerosene lamp. The scene dramatized Coolidge's appeal to the American people as a symbol of traditional American values.

By the end of 1923, the lid had blown off the scandals surrounding the Harding Administration. "Teapot Dome" became the catchphrase used to describe the whole sordid mess. Congressional and public investigations stunned the nation. A tight-lipped President Coolidge fired Attorney General Daugherty and appointed in his place the Dean of Columbia Law School, Harlan Fiske Stone. The two men had known each other since their student days at Amherst College, in Massachusetts, in the 1890s. Coolidge gave Stone a mandate—clean up the Administration—and Stone complied. The nation was reassured. The new President clearly had had nothing to do with the mess in Washington.

Coolidge won a term of his own in 1924 with the slogan "Keep Cool with Coolidge." He easily defeated the disorganized Democratic Party, whose convention had lasted for two weeks and 103 ballots before naming a Presidential candidate, a little-known corporation lawyer and former Solicitor General, John W. Davis. Disaffected liberals again split off from both parties and formed a new Progressive Party, led by Senator Robert LaFollette of Wisconsin.

Coolidge, depressed by the sudden death of his son, became the ultimate do-nothing President. He said little and slept twelve hours a day. He once woke from a long nap and asked, "Is the country still here?" He claimed that if you saw ten troubles heading for you, your best policy was to do nothing—nine would fall by the wayside, and you would have only one to deal with. He declared that "the business of America is business," and observed, "When more and more people are thrown out of work, unemployment tends to be the result." While Americans spent more and more and gambled recklessly on the stock market during the "Roaring Twenties," the President kept silent. Several economists, however, saw warning signs of a coming financial crash.

Coolidge announced in 1928, "I do not choose to run." Some historians think that he was hinting that he wanted to be drafted for the nomination, but the Republicans took him at his word, naming Secretary of Commerce Herbert Hoover as their candidate. They counted on Hoover's worldwide fame and sterling record of efficiency, brilliance, and compassion. The man who had been the mastermind of American famine relief for Europe in 1918–1919 seemed unbeatable.

The Democrats chose Governor Alfred E. Smith of New York to oppose Hoover. Smith, the first Roman Catholic to be nominated for President by a major party, had close ties to voters from urban areas and the "newer" ethnic groups from Southern and Eastern Europe. He supported repeal of Prohibition. But his views and connections disturbed voters in the South and Midwest, and his religion brought out every hate group from under every rock across the land. They were more comfortable with the familiar and safe Hoover and elected him handily.

In the late 1920s, most Americans believed that the nation's economy was booming. Indeed, as President Hoover confidently predicted in his inaugural address in March 1929, poverty might well vanish from American life once and for all. But some economists were deeply worried. They argued that the ever-rising stock market was overdue for a major tumble. A crash would bury millions of Americans who had plunged into the gamble of buying and trading stock.

The crash finally came in October 1929. On October 24 and again on October 29, the bottom fell out of the New York Stock Exchange. Within two weeks, stock prices plunged so far that $30 billion in the market value of listed stocks vanished. By mid-1932, this figure had more than doubled, to $75 billion. The Great Crash was the opening act of the severest economic catastrophe in American history.

The effects of the Crash, which eventually developed into what historians call the Great Depression, did not show themselves over-night. But as month succeeded month and the ripples from the Crash spread throughout the economy, all agreed that the economic "mira-cle" of the 1920s was finally over. Factories shut their gates and closed, and millions of frightened citizens lost their jobs. Had that "miracle" ever been real? The businessman had been the hero of the 1920s, but Americans no longer admired the businessman in the 1930s. Instead, they demanded a solution to the crisis.

President Hoover recognized the seriousness of the situation, but he believed that the free-enterprise system, like a huge and complex self-regulating machine, would fix itself. Prosperity, he kept saying, was "just around the corner." The President's promise grew ever more hollow as the promised turnaround failed to materialize.

Most Americans had never looked to government for aid in dealing with problems such as debt, unemployment, and the difficulty of find-ing an income in old age. Most people were on their own and ac-cepted this as the way of the world. But the Depression seemed too monumental a problem for too many people to rely on self-help and private charity. Financially strapped state and city governments did what they could, but they were far from able to assume the burden of relief programs. The American people remembered Hoover's accom-plishments in providing food, medicine, and other supplies to war-torn Europe in the years after the First World War. Surely Hoover would meet this challenge at home as well.

The problem was that the President believed that the federal gov-ernment should not give direct relief to the unemployed. He argued that a national relief policy would violate the Constitution's limits on the powers of the federal government. He held these views in good faith, and he had some basis for them. But as the Depression wors-ened, many Americans decided that the President did not care about their plight. They made fun of Hoover, but their jokes were filled with anger and despair. A torn jacket stuffed with newspapers to ward off the cold was called a "Hoover overcoat." A broken-down car pulled by horses was a "Hoovermobile." Most famous of all, the communities of tar-paper and balsa-wood shacks built by homeless Americans in cities across the nation were "Hoovervilles."

One incident ruined Hoover's reputation. At the end of the First World War, Congress had agreed to establish a program to pay American veterans a cash bonus. In 1931, Congress passed a law over Hoover's veto allowing veterans to get from the government loans of 50 percent of the value of their bonus. The next year, Democratic leaders in Congress suggested that the whole bonus be paid in cash. Veterans' groups marched on Washington to press for laws authorizing the payment of the whole cash bonus. The "Bonus Army" marchers brought their wives and children to show the President and Congress their collective plight. Many had no homes. The President refused to hear their pleas. The seventeen thousand marchers camped in Washington, declaring that they would not leave the city unless the bonus bill succeeded. When the bill failed in the Senate, the government offered to pay the veterans' travel costs home, but two thousand stayed put. They had no place else to go. District of Columbia police clashed with the homeless veterans; two police officers and two veterans died in the fighting. The President then called out federal soldiers under the command of General Douglas MacArthur and his aide, Major Dwight D. Eisenhower, to disperse the "Bonus Army." The soldiers used tear gas, tanks, and flamethrowers to demolish the "Hooverville." Soldiers wearing gas masks and carrying rifles with fixed bayonets arrested the fleeing veterans and their families. Motion-picture newsreels showing the violence stunned the nation.

The 1932 Republican convention grimly renominated President Hoover. There was no alternative candidate. In November, the unpopular President was turned out of office. Many voters were doubtless swayed by the Democrats' promise to repeal the Eighteenth (Prohibition) Amendment. But the real issue was the Depression. Thirteen million Americans were without employment; thousands of families were still living in makeshift shacks; farmers were rioting; hunger was rampant; and most of the nation's banks were closed or about to close. The victorious candidate, Democratic Governor Franklin D. Roosevelt of New York, seemed confident and able. No one was sure what he would do, or could do, about the Depression—but the American people were willing to give him a chance.

# CHAPTER EIGHT

# FRANKLIN D. ROOSEVELT

Franklin Delano Roosevelt set the model for all his successors, and generations of American voters have measured candidates for the Presidency by Roosevelt's standard. As with Abraham Lincoln, Roosevelt used the powers of the Presidency to lead the nation in dealing with a grave crisis.

Roosevelt was the only child of wealthy landowners in upstate New York. He was educated in private schools, at Harvard College, and at Columbia Law School. In 1905, he married his fifth cousin once removed, Eleanor Roosevelt, the niece of President Theodore Roosevelt, who gave the bride away at the wedding. He joined President Woodrow Wilson's Administration as Assistant Secretary of the Navy, the same post from which Theodore Roosevelt had begun his national political career. Unlike most other members of the family, Franklin Roosevelt was a Democrat. The handsome, charming New Yorker loyally accepted the Vice Presidential nomination on the doomed 1920 Democratic ticket, knowing that loyalty in politics is rewarded sooner or later. He seemed to have a great future.

Roosevelt's hopes disintegrated in 1921. While on a family vacation in Campobello, in New Brunswick, Canada, Roosevelt caught a chill after swimming in the Bay of Fundy that led to polio, or infantile paralysis, a dreaded disease until a vaccine was developed in the 1950s. Roosevelt lost the use of his legs for the rest of his life. His heartbroken mother told him that he should retire to the family estate at Hyde Park, New York, along the Hudson River, and give up all thought of a career in politics.

But the illness transformed Roosevelt. From an amiable but superficial aristocrat with an intellectual bent toward social justice, he became a fully committed reformer who *felt* people's suffering and burned to remedy it. He grew to share his wife's compassion and interest in reform. Eleanor became her husband's partner and tutor as he taught himself about the problems facing the United States.

Roosevelt's revived political career grew out of this new-found passion for social justice. By 1932, he was governor of New York, a central figure in national Democratic politics, and the leading candidate for his party's Presidential nomination. He triumphed at the convention in Chicago, Illinois, after a sharp and bitter contest with his rival and former friend Al Smith. Breaking tradition, Roosevelt flew to Chicago to accept the nomination in person. He wanted to prove he could get around, and he knew his appearance would electrify the convention and the nation. He was right. His promise of "a new deal for the American people" was enthusiastically received. In a whirlwind campaign, FDR spoke to audiences large and small, jousted and joked with reporters, and projected precisely the image of confidence that Hoover had called for and yet seemed so far from achieving. The Democrats overwhelmed Hoover, scoring their first lopsided victory in generations.

In February 1933, the month before his inauguration, Roosevelt narrowly escaped being murdered in Miami after a fishing vacation. As FDR sat immobilized, with ten pounds of steel braces around his legs, in an open touring car with Mayor Anton Cermak of Chicago, a bitter thirty-two-year-old brick mason named Giuseppe Zangara, who had been in constant torment from a stomach operation, shouted, "Too many people are starving to death." He fired his cheap pistol five times at the car from a park bench thirty-five feet away. The President-elect was unscathed, but Mayor Cermak was wounded, and he died two weeks later. As Roosevelt cradled the wounded man in his arms, Cermak whispered, "I'm glad it was me instead of you." (The killer was electrocuted two weeks after Roosevelt's inauguration.)

March 4, Inauguration Day, dawned cloudy and cheerless. The glum and downcast Hoover and the somber Roosevelt rode side by side in the Presidential limousine to the Capitol's East Front, where

100,000 anxious witnesses were waiting. The retiring President was bitter toward his successor, who had refused Hoover's plea to work together in the days leading up to the transfer of power. The thirty-second President had his own ideas, and he wanted to make a clean break with the past. His inaugural address, delivered in a cold wind, did not mince words. Holding tight to the rostrum, he declared what everyone knew to be the case: The American economy had all but ground to a halt, and drastic action was needed. He promised "action, and action now." He described the Depression as a crisis as serious as any war the nation had faced, a "dark hour of our national life." Crisis measures were necessary.

Roosevelt's pledge of action lifted the spirits of the American peo-

Franklin D. Roosevelt Library

*Franklin Delano Roosevelt (1882—1945; term, 1933—1945) has been the only Chief Executive to have more than two terms. He died of a cerebral hemorrhage three months after his fourth inauguration (the only one ever held in the White House). His "New Deal" guided the nation through the Great Depression. FDR, as he was popularly dubbed by tabloid newspapers, was our greatest war President, directing the Allied powers to victory over Germany, Japan, and Italy in the Second World War. He was also the first media President, making effective use of "fireside chats" over the radio to the American people and witty, jovial, off-the-cuff press conferences in the Oval Office.*

ple and gave meaning to his ringing declaration, "The only thing we have to fear is fear itself—nameless, unreasoning, unjustified terror which paralyzes needed efforts to convert retreat into advance." Happiness, he said, "lies not in the mere possession of money; it lies in the joy of achievement, in the thrill of creative effort." The family Bible on which Roosevelt took the oath of office from Chief Justice Charles Evans Hughes lay open to 1 Corinthians: "And now abideth faith, hope, charity, these three; but the greatest of these is charity."

The next three months—known as "the Hundred Days"—were a whirlwind of Presidential proclamations, bills, and executive orders. Roosevelt delivered the first of his famous radio broadcasts, the "fireside chats." The President took the American people into his confidence, explaining each new measure step by step so that the people felt that they understood and had a part in the new effort to fight the Depression. Congress cooperated with joy and relief, often passing bills the members had not even read.

Roosevelt knew how dangerous the situation was. Most people had all but despaired of any solution to the Depression that was consistent with the Constitution. Some called openly for a dictatorship, whether of the left or the right. The President's great object—and great achievement—was to convince the people that the government could cope with the country's problems without having to destroy government of, by, and for the people.

The Roosevelt Administration's program, dubbed the New Deal, swept out of the capital and through the nation like a tornado. It had two goals: (1) to get direct aid to the victims of the Depression and (2) to get the economy back on its feet. Hundreds of bright young men and women, graduates of the nation's leading universities, overran Washington to run the New Deal programs. Reporters nicknamed them "Felix's happy hot dogs," after their mentor, Professor Felix Frankfurter of the Harvard Law School. They staffed a bewildering collection of agencies—NRA, WPA, PWA, HOLC, AAA, CCC, and so forth. These were the "alphabet agencies," and the people running them and advising the President were called the "brains trust."

The centerpiece of the first wave of New Deal programs was the National Recovery Administration (NRA), whose symbol was the "blue eagle." The idea behind the NRA was that cut-throat competition among businesses had helped to drop prices and wages, making the Depression worse. If you regulated competition, the economy would recover its strength. The NRA organized industries into groups that would write *codes*, or sets of rules, governing prices and quality of goods and wages. Any company violating its industry's code could be prosecuted under federal law.

The NRA was not successful—and within two years the Supreme Court killed it. In the famous "sick chicken" case, *Schechter Poultry Corp. v. United States*, the Justices unanimously agreed that the NRA was unconstitutional because Congress had handed over its lawmaking powers to an executive agency, which in turn had handed these powers to private companies.

Secretly, the President was relieved that the Court had killed the NRA. The Justices had disposed of a failed program, saving the President the embarrassing task of shutting down the NRA himself. But the Justices sharpened their axes and went after other New Deal programs. They claimed that the programs violated private property rights protected by the Constitution and that Congress had gone too far in trying to use its power to regulate interstate commerce. The Court struck down New Deal measures designed to relieve the plight of the poor and powerless—farmers, mine workers, those who could not pay off mortgages on their homes. The small liberal group on the Court—Justices Louis D. Brandeis, Harlan Fiske Stone, and Benjamin Nathan Cardozo, occasionally joined by Chief Justice Charles Evans Hughes—protested bitterly against these decisions, but to no avail.

Roosevelt and the nation were outraged. To be sure, some of the New Deal laws were badly drafted and should have been struck down. But it seemed that the Supreme Court was standing in the way of the government's efforts to solve the problems of the Depression.

Roosevelt made the election of 1936 a referendum on his policies, and the voters rallied to his call. He carried every one of the forty-eight states except Maine and Vermont. (He was sworn in on January 20, 1937—the first President to take office under the Twentieth Amendment, which pushed back the start of the Presidential and Congressional terms from March to January to eliminate "lame duck" sessions of Congress.) The people liked the New Deal. They liked that the government had put millions of jobless Americans to work building bridges, post offices, schools, roads, libraries, and dams. They liked the new Social Security program, which gave retired and disabled Americans a source of income. They were convinced that the government now cared about and understood their problems and was willing to help.

Roosevelt decided that the people had given him a mandate to move against the Supreme Court. He made a speech in which he argued that the "Nine Old Men" were tired and overworked and needed help. He suggested that Congress adopt a law allowing the President to name a new Justice for every sitting Justice over seventy years of age who did not retire from the Court, up to a maximum of six. If enacted, the Court reorganization plan would have given the President a guaranteed majority on the Court to support his programs against the conservative Justices.

Many Americans were shaken by Roosevelt's idea, which quickly became known as the "Court-packing" plan. They believed that the proposal, if adopted, would destroy the independence of the Court and as a result might destroy the Constitution. Many members of Roosevelt's own party opposed the bill. The Justices countered with a shrewd move of their own. Chief Justice Hughes and Justice Brandeis joined with conservative Justice Willis Van Devanter to draft a response by the Chief Justice to a question from Senator Burton K. Wheeler of Montana, an opponent of the plan. Hughes explained that the Court was easily keeping up with its work and that the Roosevelt plan would actually hamper the Justices' efforts to handle their workload. At the same time, the Court announced a major decision. It upheld the National Labor Relations Act, a law that labor unions revered as "labor's Bill of Rights." The decision signaled that the Justices would not stand in the way of all New Deal measures. And then Justice Van Devanter finally resigned, giving the President his first chance to appoint a Justice to the Supreme Court. These events, and the sudden death of the Senate Majority Leader, the floor leader for the Court reorganization bill, killed the measure. It was a significant defeat for the President.

Roosevelt's second term was also complicated by foreign policy issues. He watched helplessly as the Nazi dictatorship in Germany and the Fascist dictatorship in Italy expanded their power by subversion and conquest. He also worried about Japan's efforts to carve out a Pacific empire. The American people, however, did not share Roosevelt's concerns. They had bitter memories of the "war to end all wars," the Treaty of Versailles, and the toothless League of Nations, and they wanted to stay out of foreign wars. They did feel some concern about Japan's expansionism, but they did not take the Japanese seriously as a military power.

Roosevelt urged in several of his speeches that the free powers of the world "quarantine the aggressors" through an economic boycott —an idea that other nations did not adopt. He denounced German takeovers of Austria and Czechoslovakia and the Italian conquest of Ethiopia. And his Administration applied constant pressure to the

Japanese, demanding that Japan limit its expansion into China and the Pacific islands.

In September 1939, war broke out in Europe. The line-up startled Americans, for the Soviet Union allied itself with Germany, Italy, and Japan. Germany and the U.S.S.R. carved up Poland in a few weeks, but most Americans did not care. The "America First" movement argued that the war was not America's problem and that Europe was doomed anyway. If the United States entered the war to support Britain and France, they predicted, the United States would be doomed as well.

Other Americans believed that the United States had to aid Britain and France in order to protect American interests and the cause of freedom. Many American volunteers joined British and Canadian military units. When France fell in the spring of 1940 and Winston S. Churchill became Britain's new Prime Minister, Americans were stirred by his eloquence and courage. Journalists such as Edward R. Murrow of CBS reported on the heroism of the people of London, who were enduring daily bombing raids by the German Air Force.

The 1940 Presidential campaign was not politics as usual. President Roosevelt had surveyed the field of candidates vying to succeed him and believed that none of them was up to the job. Therefore, he decided that he would have to break tradition and run for an unprecedented third term. Republicans—and some Democrats—were infuriated that he was challenging a tradition that George Washington had begun nearly 150 years earlier. Campaign buttons read: "WASHINGTON WOULDN'T. GRANT COULDN'T. ROOSEVELT SHOULDN'T." In reply, the Democrats argued that it would be foolish to "change horses in the middle of a stream." The Republican candidate, Wendell Willkie, charged that the President would drag the nation into war in Europe. Roosevelt angrily replied, "Your boys are *not* going to go off to die in foreign wars." The President did win his third term but by a narrower margin than he had amassed in 1932 or in 1936.

In 1941, President Roosevelt took two major steps closer to taking sides with the Allies. He proposed that the United States "be the great arsenal of democracy" and put forward a remarkable program called Lend-Lease. The British would receive fifty old but usable American destroyers in exchange for ninety-nine-year leases on British bases in the Western Hemisphere. Roosevelt explained his reasoning by analogy: A neighbor's house is on fire, and he asks to borrow your garden hose. All you want to do is to lend him the hose to put out the fire and get it back when the fire is out.

That summer, FDR held a secret meeting with Prime Minister Churchill. In August, American and British ships rendezvoused in Canadian waters, and the two leaders conferred amiably for two days. In a joint statement, the Atlantic Charter, they called for "final destruction of the Nazi tyranny" and affirmed their hopes for peace, freedom for the world's peoples, and a strong new international peace-keeping structure. These and other initiatives indicated that Roosevelt saw American involvement in the war as inevitable, but he did not commit the nation to war.

When America did enter the war four months later, it was not a foreign war any longer. On December 7, 1941, the Japanese Navy and Air Force staged a surprise raid on Pearl Harbor, Hawaii, the site of the largest U.S. Pacific naval base. The Japanese destroyed 19 ships, including 8 battleships, and 188 aircraft and killed 2,280 military personnel and 68 civilians. The Pearl Harbor attack was only one element of an array of Japanese strategic raids throughout the Pacific. At the time, Japanese diplomats were still in "friendly" negotiations with American Secretary of State Cordell Hull in Washington, D.C. Most historians agree that the Administration expected some sort of large-scale Japanese move somewhere in the Pacific but that Roosevelt and his aides were stunned that the Japanese would actually strike at American territory.

The next day, President Roosevelt appeared before a joint session of Congress. His speech took just six minutes. In clear, angry prose that he had written himself, the President listed the numerous attacks the Japanese had launched, declaring December 7 to be "a date which will live in infamy." Congress immediately voted to declare that a state of war existed between the United States and Japan—a formula designed to conform to a 1928 treaty under which all the nations of the world, including the United States and Japan, had renounced war as an instrument of foreign policy. A couple of days later, Germany's *Führer*, Adolf Hitler, who had not wanted the United States drawn into any war, declared war on the United States, and Italy's *Duce*, Benito Mussolini, followed suit. (In the summer of 1941, the U.S.S.R. had switched sides, because Hitler had turned on his former ally.) Congress quickly replied in kind. The war was truly a world war now.

The course of the conflict aged Roosevelt terribly. Photographs taken in 1932, when FDR was fifty, show a calm, strong, jaunty President. By 1945, he looked at least ten years older than his sixty-three years. The demands of war abroad and coordinating the war effort at home were such that he felt that he could not abandon the helm or delegate the burdens of office. Again, as with the need to frame the government's response to the economic crisis of the Depression, the Second World War concentrated vast authority in the hands of the President of the United States. But that authority was a crushing weight for even the strongest and most confident President to bear.

As the war progressed, Roosevelt set in motion two projects that were destined to shape the postwar world. The first, and more hopeful, was his dream of an international peace-keeping agency that would have the teeth that the League of Nations had lacked: the United Nations. The second, which the President approved almost casually, resulted from suggestions from leading scientists, including Albert Einstein. Einstein informed the President that major advances in nuclear physics suggested that the atom could be split—an achievement that would be a source of great energy, perhaps of a weapon using that source of energy. The President approved a secret project, code-named the Manhattan Project, to carry out research and development work on an atomic weapon. At bases in Los Alamos, New Mexico, and Oak Ridge, Tennessee, the scientists and technicians of the Manhattan Project designed and built a new weapon— the atomic bomb.

Like President Lincoln during the Civil War, President Roosevelt believed that the ordinary processes of government should carry on during wartime. Thus, the United States held a Presidential election in 1944. Roosevelt ran for a fourth term against the young, vigorous Republican nominee, Governor Thomas E. Dewey of New York. The diminutive, mustached Dewey looked to many Americans like "the man on the wedding cake," and he seemed too inexperienced to lead the United States in wartime. Roosevelt won a fourth term despite his weariness—and his failing health. He did not know that he was a dying man; his doctors were deeply concerned about the state of his health, but they could not bring themselves to tell the President that a fourth term might kill him.

Like most other Presidents, Roosevelt did not pay much attention to the selection of his Vice Presidential running mates. His first, John Nance Garner of Texas, the former Speaker of the House, described the office as "not worth a bucket of warm spit." Garner retired in 1940 and was succeeded by Secretary of Agriculture Henry A. Wallace. As the 1944 election approached, leaders of the Democratic Party began to worry about Wallace's erratic views and gushing admiration for the newest major nation to join the Allies, the Soviet Union. Roosevelt was persuaded to dump Wallace and to run with Senator Harry S Truman of Missouri, an able legislator whose investigations of government waste in the war effort had saved the United States tens of millions of dollars. Neither man realized how fateful this change would be.

Roosevelt began his fourth term with a brief inaugural ceremony at the White House, the only time since the capital moved to Washington that the Inauguration has not taken place at the Capitol. He then flew off to a meeting with Churchill and Soviet leader Joseph Stalin at Yalta, a resort on the Black Sea in the U.S.S.R. For whatever reason, he never fully briefed Vice President Truman about the war effort or the Manhattan Project. In early April, the exhausted President decided that he needed a rest. He traveled to Warm Springs, Georgia, a favorite vacation spot because he believed that its waters helped restore some feeling and movement in his wasted legs. On April 12, 1945, while his portrait was being painted, he complained of "a terrific headache." Suddenly he slumped forward, unconscious. He died later that day of a massive cerebral hemorrhage, an especially serious kind of stroke.

Roosevelt's death was the end of an era. Many Americans could not remember a time when he had not been President. The nation went into deep mourning, as did the people of Great Britain, France, and the other Allies. The new President, Harry S Truman, expressed the feelings of his countrymen when he said that it was "as if the sun, the moon, and all the planets had fallen in on me." For more than four decades, the United States has lived and governed itself in the shadow of FDR.

# CHAPTER NINE

# "GIVE 'EM HELL, HARRY" AND "I LIKE IKE"

Harry S Truman was the last man to be President who had not gone to college. He was a self-taught student of history, a pretty good piano player, a failed businessman, and a veteran of the First World War, Missouri politics, and the U.S. Senate. Most Americans could not help comparing him unfavorably with Franklin D. Roosevelt, the only President many of them had known. But Truman had a solid core of intelligence, shrewdness, and common sense that shaped his Presidency.

When Truman became President, he faced an unprecedented decision: whether to use the atomic bomb. Truman had only the faintest idea of what the Manhattan Project was. When, as chairman of a Senate committee looking into waste in government war spending, he had tried to investigate the Manhattan Project, he had been warned off with no explanation. As Vice President, Truman was still in the dark about the effort to develop an atomic weapon. President Truman was stunned when Secretary of War Henry Stimson and the directors of the Manhattan Project briefed him about the bomb. Three months later, on July 16, 1945, the first atomic bomb was tested successfully, at Trinity Site, Alamogordo, in the New Mexico desert.

At the beginning of the Manhattan Project, everyone had assumed that the bomb would be used against Nazi Germany. But the Germans had surrendered unconditionally on May 7, 1945—known as V-E Day. The Japanese were still fighting, however. Allied forces were posed for an all-out amphibious assault on the Japanese homeland, but worried generals advised the President that the attack would result in millions of casualties on both sides. Perhaps, President Truman reasoned, using the atomic bomb would actually cause fewer deaths and injuries than an all-out invasion.

Truman decided that he would order the use of the first bomb on a Japanese city. The devastation it would cause would put irresistible pressure on the Japanese to surrender. The President rejected some scientists' pleas to drop the bomb on an uninhabited island or desert. He believed that such a test would not give convincing proof to the Japanese of its power.

An American B-29 bomber, the *Enola Gay*, dropped "Little Boy" on the industrial city of Hiroshima on August 6, 1945. But the Japanese did not immediately surrender because they could not believe their own reports of what had happened. The President ordered the dropping of another atomic bomb. A second B-29, *Bock's Car*, dropped "Fat Man" on the city of Nagasaki. President Truman worried as to what he would have to do if the second bomb did not persuade the Japanese to surrender. The United States had had only two bombs in its arsenal after the July test and now had used both. The only choice remaining was a full-scale invasion. But the second bomb did its work. Emperor Hirohito overruled his generals and advisers and agreed to surrender unconditionally.

The war's end brought new problems. Truman felt an obligation to make President Roosevelt's dream of the United Nations a reality. In addition, the victorious Allies had to decide what to do about war-ravaged Europe and the old colonial empires.

The major postwar foreign-policy issue facing the President was the Soviet Union. Americans distrusted the U.S.S.R. and the U.S.S.R. feared and distrusted the West. This mutual suspicion was based partly on different ideologies and economic systems. Many Americans feared that the Communist Party in the United States was nothing more than an arm of the Soviet Union. For their part, Stalin and his successors shared the ages-old Russian distrust of the outside world and its motives.

And so a "Cold War" of spies and subversion followed the Second World War. Soviet agents had infiltrated the Manhattan Project and learned top-secret military data that gave Moscow the missing links it needed to solve the problem of making atomic weapons. (Congressional critics of the Truman Administration charged that the Soviet Union never would have developed the atomic bomb without the aid of traitors in the United States. This was not true; all the "atom spies" had done was to shave a few years off the Soviet atomic program's timetable.)

President Truman was sensitive to charges, principally Republican, that there were nests of Soviet spies and saboteurs in the government. He took vigorous anti-Communist measures, though some violated individual liberties protected by the Constitution. To monitor Soviet activities and combat Soviet espionage, he founded the National Security Council (NSC) and the Central Intelligence Agency (CIA). In his retirement, Truman declared that creating the CIA was his worst mistake as President.

President Truman proposed domestic programs as bold and inventive as anything in the New Deal. He pursued a vigorous policy of civil rights. He was the first President to appoint a Civil Rights Commission. Its tough-minded report showed the nation just how broad and how deep the stain of racism and prejudice had spread. The commission's findings scandalized the nation—and angered Southern Democrats. Truman sponsored the creation of a Fair Employment Practices Commission (FEPC). He urged the adoption of a government program to assist ordinary people in paying major medical bills. He brought former President Herbert Hoover out of retirement to lead a special commission on the reorganization of the Presidency and the executive branch of government. The Hoover Commission's report helped to bring the executive branch in line with the requirements of the postwar world.

In 1948, the Democrats were badly split. President Truman's Administration was plagued with scandal. Several of his aides had been forced to resign. Former Vice President Henry Wallace, denouncing Truman for starting the Cold War and for his hostility to the Soviets, founded a new Progressive Party and became its candidate for President. On the right wing of the party, Governor J. Strom Thurmond of South Carolina led his fellow Southerners out of the Democratic Convention when liberals led by Mayor Hubert H. Humphrey of Minneapolis, Minnesota, won the floor battle to endorse black Americans' demands for equality and justice. Thurmond and other Southern Democrats formed the "Dixiecrat" Party. What was left of the Democratic Party closed ranks behind President Truman. Some party leaders hoped that he would step aside so that they could nominate

General Dwight D. Eisenhower, the Supreme Allied Commander in Europe in the Second World War. Eisenhower dashed their hopes when he disclosed that he was a Republican.

The Republican Presidential nominee, Governor Thomas E. Dewey of New York, seemed to have a lock on the election. This time, eager to erase memories of his 1944 loss to FDR, Dewey was so confident of his coming victory that he began to act as if he were already President.

Harry Truman was the only major political figure who was convinced that the election was not over until the last ballot had been counted. He campaigned across the nation by train. During his "whistle-stop" tour, he denounced the "do-nothing" Republican-dominated Congress for blocking his programs. His supporters dubbed Truman's struggle the "Give 'em Hell" campaign. Truman replied, "I'm not giving them hell. I'm telling the truth, and they think it's hell." The *Chicago Tribune* proclaimed on the night of Election Day 1948: "DEWEY DEFEATS TRUMAN." Truman and the Democrats had the last laugh: Truman won re-election, beating Dewey, Thurmond, and Wallace narrowly in the popular vote and decisively in the Electoral College. And the Democrats took back control of both houses of Congress, which they had lost in the 1946 midterm election.

The full term of office that Truman won in 1948 was even more eventful than the preceding forty-five and a half months had been. Nothing seemed certain—not even the White House. The President discovered structural problems in the White House that threatened to cause its collapse, and ordered that it be thoroughly reconstructed. He and his family took up temporary residence in Blair House, across the street. A band of terrorists seeking independence for Puerto Rico attacked Blair House but failed to get off even one shot at the President.

On the world front, the Truman Administration stood by helplessly as Mao Zedong and Zhou Enlai led Communist forces to final victory in China in October 1949, compelling the anti-Communist Nationalists, led by Chiang Kai-shek, to flee to the island of Taiwan. Republicans gleefully charged that Truman had "lost" China to the Communists. (Truman declined the opportunity to discuss personally with Mao and Zhou, in Washington, D.C., the future of U.S.-China relations.)

Most important of all, the President led the United States into a new armed conflict in 1950. As a result of the Second World War, the Asian nation of Korea, once occupied by the Japanese, had been partitioned. North Korea was a Communist state under the domination of China and the Soviet Union, and South Korea was friendly to the West. In June 1950, the North Korean army crossed the boundary between the two nations and invaded the South. The Korean Conflict had begun.

For three years, the United States and other members of the United Nations fought a "police action" against North Korea and, ultimately, China. In 1951, President Truman locked horns with General Douglas MacArthur, the supreme American commander in Korea and the officer who had led the Army in breaking up the "Bonus Army" in 1932. MacArthur had thrown back a major Chinese attack on South Korea and then advanced far into North Korea. He wanted to cross the Yalu River and take "the preponderance of Allied power" into China. President Truman repeatedly ordered against such measures, but General MacArthur was unwilling to obey. President Truman invoked his constitutional authority as Commander-in-Chief and fired MacArthur for "rank insubordination" a few months after flying 7,250 miles to Wake Island in the Pacific to try to reach an understanding face to face. The American people reacted with anger at first, demonstrating support for the hero of the Second World War. But the President stood his ground, and in time the people came to agree with him. Truman vindicated the central principle of civilian supremacy over the military.

A problem related to the Korean Conflict led to a confrontation over the limits on Presidential power. A crippling steel strike threatened the war effort. The President issued an executive order seizing the steel mills and drafting the striking workers into the Army. The President claimed that he had inherent authority under the Constitution to protect the national security by such means. But the Supreme Court ruled that Truman had overstepped his powers. He was angered by the Court's decision but obeyed it. The strike was settled by ordinary means.

In 1952, President Truman thought about running again for a second full term of his own. In 1946, the Republican-controlled Congress had struck at the late President Roosevelt. It had proposed, and the states had ratified, the Twenty-second Amendment, which bars any future President from more than two terms in office. President Truman was exempt from the two-term limit, but decided not to run —in part because he believed that he might not win. In addition to dissatisfaction over the Korean Conflict, several scandals involving members of Truman's staff tainted the reputation of his Administration. Republicans tauntingly asked, "Had enough?"

The 1952 election became a referendum on Korea and the "Truman scandals." The Democrats nominated the eloquent liberal Governor of Illinois, Adlai E. Stevenson. (Stevenson's grandfather had been Grover Cleveland's second Vice President.) The Republicans chose former General Dwight D. Eisenhower to bear their standard; Senator Richard M. Nixon of California was his running-mate.

Eisenhower was the first Presidential candidate to make use of modern advertising methods in his campaign. His advertising agency coined the slogan "I Like Ike." The General campaigned as a peace candidate. He declared, "I will go to Korea" to end the bitter war there. He also ran as a vigorous anti-Communist. Documented charges about scandals involving Senator Nixon had no effect on Eisenhower's popularity. The Republicans swamped the Democrats and moved into the White House for the first time in twenty years.

Eisenhower served two full terms as President, contending with anti-Communist hysteria at home and the Cold War abroad. He depended heavily on his chief of staff, the cold and efficient Sherman Adams, a former Governor of New Hampshire, for the day-to-day running of his Administration, and on his combative Secretary of State, John Foster Dulles, for the conduct of foreign policy, which sometimes ran to *brinkmanship*, that is, taking disputes with the U.S.S.R. to the edge of war. His Cabinet was nicknamed "eight millionaires and a plumber [the Secretary of Labor]."

President Eisenhower had to contend with anti-Communist witch-hunts conducted by the House Un-American Activities Committee and by Senator Joseph R. McCarthy of Wisconsin. He reluctantly oversaw the federal government's enforcement of civil rights legislation and the momentous federal court decisions ordering desegregation of the nation's schools. In 1958, to enforce a Supreme Court decision resisted by the Governor of Arkansas and the state's National Guard, Eisenhower put the state's National Guard under his own command and sent the 101st Airborne Division to enforce the law of the land. During his Administration, the interstate highway system and the American space program were born. The Korean Conflict ended in an uncomfortable stalemate for both sides.

Eisenhower was one of the oldest Presidents in American history. He suffered several serious bouts of ill health, including a heart attack, that caused many Americans to worry about the problems of Presidential disability and succession. He managed to recover from

*This photograph—made on November 18, 1961, in Bonham, Texas—shows (left to right) four past, present, and future Presidents of the United States: President John F. Kennedy (1917—1963; term, 1961—1963) (Democrat-Massachusetts), then-Vice President Lyndon B. Johnson (1908—1973; term,*

these illnesses and arranged with Vice President Nixon the first detailed measures for coping with Presidential illnesses. Eisenhower was the first President to be bound by the two-term limit of the Twenty-second Amendment.

In his 1961 annual message to Congress, President Eisenhower performed one last public service to the nation, warning of the growing power in American life of the "military-industrial complex" —the network of defense contractors and government agencies that wielded ever-increasing power over American diplomatic, budget, and defense policies. The nation has been slow to heed his warning.

1963—1969) (Democrat-Texas), and former Presidents Dwight D. Eisenhower (1890—1969; term, 1953—1961) (Republican-Kansas) and Harry S Truman (1886—1972; term, 1945—1953) (Democrat-Missouri). The four were attending the funeral of Speaker of the House Sam Rayburn (1882—1961) (Democrat-Texas).

# CHAPTER TEN

# "THE CHALLENGING, REVOLUTIONARY SIXTIES": KENNEDY, LYNDON JOHNSON, NIXON

The 1960 Presidential campaign featured, for the first time, two Presidential candidates born in the twentieth century. Senator John F. Kennedy, a Massachusetts Democrat and the first Catholic Presidential candidate since Al Smith in 1928, declared himself to be in the tradition of Jefferson, Wilson, Franklin D. Roosevelt, and Truman. (Truman supported fellow Missourian Stuart Symington for the White House, and Eleanor Roosevelt preferred Adlai Stevenson.) He sparred with Vice President Richard M. Nixon, the Republican nominee, in four television "debates." In one of the closest elections in American history, Kennedy narrowly defeated Nixon and became, at forty-three, the youngest man ever elected to the Presidency.

John Kennedy's Inaugural Address was an eloquent call to battle, to service, and to achievement: "Ask not, my fellow Americans, what your country can do for you—ask what you can do for your country." He and his wife, Jacqueline, set standards of style, elegance, and culture. He inspired the young people of America to consider careers in government and public service through the creation of such organizations as the Peace Corps and the Alliance for Progress. He held frequent televised press conferences. His enthusiastic support for the American space program helped the United States to recover lost ground in the "space race" with the Soviet Union. He challenged the nation to achieve his goal of landing a man on the Moon and returning him safely to Earth before the end of the decade.

His Administration had problems as well. In 1961, a secret operation that had been planned by the Eisenhower Administration against the new, Communist leader of Cuba, Fidel Castro, led to the botched Bay of Pigs invasion. A force of 1,500 anti-Castro Cubans was overwhelmed on the beaches; 1,100 survivors were captured by Castro's army. Castro was a nagging worry for the President. Kennedy authorized several secret, illegal operations, some with Mafia aid, designed either to assassinate Castro or otherwise to discredit him and remove him from office.

There was no actual "shooting war" in Europe, but the continent became a chessboard in the Cold War. A summit meeting in Vienna, Austria, in the spring of 1961 with Soviet leader Nikita Khrushchev left Kennedy bruised and shaken. In the summer of 1962, a crisis developed in the divided nation of Germany. East Germany was ruled by a Communist government supported by Soviet army units; West Germany was allied with the anti-Communist nations of Western Europe and the United States. Berlin, the former German capital, was deep in the heart of East Germany but itself was divided into Communist and non-Communist zones. That summer, the Soviet Union built a wall that cut Berlin in two. The Berlin Wall stood until 1989, a notorious symbol of the Cold War.

During Kennedy's three years in office, Southeast Asia became the principal focus of East-West tensions. Communist forces controlling North Vietnam worked with guerrillas in South Vietnam and Laos to overthrow neutralist or anti-Communist regimes in those countries. The President supported these regimes with American aid and advisers. At the beginning of November 1963, Kennedy and his aides agreed that the President of South Vietnam, Ngo Dinh Diem, could no longer be relied on, and they encouraged a conspiracy of South Vietnamese military officers to overthrow Diem—although Kennedy was shocked when Diem and his brother were assassinated during the coup.

In October 1962, the United States discovered that the U.S.S.R. had planted Soviet intercontinental missiles in Cuba, ninety miles from Florida. A high-flying American "spy plane" provided detailed photographic evidence of the Soviet missile bases. Apparently the Soviets had acted on the request of Cuba's Fidel Castro, who believed that the bases would provide him with security against American efforts to overthrow him. President Kennedy announced a naval blockade of the island to force removal of the missiles. An "eyeball-to-eyeball" confrontation between Kennedy and Khrushchev followed. In a dramatic exchange at the United Nations, American Ambassador Adlai Stevenson displayed damning evidence that the Soviet Union had established missile bases in Cuba. Khrushchev "blinked," withdrawing the missiles from Cuba despite Castro's outrage. The Soviet leader was not prepared for the possibility that the crisis might end in nuclear war.

The Cuban Missile Crisis led both Kennedy and Khrushchev to explore ways to reduce tensions. They established a "hot line" link between Washington, D.C., and Moscow. And in the spring of 1963, both world powers and many other nations signed the world's first Test Ban Treaty, which stopped above-ground testing of nuclear weapons.

The President had to deal with serious domestic troubles as well. He tangled with Congress, specifically the wily, autocratic "Judge" Howard Smith of Virginia, chairman of the House Rules Committee. He and his brother Attorney General Robert F. Kennedy fought an ongoing battle with the director of the Federal Bureau of Investigation, J. Edgar Hoover. Attempts to enforce federal court decisions on civil rights in Southern states led to confrontations with the governors of Mississippi and Alabama. Kennedy had to call out the National Guard to enforce federal court decisions mandating that black and white students go to school together. He also forced the leaders of the steel industry to roll back a price increase that, Kennedy declared, would damage the national interest.

The President was looking forward eagerly to the 1964 Presidential election. In November 1963, he traveled to Texas to resolve a dispute that was dividing the Texas Democratic Party. Riding in an open limousine with his wife in Dallas, President Kennedy was shot twice. He died almost immediately. The police arrested a twenty-four-year-old loner, Lee Harvey Oswald, for the murder of a Dallas police officer, and accused him of Kennedy's murder as well. Two days later, a local nightclub owner named Jack Ruby shot Oswald dead in full view of television cameras in the basement of Dallas police headquarters. The horrified nation saw its first "live" murder.

The assassination of President Kennedy has been a controversial event ever since, with as many theories as there are students of it. Was there a conspiracy? Were the bullets aimed at someone other than JFK? Kennedy's assassination, the fourth murder of a President in our history, shocked the people of the United States and the rest of the world.

Vice President Lyndon B. Johnson of Texas, who had been in the motorcade in Dallas, was sworn in as President aboard Air Force One. He had been the former Majority Leader of the Senate, a renowned and foxy master of political horse-trading. Some Americans thought that Johnson was crass and vulgar by comparison with the late President. Johnson resented these contrasts. But he was determined to achieve and build on Kennedy's policy objectives, just as President Truman had wanted to carry on FDR's legacy. In his first address to the nation, President Johnson declared: "Let us continue."

Johnson used Kennedy's name as a powerful political weapon, declaring repeatedly, "I'm the only President you've got." He won enactment of many of the measures that Kennedy had not been able to get Congress to adopt—the Civil Rights and Voting Rights Acts, Medicare, the inauguration of the Public Broadcasting System, and programs designed to combat poverty and urban decay and to protect the civil rights of all Americans. In the 1964 Presidential election, Johnson piled up one of the greatest landslides ever, overwhelming the conservative Republican candidate, Senator Barry Goldwater of Arizona.

In the first year of Johnson's full term, the Twenty-fifth Amendment was ratified. This new constitutional provision set forth rules governing problems of Presidential succession, including disability resulting from illness, as had happened with Presidents Garfield, Cleveland, Wilson, and Eisenhower. It also set forth rules on how to fill a vacancy in the office of Vice President. When a Vice President must assume the Presidency, he, with Congress, can fill vacancies in the line of succession.

Johnson cared profoundly about his domestic programs, but events forced him to become a war President. The Vietnam Conflict was perhaps the most unpopular war in the nation's history. Johnson remembered that such experts as General MacArthur had declared the United States should never fight a land war in Asia. For several weeks, he resisted pressure by his aides to commit American combat forces to Vietnam. But he was determined not to let another nation fall to the Communists. He also believed that supporting the new South Vietnamese government had been a major priority of the Kennedy Administration and that it was his responsibility to uphold it as well. In August 1964, an American destroyer was supposedly attacked by North Vietnamese boats in international waters in the Gulf of

Tonkin off North Vietnam. Invoking this incident, President Johnson won from Congress the Tonkin Gulf Resolution, a virtual blank check authorizing direct American military action in South Vietnam.

In the Vietnam Conflict, the U.S. Air Force conducted bombing raids on North Vietnamese cities, and more than 500,000 American soldiers served in ground combat. The war tore the United States apart. It was the first televised war. The millions of Americans confronting the brutal realities of combat in their living rooms were horrified by what they saw. Antiwar protests increased in number and passion during the late 1960s. Students protested the draft that would send many of them to fight in an "immoral war." They chanted, "Hey, Hey, LBJ, how many kids have you killed today?" At the end of January 1968—the month of Tet in the Vietnamese religious calendar —Communist forces staged surprise attacks throughout South Vietnam. They attempted to storm the American Embassy in South Vietnam's capital, Saigon. The Tet Offensive was a military failure for the Communist Vietcong, but it showed that American predictions of victory were equally hollow.

In 1968, Senator Eugene McCarthy of Minnesota emerged as a peace candidate in the Democratic Party, and he almost outpolled the Administration ticket in the New Hampshire Democratic primary in February. At the end of March, President Johnson declared that he would not seek or accept the Democratic nomination.

The campaign for the nomination was marred by tragedy. In April, the great black civil rights leader, Reverend Martin Luther King, Jr., was assassinated in Memphis, Tennessee. Two months later, Robert F. Kennedy, a freshman Senator from New York who was the Democrats' front runner, was shot dead in Los Angeles on the night he had won the California primary. The murders of King and Kennedy deprived the nation of two leaders who could have moderated among the contending factions of American society. The slaying of Robert Kennedy was particularly shocking because his brother John had been murdered less than five years earlier. Unrest in the nation's slums and ghettos had plagued the United States in the three years before 1968, and resurfaced that summer as well. Both the Republican convention in Miami, Florida, and the Democratic convention in Chicago, Illinois, were marred by violence by demonstrators and rioters and by the police. A horrified public watched the bloody street battles on television.

The splintered Democratic Party joylessly nominated Vice President Hubert H. Humphrey. He wanted to repudiate President Johnson's Vietnam policy but feared vindictive reprisals by the President. Southern conservatives and right-wing Democrats formed the American Independent Party and nominated Governor George C. Wallace of Alabama. By contrast, the Republicans seemed organized, confident, and moderate. They nominated former Vice President Richard M. Nixon. He seemed to have matured in retirement after losing the Presidential election of 1960 and the gubernatorial election in California in 1962, and he pledged to end the war in Vietnam and "bring us together." In an extraordinarily narrow election, Nixon defeated Humphrey and Wallace; the nation had to wait a day after Election Day to learn the outcome.

President Nixon offered gestures of conciliation, but when he did not act immediately to end the war, protests began anew. Nixon and his aides feared and distrusted domestic dissent. They took stern measures against it, including covert infiltration of antiwar groups by government agents.

In the spring of 1970, President Nixon ordered American forces to carry out "incursions"—raids—into the territory of Cambodia, the neutral nation adjoining South Vietnam. At the end of April 1970, he announced to the nation that Cambodia had agreed to permit these raids because North Vietnam's forces and materiél were in hiding there. College campuses erupted in protest. Two demonstrations in May led to clashes with state National Guard units that left six students dead at Kent State University, in Ohio, and Jackson State University, in Mississippi. Protests continued throughout Nixon's first term in office.

On July 20, 1969, two American astronauts landed and walked on the Moon, fulfilling President Kennedy's challenge to the nation in 1961. President Nixon joyfully declared the Apollo XI mission to be the greatest week in the history of the world since Creation. The several Apollo flights confirmed the success and the value of the American space program, but they did not distract the American people from serious problems closer to home.

For most of his political career, Nixon had been known as the fiercest of anti-Communists. Thus, his dramatic overtures to the People's Republic of China and the Soviet Union in 1971 and 1972 were all the more surprising. Many historians have pointed out that only a President with an unwavering anti-Communist record could have undertaken these initiatives successfully. Nonetheless, President Nixon, in fruitful partnership with his National Security Adviser, Dr. Henry Kissinger, demonstrated the imagination and resourcefulness to score

*Richard M. Nixon (1913—; term, 1969–1974), is the only Chief Executive to resign. He was one of the most complex Presidents, and his legacy mixed distinguished achievements—such as his 1972 "journey for peace" to the People's Republic of China—with abuses of power, the most famous of which was the Watergate scandal that forced him from office to escape impeachment. A month after his resignation, he was pardoned by his successor, Gerald R. Ford, for all offenses he had committed or might have committed during his Presidency.*

*This photograph, taken on December 21, 1970, in the Oval Office in the White House, shows President Nixon shaking hands with Elvis Presley (1935—1977), "the king of rock 'n' roll." Nixon presented Presley with an Outstanding Young American Award; Presley gave Nixon a World War II Colt .45 revolver and seven silver bullets. In a 1993 interview, Nixon commented, "Well, [Elvis Presley] was very flamboyant. My daughters knew him and heard him. I didn't know that much about him except what I read. But as I talked to him, I sensed that basically he was a very shy man. Flamboyancy was covering up the shyness."*

notable foreign policy triumphs. Nixon's state visit to China in February 1972, which included face-to-face meetings with Chairman Mao Zedong and Premier Zhou Enlai, won him new accolades as a statesman. The President always was more comfortable dealing with issues of foreign policy than he was in facing domestic issues, and this inclination in turn shaped his Presidency.

President Nixon tangled repeatedly with Congress over economic policy, judicial appointments, and foreign affairs. He insisted that he had inherent Presidential power to impound funds appropriated by Congress. He wrestled with the economy's problems but could find no solution for the twin problems of inflation and recession. He worried about "our political enemies," the prevalence of dissent, and what he and his aides saw as threats to the stability of the government and the national security. He was outraged when a former government official, Daniel Ellsberg, leaked to leading newspapers the Pentagon's secret history of American involvement in the Vietnam Conflict. He was disgusted when the Supreme Court upheld the newspapers' right to publish these "Pentagon Papers." He launched secret government programs to close off any future leaks. Working out of the White House basement, aides known as "plumbers" monitored dissent as other aides prepared an "enemies' list."

Above all, the President worried about the 1972 election. Most observers believed that Nixon would have no trouble winning a second term against even the strongest Democratic challenger. But the President did not feel so confident. Not even Nixon's greatest foreign policy triumph—his reopening of communications between the United States and China—eased his concern. In its efforts to help Nixon secure re-election, the Committee to Re-Elect the President (CREEP) carried out acts of sabotage against Democratic Presidential candidates and spied on Democratic Party officials. A wiretap was placed on the office telephone of the chairman of the Democratic National Committee (DNC). When five officials of CREEP, acting under the supervision of two White House aides, were arrested in the DNC offices in the Watergate apartment complex in Washington, D.C., on June 17, 1972, most people did not notice. It seemed to be only a police-court story, a matter of low comedy. It turned out to be the first act in one of the greatest scandals in American political history.

Nixon was re-elected in a landslide—in part because agents of CREEP had managed to sabotage campaigns of most leading Democratic politicians who had a chance to defeat the President. The

Democratic candidate, Senator George McGovern of South Dakota, was a decent and honest man who urged an immediate end to the Vietnam Conflict. But most Americans were persuaded to distrust McGovern because he was "too left-wing." He was able to carry only Massachusetts and the District of Columbia. (During the campaign, Governor George Wallace of Alabama, who had scored impressive victories in several Democratic primaries, was seriously wounded by a gunman in a Maryland shopping center and compelled to withdraw from the race.)

Most Americans soon forgot about the election. They were more interested in the efforts of President Nixon's chief foreign policy adviser, Henry Kissinger, whose negotiations with the North Vietnamese promised to bring an end to American involvement in Vietnam, just as Kissinger's efforts in 1971 had helped to "reopen" China. After one last, brutal series of American bombing raids on North Vietnamese cities at the end of 1972 and at the beginning of 1973, the United States, North Vietnam, South Vietnam, and the Provisional Revolutionary Government or Viet Minh (the organization representing Communist Vietcong guerrillas in South Vietnam) signed agreements that made it possible for the United States to withdraw its combat forces.

While most Americans were paying attention to the last stages of direct American involvement in the Vietnam Conflict, the press, led by the *Washington Post,* had begun to dig into the Watergate break-in. They found a web of corruption and dirty tricks. The more they found, the dirtier and more complex the scandal seemed to be.

In the spring of 1973, the Senate appointed a select committee to investigate Watergate. The committee's hearings soon became a major television event. Even before the committee began its work, the President was forced by public opinion to accept the resignations of Chief of Staff H. R. Haldeman, Domestic Adviser John Ehrlichman, and Attorney General Richard Kleindienst, and to fire a fourth, Presidential Counsel John Dean. The new Attorney General, Elliot Richardson, pledged to appoint a special prosecutor to investigate the Watergate scandal and to back him fully. Archibald Cox, Richardson's former constitutional law professor at Harvard Law School and a Solicitor General under President Kennedy, got the job.

The Senate investigation disclosed that the President had taped conversations in the Oval Office. Cox demanded that the President turn over the tape recordings to him for use as evidence in the grand jury investigation of Watergate. Nixon resisted. He cited as grounds the doctrine of *executive privilege*—a legal principle protecting the confidentiality of Presidential discussions with aides and advisers. Cox filed suit in the federal district court in Washington for a *subpoena*, or formal court order, directed to the President. Judge John Sirica issued the subpoena. The District of Columbia Court of Appeals upheld Sirica's decision.

The President then proposed a compromise, and his advisers issued veiled threats should Cox refuse to accept the deal. They appealed to Cox's patriotism: The President was dealing with a major war in the Middle East between Israel and Arab states. Cox's efforts, they said, would weaken Nixon's authority. Cox remained firm. He argued that he had a responsibility to uphold the law and that even the President had to bow to the rule of law. The President determined that Cox had to go, but Attorney General Richardson refused to fire him and resigned. Assistant Attorney General William Ruckelshaus also refused to fire Cox and was himself fired, although he tried to resign first. Finally, Solicitor General Robert H. Bork agreed to fire Cox, and he did.

This "Saturday Night Massacre," in October 1973, stunned the nation. The firestorm of criticism prompted the President to reverse his course. In April 1974, the White House staff prepared transcripts of the tape recordings for release to the special prosecutor and the public. But Cox's successor, Leon Jaworski, continued the legal battle for the tapes, and he took the case to the Supreme Court.

On July 24, 1974, the Court unanimously ruled (in an opinion written by Chief Justice Warren E. Burger, a 1969 Nixon appointee) that the President had to turn over the tapes to Judge Sirica. (Only Justice William H. Rehnquist, a 1971 Nixon appointee who had helped to develop the doctrine of executive privilege during his service in the Justice Department, did not participate.) Judge Sirica and Special Prosecutor Jaworski then agreed that the tapes should be made available to the House Judiciary Committee, which had begun hearings on the question of impeaching the President. These hearings became the focus of American public life that summer.

On July 27, 1974, three days after the Supreme Court decision, the committee adopted three articles of impeachment for discussion by the full House. The first article charged the President with obstruction of justice for his role in covering up the activities of CREEP agents in the Watergate scandal. The second accused the President of violating the constitutional rights of American citizens by authorizing secret illegal government investigations. The third focused on the

President's refusal to obey subpoenas issued by the committee to obtain documents needed for its investigation.

At the beginning of August, the President released three more transcripts indicating that he had ordered CIA officials to sidetrack and mislead FBI investigations of the Watergate break-in. This "smoking gun" confirmed that there was enough evidence for the House to impeach and the Senate to convict the President on the charge of obstructing justice. Even die-hard supporters of the President in the House and the Senate abandoned his cause. Confronted with the inevitable, Nixon announced that he would resign the Presidency.

Richard Nixon's resignation, on August 9, 1974, marked the end of an era in the history of the Presidency. From the end of the Second World War to the assassination of President John F. Kennedy, the American people had tended to believe that the government was telling them the truth, automatically assuming that the President knew best and that his decisions about policy should not be doubted. The questions raised by President Kennedy's murder, the public disenchantment with the Vietnam Conflict, and the Watergate scandal shattered public confidence in government. These crises also seemed to indicate that one of the greatest problems facing the nation was an "imperial Presidency" that had to be brought back under control to preserve the Constitution.

# CHAPTER ELEVEN

# PUTTING THE PRESIDENCY BACK TOGETHER: FORD AND CARTER

Nixon's first Vice President, Spiro T. Agnew, also had resigned. He had quit in October 1973 when it became clear that he would be indicted for bribery and other charges unrelated to Watergate. The Twenty-fifth Amendment was used for the first time to deal with the Agnew vacancy.

President Nixon nominated and Congress confirmed the Minority Leader of the House of Representatives, Gerald R. Ford of Michigan, as the new Vice President. When Nixon resigned the Presidency ten months later, Ford succeeded him as President, declaring, "Our long national nightmare is over." President Ford appointed and Congress confirmed Nelson A. Rockefeller, the former governor of New York and a perennial Republican Presidential candidate, to the Vice Presidency. For the only time in American history, the nation's two highest officeholders were men who had not been elected to their offices.

Gerald R. Ford has been the only President to survive two assassination attempts during his time in office. His two assailants, in separate incidents in the late summer of 1975, were the first women to attempt to kill a President. Lynette "Squeaky" Fromme was a disciple of the convicted mass-murderer and cult leader Charles Manson. Sara Jane Moore was a follower of a 1970s radical splinter group, the Sym-

*On September 23, 1976, President Gerald R. Ford (1913—; term, 1974—1977) (Republican-Michigan) (right) met former Governor Jimmy Carter (1924—; term, 1977—1981) (Democrat-Georgia) in the first Presidential debate since the 1960 Kennedy-Nixon debates. A technical problem silenced both men for nearly half an hour. In the election, six weeks later, Carter narrowly defeated Ford, bringing to an end Ford's caretaker Presidency.*

bionese Liberation Army. Fromme's pistol did not fire when she pulled the trigger, and Moore missed when an alert bystander spoiled her aim.

In April 1975, two years after the signing of agreements ending American involvement in Vietnam, the South Vietnamese government crumbled in the face of North Vietnamese invasion and Vietcong uprisings. The collapse startled the world by its speed and completeness. At the end of that month, Saigon, the South Vietnamese capital, fell. Television reports showed the last American helicopters taking off from the roof of the U.S. embassy as hundreds of South Vietnamese citizens begged to be evacuated. All the places that had become landmarks for thousands of American soldiers and millions of citizens watching the televised war at home—Da Nang, Hue, Cam Ranh Bay—were now in the hands of the victorious Communists. (Saigon was renamed Ho Chi Minh City to honor the founder of North Vietnam.)

President Ford's great achievement was to restore a measure of faith in the government after the Watergate scandal. He also tried, with less success, to bring inflation under control. But the President angered many Americans when he granted a pardon in September 1974 to former President Nixon for any offenses against the law that he had committed or might have committed during his years as President.

It became clear that President Ford would not automatically be nominated by the Republicans as their candidate in the 1976 election. Former Governor Ronald Reagan of California mounted a challenge to Ford from the right wing of the party, which Ford barely managed to overcome. The Democrats nominated a political unknown, former Governor Jimmy Carter of Georgia. Carter described himself as a political outsider and promised "a government as decent, compassionate, competent, and full of love as the American people." Carter defeated Ford by a narrow margin. It was the first time in forty-four years that an incumbent lost a Presidential election.

Jimmy Carter's Administration scored several notable foreign policy achievements. He established formal diplomatic relations with the People's Republic of China. He negotiated a major strategic arms limitation treaty with the Soviet Union. He negotiated and got the Senate to ratify a treaty returning sovereignty over the Panama Canal to Panama at the end of the century. With justifiable satisfaction, the President hailed the Panama Canal treaty as "the most significant advance in political affairs in the Western Hemisphere in this century." He pursued a vigorous policy of pressuring other nations to recognize and expand protections for human rights. And in 1978, with Israeli Prime Minister Menachem Begin and Egyptian President Anwar el-Sadat, he worked out the "Camp David accords," which he hoped would become the foundation for future efforts to achieve peace in the Middle East. On the domestic front, the Carter Administration promoted energy conservation, limited strip mining, adopted stricter ethical standards for government officials, increased federal commitment to protecting the environment, and limited the power and discretion of federal intelligence agencies.

But the Carter Presidency was also a period of frustration and complexity. He and his aides never mastered the delicate task of maintaining good relations with Congress. The Panama Canal treaty offended American conservatives of both parties. The strategic arms limitation treaty was stalled in the Senate and never achieved ratification. The Middle East remained a tinderbox in international politics, despite the President's best efforts, for no other country in the region would join Israel and Egypt in the Camp David accords. The economy's problems continued, defeating the efforts of a third President in a row. The Soviet Union invaded Afghanistan at the end of 1979; Carter's efforts to forge an international trade embargo against the U.S.S.R. failed and drew the fury of American farmers who depended on grain sales to the Soviet Union. But the problem that eventually cost President Carter a second term was the Iran crisis.

Iran is a significant nation in the Middle East. Its history stretches back more than 2,500 years to the days of the Persian Empire. In the 1950s, the United States had helped to topple Iran's popular, democratically chosen leader, the neutralist Prime Minister Mohammed Mossadegh, and restored the monarch, or *Shah*, to his throne. For nearly thirty years, the Shah ruled with an iron hand, backed by the dreaded secret police, the SAVAK. In the 1960s and 1970s, many Iranian students, some with leftist views and others allied with extremist Muslim clergymen, demonstrated throughout the Western world against the regime of the Shah. Carter, like all other Presidents since Eisenhower, was reluctant to criticize the Shah. American criticism might suggest that the United States would not object to his overthrow. Keeping the Shah on his throne seemed vital to American interests in the Persian Gulf region.

In 1979, protests uniting the radical left, the religious right, and moderate opposition political parties toppled the Shah's regime. An interim government led by a respected moderate, Prime Minister Shapur Bhaktiar, also fell, and the religious right's leader, the Ayatollah Ruhollah Khomeini, flew in from exile in Paris to lead the Iranian "Islamic revolution." The new Prime Minister, Mehdi Bazargan, stepped down in frustration, and the religious faction took over the government of the country.

The Shah was given refuge in the United States. In revenge, a group of fundamentalist Iranian students, with the behind-the-scenes backing of the Iranian government, seized the U.S. embassy in Teheran and took about one hundred hostages, but released nearly half of them. President Carter declared that the United States would never negotiate with terrorists. He also declared that his top priority was the release of the hostages. These two positions left the United States helpless and frustrated.

The Iranians repeatedly captured the attention of the international news media. They staged "media events" with the remaining fifty-three hostages. The hostages' pleas for release and the lobbying of their families with Washington and the news media created the impression that the Carter Administration was powerless to win the hostages' freedom or to punish violations of international law.

The Carter Administration's helplessness was made evident in the spring of 1980 when a military rescue mission ordered by the President dissolved in failure with the deaths of eight American servicemen in a helicopter accident at a desert site in Iran. Secretary of State Cyrus Vance, who had opposed the idea of what many considered a "suicidal" rescue mission in favor of diplomatic negotiations, resigned in protest.

Like his predecessor in the White House, Carter faced a tough challenge for his party's Presidential nomination, but he managed to turn aside the bid of Senator Edward M. Kennedy, the brother of John and Robert Kennedy. Still, the contest within the party hurt the President's chances for re-election.

The front runner for the Republican Presidential nomination, Ronald Reagan, denounced President Carter's handling of the hostage crisis. He promised a return to traditional American values. Reagan won his party's nomination and defeated Carter in a landslide almost as lopsided as the Nixon-McGovern race of 1972. The Republican victory was so overwhelming that the party took control of the Senate from the Democrats for the first time in a generation.

During the election campaign, negotiations dragged on between the United States and Iran for the release of the hostages. The Iranians were paying close attention to the Presidential election. They despised Carter and wanted to deny him even the slightest satisfaction. They waited until the moment that President Reagan was sworn into office to release the hostages.

Jimmy Carter at first was devastated by his defeat. He busied himself with consoling his family, building his Presidential library at Emory University in Atlanta, and pursuing his interests in international human rights. Carter has led teams of inspectors to oversee elections in countries trying to build or rebuild democratic government, and has worked tirelessly to lead efforts to build low-cost urban housing. Carter has been the greatest ex-President since John Quincy Adams, and his popularity has begun to rebound from the nadir of 1980.

# CHAPTER TWELVE

# THE RISE AND FALL
# OF THE
# REAGAN–BUSH ERA

Ronald W. Reagan, the oldest man ever elected to the Presidency (he was sixty-nine when he took office), argued that most of the nation's economic and domestic problems flowed from the mistaken belief that government could solve these problems. In fact, he declared, government *was* the problem.

Reagan promised to reduce taxes, balance the budget, and increase defense spending—all at once. Critics declared this set of goals to be impossible and mutually inconsistent. (Even George Bush, who had lost the nomination to Reagan but became his Vice President, had denounced Reagan's policy as "voodoo economics.") But Reagan persevered.

President Reagan almost did not get the chance to govern. Two months after taking office, he was shot by John W. Hinckley, Jr., a mentally disturbed young man. The wound was serious—more serious than the White House disclosed at first—but the President recovered.

More than any other President since Franklin D. Roosevelt, whom he claimed as his hero and model, Reagan used as his favorite political strategy direct appeals to the American people. They welcomed his folksy and candid style. They forgave his habit of making mistakes of fact and law in his speeches and news conferences. But he was one

UPI/Bettmann

*On January 20, 1981, Ronald W. Reagan (1911—; term, 1981—1989) (Republican-California) became the fortieth President of the United States. He soon won the nickname "the Great Communicator," for his skill in persuading voters and legislators to adopt his programs. Reagan's 1981 Inaugural Address was a bold, vigorous, and eloquent attack on the role of government in American life.*

of the most inaccessible of modern Presidents. He held fewer formal news conferences even than Richard Nixon had held in the worst days of the Watergate scandal.

Reagan's first term seemed to be phenomenally successful. He secured the largest peacetime defense buildup in history, as well as a significant tax cut. But these victories carried with them enormous increases in the yearly and cumulative budget deficits. Congress and the American people did not want to make the deep cuts in social programs that the President sought to offset the increase in defense spending. The budgetary process broke down year after year. Congress abandoned the effort to adopt a compromise budget. Further borrowing and "continuing resolutions" were the tools that Congress had to use to keep the government going. The national debt under President Reagan doubled, as "Reaganomics" turned out to be a poor predictor of how the economy would respond to tax cuts and increases in defense spending. Another indication that the President's economic formula was not succeeding was the "Reagan recession" of 1982.

The President's proposed budget cuts dramatized his belief in a severely limited role for the federal government in national life. Even where he could not eliminate major government agencies, such as the Departments of Education and Energy, he hampered their work by staffing them with officials hostile to their purposes. But internal fighting among his aides at times hamstrung the Administration's efforts to articulate and achieve policy goals.

President Reagan's foreign policy was built around his opposition to Communism. During his first term, he often resorted to angry rhetoric. He declared that the Soviet Union was an "evil empire." Not since the period between 1917 and 1933, when the United States did not even recognize the U.S.S.R., had relations between the two countries been so cold. But Reagan tempered his rhetoric with shrewd recognition of domestic politics. For example, to placate American farmers who had backed his successful 1980 bid for the Presidency, he lifted President Carter's embargo on trading with the U.S.S.R.—even though Soviet armies still occupied Afghanistan.

The President's efforts to bring peace to the Middle East were unavailing. They betrayed a fundamental lack of understanding of the region's problems. Indeed, his approaches to the problems of the disintegrating nation of Lebanon produced two of the greatest calamities of his Administration. He sent a peacekeeping force of American Marines to Lebanon. They were headquartered in an isolated building in the capital city of Beirut. A suicidal car-bomb attack on a Sunday morning demolished the structure, killing 220 Marines and other Americans. A second terrorist attack, on the American embassy, killed more Americans and persuaded the President after eighteen months to withdraw U.S. Marines from Lebanon.

Reagan's greatest concern in foreign policy was the assertion of the Monroe Doctrine in the Western Hemisphere against Communism.

He charged that the guerrilla movement in the Central American nation of El Salvador was a Communist conspiracy against a friendly democratic nation, but he ignored the many human rights violations by El Salvador's government. He denounced the Sandinista regime in Nicaragua as a Communist dictatorship. He declared its opponents, the *contras*, to be the "moral equivalents of our Founding Fathers," despite extensive evidence that the *contras* were corrupt and just as willing to violate human rights as the government. In 1983, the President joined with leaders of Caribbean nations to send military forces to overthrow the Communist-backed government of the 120-square-mile island nation of Grenada in the West Indies.

Reagan won renomination for a second term easily. The Democrats named Walter F. Mondale of Minnesota, who had been Vice President in the Carter Administration, to oppose Reagan. The Democratic Vice Presidential nominee, Representative Geraldine Ferraro of New York, was the first woman to be part of a major party's national ticket. Campaigning on the upbeat slogan, "It's Morning in America," the Republicans buried the Democrats in a second "Reagan landslide."

Almost immediately, Reagan's new term ran into trouble from many of the same causes that had plagued his first term. Congress had enacted legislation forbidding direct governmental aid to the *contras*. The President's aides decided to evade the law by establishing private channels of privately-raised funds. They argued that the Congressional legislation violated the President's inherent power under the Constitution to conduct foreign policy and protect the national security. The secret networks of aid included an elaborate conspiracy to sell weapons at marked-up prices to Iran, then embroiled in the fifth year of a bitter war with its neighbor Iraq. The conspiracy used the profits from the Iran arms deals to aid the *contras*. A second purpose for the Iranian weapons deals was to secure the release of American hostages held by Iranian-backed terrorist groups in Lebanon.

The scandal, which became public in November 1986, prompted another outcry across the land. Investigations and congressional hearings dominated most of 1987—the bicentennial year of the U.S. Constitution—as did the investigations and report of the President's own study group chaired by former Senator John Tower (Republican-Texas). One especially confused issue was whether the President had authorized or approved—or even known about—the diversion of funds to the *contras*. The controversy damaged the President's formerly unparalleled ability to persuade the public to support his policies, crippling his Administration.

Other initiatives failed abruptly, dramatizing Presidential insensitivities and inattentiveness. The most noteworthy was the President's attempt to fill a critical vacancy on the Supreme Court left by the sudden retirement of Justice Lewis F. Powell, Jr., a 1971 Nixon appointee. President Reagan hoped that this appointment would give the conservative bloc on the Court a five-vote majority to overturn many significant decisions long criticized by the right wing, such as the 1973 landmark abortion decision, Roe v. Wade. In July 1987, President Reagan nominated Judge Robert H. Bork, a scholarly and combative former law professor. Bork's explanations of his views led to his rejection by the Senate by the largest margin ever to turn down a nominee to the Court. Reagan tried again. His second nominee, Judge Douglas H. Ginsburg, suddenly withdrew his name under pressure from Administration officials after confirming news reports that he illegally had smoked marijuana as a student and a law professor. (The Administration never had a chance to submit Ginsburg's name formally.) At last, in early 1988, Judge Anthony Kennedy of California, the President's third nominee, was confirmed by the Senate.

The President tried to shore up his Administration by making new overtures to the Soviet Union—moves that were reciprocated by the new Soviet leader, Mikhail Gorbachev. Two summit meetings, one in late 1987 and the second in the spring of 1988, revived the stalled talks between the two superpowers on limiting the growth of their nuclear arsenals.

But whatever benefit the President enjoyed as a result of these summit talks was eroded by the continuing Iran-contra investigations and by damaging revelations contained in "kiss-and-tell" memoirs published by key former Presidential aides. For most of his political career, Reagan had frustrated opponents and skeptical journalists alike, for none of their charges or criticisms seemed to "stick" to him. For this reason, he won the nickname of "the Teflon President." But the "kiss-and-tell" memoirs managed to cut through the President's Teflon surface. Not only their content, but their mere existence proved damaging to him, for never before in American political history had present or former members of an Administration published memoirs of their White House experiences before their President had stepped down.

Former Secretary of State Alexander Haig, former Budget Director David Stockman, former Education Secretary Terrell Bell, former

Deputy Chief of Staff Michael Deaver, former Press Secretary Larry Speakes, and former Treasury Secretary and Chief of Staff Donald Regan were sharply criticized for breaching confidences. But these attacks on the moral "sleaziness" of the authors of these books did not obscure the common theme of the accounts—that President Reagan was the single most passive President in the sixty years since Calvin Coolidge (a President for whom Reagan professed deep admiration). The books painted a picture of the President as uninterested in detail, unwilling to give direction to his aides and advisers, comfortable only with a completely scripted day that left him no need or chance to express himself on major issues, and unable to assimilate new information, to comprehend complex issues, or to take charge of his Administration. In fact, Mrs. Reagan, rather than her husband, seemed to be a leading source of political insight and executive decisiveness.

But the critics of the Reagan Administration overlooked two vital ways that Ronald Reagan was more successful than any President since Franklin D. Roosevelt: first, his command of the symbolic language of American politics and, second, his success at persuading the American people that it was a bad idea to use government to solve national problems.

Through his speeches and his public appearances, Reagan labored to rebuild national morale. He and his advisors created a series of compelling images—whether of the President helping flood-control workers to stack sandbags along the Mississippi River, or leading national mourning for the astronauts of the ill-fated 1986 *Challenger* space-shuttle mission, or embracing Olympic athletes—that identified the nation's highest office (and the man who held it) with the best that Americans could do or aspire to.

Reagan used his success in restoring the American people's self-confidence as the basis for his governing agenda. He convinced the electorate that a runaway government *was* the main problem facing America. He hammered home his belief that bloated, intrusive government caused the American economic slump and the nation's failure to solve its domestic problems. For the first time in half a century, a President persuaded the American people to change their minds about the role of government in American life. In the 1930s, Reagan's idol, Franklin D. Roosevelt, had spearheaded a sweeping campaign to use the powers of government to solve pressing national problems. In the 1980s, Reagan tried to lead an equally far-reaching effort to abolish what he derided as needless, wasteful, and even ridiculous government programs. His stated goal was to clear the way for forces of the marketplace and the natural good will of individual citizens to solve the nation's problems.

Analysts disagree on the effects of the Reagan policies on American life. His supporters claim that the 1980s were a decade of unparalleled prosperity and confidence, but his critics point to the staggering growth of the nation's budget deficit and the untold human costs of government cuts in social services and regulatory enforcement. Whatever the historical verdict on the "Reagan Revolution," however, Ronald Reagan has established for himself a major place in the history of American political thought.

As the 1988 election approached, the Democrats hoped that they could recapture the Presidency. But their quest for a Presidential nominee was plagued by confusion, political ineptitude, and personal scandals that disabled such leading candidates as former Senator Gary Hart of Colorado and Senator Joseph Biden of Delaware.

The Democratic nominee was not a clear winner, but the last survivor—Governor Michael S. Dukakis of Massachusetts. Dukakis presented himself as a tough, efficient manager who promised to bring to America the same prosperity and justice that he claimed to have brought to Massachusetts in the much-praised "Massachusetts miracle." Dukakis, the first major-party nominee who was not of Northern European ancestry (his family came from Greece), seemed to be an ideal candidate for a Democratic Party seeking to bring together Americans of all races, colors, and creeds.

Dukakis chose the courtly Texas Senator Lloyd Bentsen for his running mate; he hoped to evoke memories of the same "Boston-Austin" axis that had produced the winning Kennedy-Johnson ticket in 1960. Dukakis and Bentsen accepted their nominations against a comforting background of public-opinion polls that had them well ahead of the likely Republican nominee, Vice President George Bush.

On paper, at least, George Bush was a formidable candidate, with an impressive record of public service. The youngest American fighter pilot in the Second World War, he was a bona-fide war hero. After pursuing a career in the Texas oil business, Bush won election to the U.S. House of Representatives, where he served two terms (1969–1973). During the Nixon Administration, he had been Chairman of the Republican National Committee; under President Ford, he had served as U.S. Representative to the United Nations, U.S. Representative to the People's Republic of China, and Director of the Central Intelligence Agency.

But Bush had a reputation as a "wimp." Some Republicans, remembering how Ronald Reagan had clobbered him in the 1980 campaign for the Republican Presidential nomination, questioned Bush's ability to run a winning campaign. The son of the late Connecticut Senator Prescott Bush, a graduate of elite private schools and Yale University, Bush seemed somehow out of touch with most Americans.

Bush surprised political professionals and the public. Stressing his record of public service and his loyalty to the record of Ronald Reagan, Bush based his campaign on themes of patriotism and national pride. He pledged to continue the Reagan Revolution and promised, "Read my lips—no new taxes!"

Bush campaign officials also decided that they had to "go negative." They focused their energies on reshaping what the public thought of Dukakis's record. Bush campaign commercials painted the Massachusetts governor as an ultra-liberal candidate who believed in releasing convicted murderers and rapists on weekend furloughs, a hypocrite on the environment who let Boston Harbor become a waste dump, and a man so dangerously soft on defense that "he never met a weapons system he liked."

The strategy succeeded beyond Bush's hopes. Even Bush's most obvious weakness—his choice of Indiana Senator Dan Quayle as his running-mate—had no effect on the Republican boom. At forty-one, Quayle was the youngest Vice Presidential nominee since Richard Nixon in 1952. Quayle was a political unknown whose tongue-tied performance during the campaign made him a national laughingstock. Some observers suggested that Bush chose Quayle because he made Bush look Presidential; others guessed that Quayle was Bush's "impeachment insurance." In the Bentsen-Quayle debate, the Texan humiliated his opponent; when Quayle tried to defend himself from charges of inexperience by citing the example of John F. Kennedy, Bentsen said, "Senator, I knew Jack Kennedy. He was a friend of mine. Senator, you're no Jack Kennedy." But Quayle never became a make-or-break issue for the Bush campaign.

The ferocity of the Bush media campaign, masterminded by political strategist Lee Atwater, stunned the electorate. But they were even more amazed, and disturbed, by Dukakis's failure to answer the Republicans' charges, and by Dukakis's cold, aloof performance in the Presidential debates. Dukakis seemed to consider himself so far above the fray that he did not have to answer the charges; he did not change tactics until it was far too late to save his campaign. Although Dukakis was the first Democratic presidential nominee since Jimmy

Carter in 1976 to score more than 100 electoral votes, he was no match for the Bush juggernaut.

In his inaugural address, President Bush pledged "a kinder, gentler nation" while, at the same time, promising continuity of purpose and principle from the Reagan Administration. He also committed himself to work with Congress and to reach out to political adversaries.

Bush was more focused on foreign affairs than domestic policy, and more interested in managing the existing state of affairs than in formulating new policies. He answered critics' charges that he had no larger vision of his Administration or his goals by dismissing the question as "the vision thing." Bush formed close personal friendships with world leaders, and regularly telephoned them to consult them on current issues or to give them advance word of American initiatives. He extended cautious but friendly support to Mikhail Gorbachev, the Soviet leader whose policies of *glasnost* (openness) and *perestroika* (a new beginning) promised a rebirth of democracy in the Soviet Union. He and Secretary of State James Baker hoped to find a formula to achieve lasting peace in the Middle East.

But Bush's critics charged that the Administration was excessively cautious and had no clear sense of direction. Their principal example was Bush's reaction to the end of Communist domination of Eastern Europe. When, in the fall and winter of 1989, Eastern European Communist regimes began to crumble and collapse, Bush waited for months before extending American support and encouragement to the fledgling democracies of the region.

By contrast, in December 1989, when the Panamanian dictator, General Manuel Noriega, refused to accept his defeat in a presidential election and threatened to seize control of the Panama Canal, Bush took command of the situation. He ordered American naval and ground forces to invade Panama to safeguard American interests in the Canal Zone, to overthrow Noriega (whom he denounced as a dictator who conspired with drug traffickers and Communist regimes), and to help the people of Panama restore democratic government.

"Operation Just Cause" at first looked like a complete success. Noriega was captured and brought to the United States to stand trial, and American forces enabled the actual victor in the Panamanian election, Guillermo Endara, to take office as President. But, in the three years following Operation Just Cause, the people of Panama lost confidence in their government, and many of the charges against Noriega turned out to be without foundation.

In 1990, the Bush Administration ventured into the domestic policy arena. After the savings and loan crisis and budgetary problems threatened to produce deficits far beyond previous records, President Bush reluctantly hammered out a budget compromise with Congressional leaders of both parties. Part of that compromise was a set of tax increases—a step that flew in the face of the President's pledge of "no new taxes." Bush also promised to be "the environmental President" and the "education President," but his proposed policies in these fields failed to satisfy his critics.

The Persian Gulf crisis of 1990–1991 offered Bush an opportunity to demonstrate the need for a President experienced in foreign affairs. In August 1990, Iraqi forces invaded and conquered the oil-rich country of Kuwait. Iraq's President, Saddam Hussein, claimed that Kuwait historically had been part of Iraq and vowed never to give it up. The world was appalled by reports of atrocities carried out by Iraqi forces against Kuwaiti civilians, and President Bush denounced Saddam Hussein as an aggressor. (Forgotten were American efforts throughout the 1980s and into 1990 to befriend the Hussein regime as a counterweight to neighboring Iran.)

The President assembled an international coalition, organized an international boycott and blockade of Iraq, and procured United Nations authorization for military operations to liberate Kuwait and deprive Saddam Hussein of the power to threaten his neighbors in future. Bush committed several hundred thousand American military personnel to Operation Desert Shield, designed to safeguard Saudi Arabia from Iraqi attack. He warned Iraq that coalition forces were prepared to liberate Kuwait from Iraqi occupation. In early January, as the President's January 15 deadline for Iraqi withdrawal approached, he reluctantly agreed that Congress should vote on whether to authorize American forces to be used against Iraq. Once Congress approved military action (52–47 in the Senate, 250–183 in the House), Bush was free to act.

On January 15, 1991, Bush ordered the beginning of Operation Desert Storm. Coalition forces quickly liberated Kuwait, shattered the Iraqi occupation forces, and penetrated deep into Iraqi territory. Some American politicians demanded the overthrow of Saddam Hussein, but coalition partners such as Saudi Arabia opposed this action, fearing that the total collapse of Iraq might be a source of conflict in the Persian Gulf for years to come. For these reasons, Bush ordered the end of Operation Desert Storm.

That spring, with the President's approval ratings at an all-time high of 88 percent, most Americans assumed that George Bush was guaranteed a triumphant re-election in 1992. Several potential Democratic challengers decided to forego the campaign. But other Democrats sensed weaknesses in Bush's position.

The first sign of trouble for Bush was the economic downturn that began that summer and persisted through 1991 and into 1992. What made matters even worse was Bush's apparent indifference to the weakness of the economy.

In August 1991 came a short-lived Soviet coup against Mikhail Gorbachev. The Bush Administration's hesitant response surprised many Americans. Not until after the people rallied behind Russian President Boris Yeltsin in opposition to the hard-line Communist leaders of the coup did the Bush Administration abandon its cautious wait-and-see approach. (Bush tried but failed to take credit for winning the Cold War.)

The third major blow was the bitter controversy over the nomination of Judge Clarence Thomas to the Supreme Court and the nationally-televised Senate Judiciary Committee hearings pitting Thomas against Anita Hill, the law professor who accused him of sexual harassment.

Bush's main problem remained the economy. In the fall of 1991, after the death in a plane crash of Senator H. John Heinz (Republican-Pennsylvania), Bush's Attorney General, Richard Thornburgh, resigned to run for Heinz's seat against Heinz's successor, Harris Wofford; politicians and journalists agreed that the popular Thornburgh, a former governor of the state, would easily defeat Wofford, a liberal Democrat with little apparent public appeal. But Wofford ran a vigorous campaign based on two themes—the ailing economy and the need for a program of national health insurance. Wofford's surprise upset of Thornburgh sent danger signals to Bush campaign strategists.

Bush tried to convey to the American people that he "got the message" of public anger and dissatisfaction, and his aides promised that his 1992 State of the Union message would be the speech that would turn his re-election campaign around. But Bush's lackluster oration contained nothing new; his major recommendation was a technical change in the tax laws that would cut the taxes of investors on profits they made from their investments. Bush considered this capital-gains tax cut a vital step toward economic recovery, but he could not persuade Congress or the electorate that he was right.

Ultra-conservative news commentator Patrick Buchanan mounted a challenge from the far right to Bush's renomination. Buchanan never defeated Bush in any Republican primary, but he regularly scored between twenty and thirty percent, indicating Bush's weakness among "true believers." Bush's advisers, therefore, decided to woo back the right wing; they believed that they had to consolidate the President's political base before mounting a national campaign.

The major Democratic contender was Governor Bill Clinton of Arkansas, whom the media anointed early as the "front runner" in the campaign for the party's Presidential nomination. Clinton was a veteran governor (six election victories) who had made a genuine difference for the better in a state plagued by economic and environmental problems. (The nation's other governors repeatedly named him the nation's most effective governor.) He also was an effective face-to-face politician with a talent for building consensus and a master of the arcane details of a wide range of domestic issues. A founder of the moderate Democratic Leadership Council, he was the choice of the moderate and conservative wing of the Democratic Party. He hired James Carville and Paul Begala—the architects of Harris Wofford's victory in Pennsylvania—as his campaign strategists.

Early in the campaign, Clinton seemed to be damaged by charges that he had had an extramarital affair. He and his wife, the respected attorney Hillary Rodham Clinton, acknowledged that there had been problems in their marriage, but maintained that they had overcome them and refused to provide any details or to discuss the question further. Clinton lost the New Hampshire primary, but bounced back, winning most of the later primaries. In a series of televised debates, he displayed his mastery of issues and his ability to reach out directly to voters.

While Bush sought to firm up his political base and Clinton struggled to clinch the Democratic nomination, it became evident that 1992 would not be a typical Presidential election. Beginning in February, Texas billionaire and political gadfly H. Ross Perot tantalized voters with his blunt-spoken criticisms of "politics as usual." When asked by talk-show host Larry King if he would consider entering the campaign, Perot pledged that he would do so—but only if volunteers put his name on the ballot in all fifty states. In response, a "Draft Ross" movement sprang up throughout the nation, and Perot was well on his way to his goal. Politicians and journalists, hypnotized by "the Perot factor," threw conventional political calculations into wastebaskets across the nation.

Hovering on the edge of declaring his candidacy, Perot assembled a "world-class" team of advisers, including Edward Rollins (Ronald Reagan's 1984 campaign manager) and Hamilton Jordan (Jimmy

Carter's chief strategist in 1976). But reports leaked out that he was unwilling to follow their advice. Close media attention to Perot's spotty record and his personal eccentricities infuriated him and made him look less and less Presidential. In July, Rollins quit in disgust, amid reports that the Perot campaign was disintegrating even before it was officially to begin. On the day that Clinton was to accept the Democratic nomination, Perot announced that he was suspending his campaign. The Texan went out of his way to praise Clinton and the Democratic Party.

Perot's surprise decision focused national attention on the Democrats. Clinton reaped the benefits. He defied the conventional wisdom by picking as his running mate Senator Al Gore, Jr., of Tennessee, who came from his region and shared his views. Gore had run a failed campaign for the Democratic Presidential nomination in 1988, but he had emerged in the years that followed as a internationally-recognized expert on environmental issues and a vigorous critic of Reagan's and Bush's environmental policies. The Clinton-Gore ticket symbolized the qualities of youth, energy, and commitment to new approaches to government that Clinton and his advisers set at the core of the campaign. Clinton and Gore hit it off to such a degree that commentators speculated that the two men might reinvent the relationship between the President and the Vice President.

Clinton and Gore stated their theme as "Putting People First." (The acerbic James Carville defined the theme as: "It's the economy, stupid!") The Democratic ticket emphasized the need to bring government into regular contact with the American electorate. Just after the highly successful Democratic convention, Clinton and Gore and their wives launched the first of what became their trademark bus campaigns. The bus caravans, moving through small towns and dominating the nightly news broadcasts, locally and nationally, captured national attention and gave Clinton a sixteen-point lead over President Bush in opinion polls.

Scrambling to recover lost ground, the Republicans decided to recycle the 1988 strategy they had used so effectively against Michael Dukakis. With great fanfare, President Bush announced that the victorious strategist of 1988, James Baker, was stepping down as Secretary of State to lead the campaign. But the Republican National Convention, dominated by the party's right wing, was a public-relations disaster. Convention speakers such as Patrick Buchanan declared a cultural war on those who did not share their conservative family, religious, and moral values. They attacked Bill Clinton as an ultra-liberal, mocked Al Gore as a "tree-hugger," and denounced Hillary Rodham Clinton as an extreme feminist who would impose a radical domestic agenda on the nation. They also tried to define the election as a competition between those who stood for America (supporters of the President) and those who were against America (opponents of the President). Not even the popular First Lady, Barbara Bush, or former President Reagan were able to repair the damage. Bush's acceptance speech—the long-anticipated keynote for the fall campaign—was lifeless, rambling, and ineffective. And Baker (who Bush had announced would become the "domestic policy czar" in a second term) was all but invisible throughout the fall.

In early October, Ross Perot stunned the nation by re-entering the Presidential race, having achieved his goal of being put on the ballot in all fifty states. Perot chose as his running mate Admiral James Stockdale, a former prisoner of war in Vietnam and a genuine national hero. Perot broadcast several successful television programs in which he spelled out his diagnosis of the nation's economic problems and sketched policies that he might put into effect if he were elected President.

After bitter wrangling over petty details, Bush, Clinton, and Perot met in three televised debates, and Quayle, Gore, and Stockdale took part in a fourth. Clinton maintained his posture as an able, articulate speaker with a command of policy details and an ability to connect directly with ordinary citizens. Perot at times "stole the show" with folksy humor but disappointed voters when he did not spell out the details of his proposed solutions. President Bush startled television viewers with his lackluster performance and his repeated failure to reassure the electorate that he understood their problems. In the second debate, cameras caught the President furtively looking at his watch, as if counting the minutes until the end of his ordeal. In the Vice Presidential debate, Quayle and Gore scrapped repeatedly and heatedly, leaving Admiral Stockdale looking and sounding like a befuddled grandparent who had walked into a teenage fistfight.

On the campaign trail, Clinton and Gore continued to practice their winning brand of campaign politics. Vice President Quayle often was a more effective advocate of his party's ticket than President Bush, who on occasion drifted into shrill rhetoric against Democratic "bozos." Perot, injured by Stockdale's lackluster performance in the debate with Quayle and Gore and by his own charges that Republican operatives were out to sabotage his campaign, continued to fade in popularity, despite his brave predictions that he would win all fifty states.

Throughout the fall, journalists speculated about what might happen should the three-way race prevent any candidate from receiving a majority of electoral votes. Despite these conjectures, and despite apparent surges in the President's support reported by public-opinion polls, the Clinton-Gore ticket (the first victorious all-Southern ticket since Andrew Jackson and John C. Calhoun in 1828) racked up a comfortable 370 electoral votes, with 168 for the Republicans. Perot did not carry a single state, and thus did not receive a single electoral vote. Clinton received 43 percent of the popular vote, to Bush's 38 percent and Perot's 19 percent. Political commentators agreed that Clinton and Gore had run the best Democratic presidential campaign —and the Bush team had run the worst campaign—in living memory, and that Perot had squandered the promise of his early days in Presidential politics.

In a year that broke all the political rules, the election shattered the record of every previously-reliable electoral predictor—from Crook County, Oregon (which had picked the winner in the previous twenty-seven elections) to the Weekly Reader poll (right in nine straight elections), from the New Hampshire rule (that the winner of the election must have won his or her party's New Hampshire primary) to the Texas test (that no candidate could win the Presidency without carrying Texas). Not even the World Series axiom (an American League World Series equals a Republican victory, a National League Series means a Democratic triumph) and the wine-taster's dogma (a poor Beaujolais harvest means a Republican victory) survived Clinton's victory.

Following the election, two major questions dominated public attention: First, what had gone wrong with President Bush's attempt to seek a second term? Second, what would the new Clinton Administration do about the sluggish economy and the growing budget deficit?

Analysts agreed that Bush and his aides repeatedly missed opportunities to define the reasons why the President should win a second term, assuming until far too late in the game that there was no need to do so and that negative campaigning against the President's opponents would be enough. Peggy Noonan, the former Reagan Administration speechwriter who had crafted Bush's 1988 acceptance speech, pointed out, "The public part of the Presidency, the persuading-in-the-pulpit part, is central to leadership. The worst thing is to lie to the people, but the second worst is to ignore them and not tell what you are doing and why." Noonan's judgment covered the host of specific problems, blunders, and missed chances that other commentators spent weeks cataloguing after Election Day.

The Clinton campaign began to shift from electoral politics to transition to governance soon after the election. Occasional difficulties in finding the right appointees sparked media disapproval of the new Administration. Critics also reproached Clinton and his advisers for their alleged slowness in putting forward new policies on the budget, deficit reduction, and economic renewal. Presidential scholars pointed out, however, that the pace of the transition from Bush to Clinton was about the same as that of earlier transitions.

January 20, 1993—Inauguration Day—dawned brisk and clear. At noon, in a simple ceremony that emphasized the dignity of the occasion and the smoothness of the transfer of power, William Jefferson Clinton took the oath of office as the forty-second President of the United States. The sixty-eight-year-old Bush, the last veteran of the Second World War to occupy the Presidency, yielded to the forty-six-year-old Clinton, who was born the year after the war ended and who as a student opposed the Vietnam Conflict.

Sometimes mocked during the campaign for his tendency to deliver verbose speeches, Clinton surprised the nation with an inaugural address that lasted barely fifteen minutes. Calling for "the vision and courage to reinvent America," the new President challenged the nation: "Our democracy must be not only the envy of the world but the engine of our own renewal. There is nothing wrong with America that cannot be cured by what is right with America."

Drawing on the inaugural addresses of Washington, Jefferson, Lincoln, Wilson, Franklin D. Roosevelt, Reagan, and his personal hero John F. Kennedy, President Clinton set the themes that his Administration would follow in the years to come:

> We must do what no generation has had to do before. We must invest more in our own people, in their jobs, in their future, and at the same time cut our massive debt. And we must do so in a world in which we must compete for every opportunity.
>
> It will not be easy; it will require sacrifice. But it can be done, and done fairly, not choosing sacrifice for its own sake, but for our own sake. . . .
>
> . . . I say to all of us here, let us resolve to reform our politics, so that power and privilege no longer shout down the voice of the

people. Let us put aside personal advantage so that we can feel the pain and see the promise of America.

Let us resolve to make our government a place for what Franklin Roosevelt called "bold, persistent experimentation," a government for our tomorrows, not our yesterdays.

Let us give this capital back to the people to whom it belongs.

*"The torch is passed to a new generation": On January 20, 1993, Bill Clinton (1946—; term, 1993—) (Democrat-Arkansas), who used his full name, William Jefferson Clinton, in taking the oath of office, became the forty-second President of the United States. This photograph of the ceremony shows (left to right): Chelsea Clinton, the new President's daughter; President Bill Clinton; First Lady Hillary Rodham Clinton; former President George Bush (1924—; term, 1989—1993) (Republican-Texas); and Chief Justice William H. Rehnquist. Clinton is the first President to take office following the end of the Cold War and the first President to have been born since the end of the Second World War.*

# CONCLUSION:

# DOES THE PRESIDENCY NEED FIXING?

Political observers and historians who compare the quality of our present and potential Presidents with that of George Washington and his Administration in 1789 find much reason for concern and disappointment. Lackluster campaigns cause many journalists and citizens to ask: "Isn't there some better way to pick our President?"

Several constitutional scholars, as well as former Presidents Nixon, Ford, and Carter, have proposed that the Constitution be amended to give the President a single, six-year term of office. This idea, they claim, would relieve the President of the burden of constantly worrying about re-election and permit him or her to focus on the nation's needs, hopes, and problems. Opponents of the idea charge that it would deprive the President of the political power that he or she would have as a candidate for re-election; they claim that a six-year President would be a "lame duck" from the moment of the swearing-in ceremony.

Another proposal focusing on the length of the Presidential term calls for repeal of the Twenty-second Amendment. Ratified in 1951, this Amendment (as we have seen) was in large part a slap at the memory of Franklin D. Roosevelt. The Amendment's critics charge that it is a shameful and partisan attempt to limit the people's right to choose whomever they wish to lead the nation. However, this Amendment, despite its unsavory origins, finds defenders who claim that it has become vital to the Presidency. They argue that a President cannot survive more than two terms of the stresses and strains of the modern Presidency. They maintain that a President who serves more than two terms would thwart the rise of men and women who could succeed him or her in the White House. Would the people not run the risk of electing Presidents for life because no alternatives would appear on the horizon until the incumbent dies?

Still another question about the way Americans choose the President has to do with the ways that our votes are counted. Voters do not vote directly for Presidential candidates. They vote for *electors*— men and women who cast votes in the Electoral College. To win the Presidency, a successful candidate must amass 270 electoral votes of the 538 cast—a bare majority.

If Candidate A gets 50.1 percent of the popular vote in State X and Candidate B gets 49.9 percent, candidate A gets all the electoral votes of State X, and those who voted for Candidate B might as well have stayed home. Thus, a candidate can win the popular vote nationwide but lose in the Electoral College, as Grover Cleveland did in 1888. Also, it is possible for an elector to vote for somebody other than the candidate he or she is pledged to vote for. This happens rarely and so far has not affected the outcome of any Presidential election. That could change someday.

Many politicians and scholars have called for an amendment to the Constitution to deal with the problems of the Electoral College. The most modest amendment would do away with the electors; the electoral votes would be cast automatically once it is known which candidate has won the popular vote in each state. A broader amendment would split each state's electoral vote based on the percentage of the popular vote by the candidates.

The most sweeping and most often proposed amendment would do away with the Electoral College once and for all, replacing it with a system of direct popular vote. Its advocates point to the success of direct popular voting for Senators. Its opponents charge that abolishing the Electoral College would cause Presidential candidates to focus on only those states where the most voters can be found; as a result, states with smaller populations, such as Vermont, Alaska, and Nevada, would be slighted in favor of states such as New York, California, Illinois, and Texas. The argument has not produced an amendment to be sent to the states, nor is it likely to in the years ahead, unless something goes terribly wrong with the Electoral College.

Still other students of the Presidency focus on the powers of the President and whether the office has become too much for one person under the present system. Some argue for removing some powers and responsibilities from the President—vesting them in the Vice President (to give him or her something important to do) or in Congress or in the Cabinet or elsewhere.

Others say that the problem is not Presidential power but lack of power. Theodore Roosevelt once lamented: "Oh, if I could only be President and Congress together for just ten minutes!" His distant cousin and eventual successor, Franklin D. Roosevelt, observed: "Lincoln was a sad man because he couldn't get it all at once. And nobody can." Several scholars claim that the Constitution's system of checks and balances strangles Presidents. Therefore, they argue, Americans must make the Presidency even more powerful. Perhaps the President should have the power to veto only parts of bills that he or she does not like rather than the whole bill. (Presidents Reagan and Bush frequently called for such a "line-item veto" amendment.) Perhaps the Senate's power to approve treaties should be changed so that a simple majority of the Senators can ratify a treaty, rather than the two-thirds vote now needed. These and other changes are interesting and often discussed, but no serious proposal has emerged to date.

The problems of electing a President—for how long, how many times, in what way—are fertile sources of ideas to change the Constitution. In fact, such problems plagued the men who created the Presidency in 1787, the ratifying conventions that adopted the Constitution in 1787–1788, and all later students of the Constitutional system.

The American experiment in government had as its most daring feature the creation of a popularly-elected Chief Executive. The Presidency is the one political office in which all Americans have a stake and in the filling of which all Americans can have a voice. It is an office of great power and prestige. In the twentieth century, Presidents have assumed the role of identifying the nation's problems and goals and proposing policies to solve those problems and achieve those goals.

But another issue remains unresolved: Now that the Presidency is the "bully pulpit," as Theodore Roosevelt called it, have the American people come to believe that it is the only office of government with legitimacy and authority? Must the people rein in the Presidency? Do Americans expect too much from their Presidents? Is the ongoing search for Presidential leadership a wild-goose chase that damages Americans' ability to govern themselves?

# THE SUPREME COURT

The judicial Power of the United States, shall be vested in one supreme Court, and in such inferior Courts as the Congress may from time to time ordain and establish.
—Constitution of the United States
Article III, Section 1

*The Supreme Court*

For Christa Tillman-Young, Adam Tillman-Young, Noah Tillman-Young, Luke Tillman-Young, Mary Maya Tillman-Young, and a sixth-round draft choice to be named later . . . future leaders of the rising generation.

R. B. B.

*The Supreme Court did not acquire a permanent home of its own until October 7, 1935, when the Supreme Court building on East Capitol Street in Washington, D.C., opened its doors. The noted architect Cass Gilbert designed the building as a monumental temple of justice. Carved over the entryway are the words "Equal Justice Under Law."*

# CHAPTER ONE

# THE BIRTH OF THE SUPREME COURT

Throughout our history, the value at the heart of the American political system has been "Liberty under Law." In 1776, the Revolutionary pamphleteer Thomas Paine boasted: "In America the law is king." The Constitution of the United States, written eleven years later, is a special kind of law—a *fundamental* law. It is different from, more important than, ordinary laws. Article VI of the Constitution says, "This Constitution . . . shall be the supreme law of the land."

Chief Justice John Marshall declared in 1803, "It is emphatically the province and duty of the judiciary department to say what the law is." Article III of the Constitution assigns this power, the judicial power, to the United States Supreme Court and to whatever lower federal courts Congress sets up. How the federal courts have shaped American history—and have been shaped by that history—is the subject of this third part.

The first charter of government for the United States, the Articles of Confederation, did not provide for a federal court system. (The Articles were proposed in 1777, a year after the Declaration of Independence, and adopted by all thirteen states by March 1781.) The Confederation Congress appointed committees of its members to work out boundary and other disputes between states. A special body, the Court of Appeals in Cases of Capture, was created to hear cases having to do with piracy, shipping, and maritime law.

One reason that many Americans came to believe in the 1780s that the Articles needed to be revised or replaced was that there was no impartial system of courts where citizens of different states or subjects of foreign countries could get fair decisions in their lawsuits.

When they wrote the Constitution in Philadelphia in 1787, the delegates to the Federal Convention did not spend much time on the federal judiciary. They agreed to provide for a Supreme Court, but they did not say how many members the Court should have. They left it to Congress to decide this question and to decide whether there would be any federal courts below the Supreme Court and how these courts would fit together. The delegates also decided that the President would appoint all federal judges, but that the Senate would have to *confirm* these appointments. These judges would serve for life unless removed from office for serious misdeeds. The delegates also defined the "judicial power" of the United States. They figured that if the Constitution were adopted, the first Congress would fill the gaps. This is exactly what happened.

On September 24, 1789, President George Washington signed into law the bill now known as the Judiciary Act of 1789, the most important federal statute ever adopted under the Constitution. It established the structure and authority of the federal courts that would interpret the U.S. Constitution and federal law. Although the Judiciary Act of 1789 has been amended many times since it was enacted, it is still law.

Think of the federal court system as a pyramid. In keeping with the Constitution, the original Judiciary Act put the Supreme Court at the top of the pyramid. (It is still there today.) Under the 1789 law, the next level was the *federal circuit courts*, and the third, or bottom, level was the *federal district courts*. The federal court system exists side by side with the state court systems. Each state has its own system of trial courts and appeals courts. Although many issues of law are ultimately settled by the federal courts—and, specifically, by the U.S. Supreme Court—many issues of law that don't raise problems under the Constitution or federal law are handled by the state courts. This complex system of federal courts and state courts protects the constitutional value of *federalism*—the division of authority between the federal government and state and local governments.

Both the federal circuit courts and the federal district courts were *trial courts*. People could sue each other in circuit court or in district court. However, the district courts were authorized to hear only a few limited types of cases under the customs laws passed by Congress. The main trial courts in the federal system were the circuit courts.

The Judiciary Act of 1789 divided the United States into three *circuits:* the Eastern (New York, Massachusetts, Connecticut, New Hampshire, and Maine [then still part of Massachusetts]); the Middle (New Jersey, Pennsylvania, Maryland, Delaware, Virginia, and Kentucky [then part of Virginia]); and the Southern (South Carolina and Georgia). North Carolina and Rhode Island had not yet ratified the Constitution by September 1789 and therefore could not be included within the judicial system.

Each state had its own federal district court and judge. Kentucky and Maine also had their own district courts and judges, even though they were not yet states. They were *territories*, waiting for Congress to decide that they were ready to become states.

The three circuit courts consisted of two Supreme Court Justices and the district judge for each state or territory where the circuit court would meet. The Justices had to travel around each circuit— "ride" the circuit, by horse or stagecoach—twice a year. Justice James Iredell, assigned to the Southern Circuit, calculated that he had to travel nearly 2,000 miles on each trip. When North Carolina (in 1789) and Rhode Island (in 1790) ratified the Constitution, Congress amended the Judiciary Act to create district courts for each state and to add them to the Southern and Eastern Circuits, respectively. Congress continued to restructure the federal courts as more states joined the Union.

The Judiciary Act created a six-member Supreme Court, with a Chief Justice and five Associate Justices. They set the number of Justices at six to provide two Justices for each of the three circuits. Later, as more states joined the Union, Congress added Justices to the Supreme Court.

The Supreme Court was given the authority to hear and decide appeals from lower federal courts and to hear and decide appeals from decisions of state courts on matters affecting the Constitution or federal laws. Because the government created by the Constitution was so new, the Justices had to wait several years for their first case.

President Washington named the first Justices of the Supreme Court, and the Senate quickly approved his choices. John Jay of New York was the first Chief Justice. He was forty-four years old, a veteran of state and national politics and foreign diplomacy. He had been the

Confederation's Secretary for Foreign Affairs, the principal author of the New York constitution of 1777, and New York's first chief justice under that constitution. In 1787–1788, he had also helped to lead the battle in New York to adopt the Constitution. As part of that battle, he had written five of the famous *Federalist* essays explaining and defending the Constitution.

James Wilson of Pennsylvania had wanted to be Chief Justice but had to be content with an appointment as an Associate Justice. He was one of the greatest lawyers in America—some said that his mind was a blaze of light—and a principal member of the Federal Convention. Two other veterans of the Convention were also named to the Court: John Rutledge of South Carolina and John Blair of Virginia. Washington also nominated William Cushing, a notable Massachusetts lawyer and judge who was a leading supporter of the Constitution, and Robert Hanson Harrison of Maryland, a respected judge and a comrade-in-arms from the Revolution. But Harrison had just been named to Maryland's highest judicial post and was in poor health. So he declined the appointment to the Supreme Court, even though the Senate had already confirmed him. (As it turned out, he died the week before the Supreme Court was to begin its first session.) By this time, North Carolina had ratified the Constitution, so President Washington nominated James Iredell, the leader of that state's pro-Constitution forces, to the seat refused by Harrison, and the Senate confirmed him.

The Supreme Court convened for the first time on February 4, 1790, in New York City, the first capital of the United States. This first session was one of ceremony rather than serious business. The Court began to hear and decide cases only after it moved with the rest of the federal government to the new capital at Philadelphia at the end of 1790.

In 1793, President Washington wanted advice about measures he planned to take to keep the United States from being drawn into the war between Great Britain and France. He asked his Secretary of State, Thomas Jefferson, to send a letter to the Justices asking whether his plans were constitutional. To Washington's and Jefferson's surprise, the Justices refused this request for advice. They reminded the President that the Constitution authorized them only to hear actual cases and controversies. Under the Constitution, the phrase "cases and controversies" means disputes where actual rights, injuries, or claims of authority are at stake and the parties to the case or controversy have something to gain or lose. The Justices reminded

Collection of the Supreme Court of the United States

*John Jay, the first Chief Justice (1745—1829; term, 1789—1795), was an able judge but disliked circuit riding, because it was an excessive burden on the Supreme Court. Six years after tendering his resignation to President George Washington, Jay refused to become Chief Justice again, even though the Senate had confirmed his reappointment by President John Adams.*

the President that they could not use their power as Justices of the Supreme Court to answer questions before there was a real dispute for them to decide. This decision *not* to act was extremely important. It confirmed that the courts were independent from the other parts of the government.

The circuit courts were the most active part of the new court system in its first decade. As the Justices traveled throughout the country, they confirmed to the people that the government created by the Constitution was real and powerful.

Each session of the circuit courts opened with pomp and pageantry. The judges (the Supreme Court Justices riding that circuit and the local federal district judge) convened federal *grand juries*—bodies of citizens who were to inquire whether the laws of the United States had been violated and who should be tried in court for violating those laws. The presiding Justice would deliver a speech to the members of the grand jury instructing them about their duty and explaining to them and the people generally the principles of the Constitution.

One of the first cases to reach the Supreme Court caused a major controversy. Chisholm, a citizen of South Carolina, was the executor of an estate. (An *executor* is the person having legal responsibility for the possessions, or *estate*, of a dead person.) He discovered that the state of Georgia still owed his late friend money for war supplies that the dead man had sold to the state during the Revolution. To recover this money for his friend's estate, Chisholm sued the state of Georgia in federal court.

In 1787–1788, during the ratification controversy, the Constitution's supporters had assured the people that the Constitution would not allow federal courts to hear a suit by a citizen of one state against another state. But the Supreme Court surprised the nation—the Justices upheld Chisholm's claim.

*Chisholm v. Georgia* caused a huge public outcry. The states feared that they would be buried in lawsuits. During the Revolution, the new state governments had forced people who were still loyal to Great Britain and King George III—the Loyalists—to give up their land and their money and flee the country. The states treated them this way because the Loyalists had refused to swear to support the Revolution. Now, the state governments worried, the *Chisholm* case would be a green light for the Loyalists to sue to get their land and their money back. Congress therefore proposed a constitutional amendment to strip the federal courts of the power to hear suits against a state by citizens of another state or of foreign countries. The states quickly ratified the proposal, and in 1798 it became the Eleventh Amendment. It was the first amendment to be added to the Constitution since the adoption of the Bill of Rights, the first ten amendments, in 1791. The Eleventh Amendment is the only Amendment limiting the powers of the federal courts, and it was the first Amendment to overturn a decision of the Supreme Court.

Chief Justice John Jay was an able and respected judge, but he did not like having to travel throughout several states twice each year. In 1792, he let his friends put his name forward as a candidate for governor of New York. If Jay had won, he would have resigned from the Court to become governor. Although Jay did not campaign, he lost the election only because his opponents "fixed" the counting of the votes.

In 1794, George Washington wanted to ease American relations with Great Britain. He asked Chief Justice Jay to go to Great Britain to negotiate a commercial treaty. Jay was abroad for more than a year. He returned from London in 1795 with a treaty that pleased Americans who liked Great Britain but outraged those who distrusted their old enemy. On his arrival in New York City, the Chief Justice discovered to his surprise and delight that he had been put forward again as a candidate for governor of New York, and that this time the voters had elected him. Jay immediately resigned from the Court.

The President chose former Associate Justice John Rutledge to succeed Jay as Chief Justice. "Dictator John" was a powerful South Carolina politician who had resigned from the Court in 1791. He had never served with his fellow Justices in sessions of the Supreme Court, although he had carried out his duty to "ride circuit" in the South. The Senate was not in session when Chief Justice Jay resigned, so Washington made a *recess appointment*. This device, authorized by the Constitution, meant that Rutledge could hold the job of Chief Justice until the Senate met to vote on his confirmation.

Rutledge's nomination ran into trouble almost immediately because of speeches he had made attacking the Jay Treaty. President Washington was astonished and annoyed but did not withdraw Rutledge's nomination. Also, rumors spread that the nominee was losing his mind. The Senate rejected Rutledge. Scandalmongers whispered that "Dictator John" tried to kill himself when he heard that the Senate had turned him down. Rutledge indeed went mad in the last five years of his life. He was a shattered wreck when he died in 1800.

Washington tried again—this time with Oliver Ellsworth of Connecticut, another veteran of the Federal Convention and one of the three Senators who had drafted the Judiciary Act of 1789. Ellsworth won quick confirmation by the Senate. The Senators decided to ignore his odd habits of taking snuff constantly and talking to himself.

Under Ellsworth, the Supreme Court decided another major case, known as the "Carriage Tax Case." Congress had passed a law at the suggestion of Secretary of the Treasury Alexander Hamilton imposing a tax on carriages—which in the 1790s were what limousines are today, a means of travel available only to the rich. Some Americans refused to pay the tax, charging that it was unconstitutional because it violated the Constitution's ban on "direct" taxes (Article I, Section 9). But no one knew what the Constitution's ban on direct taxes meant; in 1787, delegate Rufus King of Massachusetts had raised the question in the Federal Convention, but nobody could give him an answer.

At the invitation of Attorney General William Bradford, Hamilton came out of retirement to defend the constitutionality of the carriage tax before the Supreme Court. Hamilton's formal presentation—what lawyers call *arguing the case*—was a great success with the Justices, and with the fashionable people of Philadelphia who had come to hear him. The Justices upheld the tax. This was the first time that the Supreme Court had exercised the power of *judicial review*—the power to say whether a statute properly adopted by the United States or a state is nonetheless invalid because it violates the Constitution.

For several reasons, the Court declined in popularity and prestige in the late 1790s. The Rutledge controversy had not helped. The Eleventh Amendment, overruling *Chisholm v. Georgia*, had not helped, either. Also, Justice James Wilson died in 1798, bankrupt and broken in mind and spirit, in an inn in Edenton, North Carolina. Wilson had been a friend and adviser of the richest man in the United States, Robert Morris, a fellow Pennsylvanian, who had been at the Federal Convention and in the 1790s was a Senator. Morris was a daring speculator in land, stocks, and bonds, and Wilson followed Morris's advice with his own investments. When Morris's financial empire collapsed, Wilson fell with him. The Justice's creditors hounded him from place to place with demands for repayment and threats of lawsuits and debtors' prison—a special jail where those who could not pay their debts were held behind bars until they could pay. Wilson's fate seriously damaged the reputation of the Supreme Court.

Finally, the Supreme Court was being drawn into politics as political parties developed and the Federalists and Republicans (*not* the Republican party of today) fought bitterly with each other. In 1798, during an undeclared naval war with France, the Federalist-dominated Congress passed the Alien and Sedition Acts. The Alien Act made it hard for people from foreign countries to become American citizens, and it gave the government sweeping power to throw them out of the country. The Sedition Act punished anyone who said or published anything that might injure the reputation of the President or other government officials. Under the Sedition Act, Federalists prosecuted many Republicans, including editors and printers, for their writings against government policy, even though Thomas Jefferson, James Madison, and their supporters argued that the law was unconstitutional. The Republicans grew to distrust and fear Federalist judges like Supreme Court Justice Samuel Chase of Maryland, and planned to revenge themselves someday.

In 1800, President John Adams dramatically turned government policy upside-down. He cleared out his Cabinet and appointed Chief Justice Ellsworth to make peace with France. While in Europe, Ellsworth resigned this appointment and the Chief Justiceship because of poor health. Adams offered the post to Governor John Jay, and the Senate confirmed the nomination, but Jay turned the President down. He would not go back to the federal courts as long as the exhausting system of circuit riding was in force. Adams then turned to his new Secretary of State, John Marshall of Virginia, and the Senate confirmed Marshall without protest.

# CHAPTER TWO

# JOHN MARSHALL

John Marshall was born in Virginia in 1755. He was a veteran of the Revolutionary War who had been with George Washington at Valley Forge. His entire legal education was six months of law lectures at the College of William and Mary in Virginia. (Law schools—the way lawyers are trained today—were not developed until the nineteenth century.) Marshall was a leading supporter of the Constitution in the Virginia ratifying convention of June 1788. He was also a national hero, having been one of the three American diplomats who refused French attempts of bribery during a failed diplomatic mission that was a major cause of the undeclared war between the United States and France (1798–1800). Marshall's popular role in the "XYZ Affair" won him election to the House of Representatives. He served there until Adams named him Secretary of State in 1800.

Marshall was the most important of a series of appointments made by John Adams in the last days of his Presidency. Adams and the Federalists had been defeated at the polls by Thomas Jefferson and the Republicans in 1800. But, as they endured the swamps and muddy roads of the new capital city of Washington, D.C., they were determined to hold on to at least one branch of government. In a *lame-duck session* between the elections and the end of their terms of office, the Federalist-dominated Congress passed the Judiciary Act of 1801. It reformed the 1789 statute and created many new judgeships for Federalists. Adams then nominated judges and the Senate confirmed them, and Adams supposedly stayed up until long after midnight on March 3, 1801, his last full day in office, signing the commissions for these "midnight judges."

In the weeks before President Thomas Jefferson's new Republican Administration took office, John Marshall was Secretary of State and Chief Justice at the same time. He was so busy that he forgot to deliver *commissions* (a formal certificate declaring the person named in it to have been appointed to a federal office) to some of the "midnight judges," one of his duties as Secretary of State. James Madison, Jefferson's new Secretary of State, found the undelivered commissions in Marshall's desk, and he and Jefferson decided not to deliver them. Because the commissions had not been delivered, the uncommissioned judges could not take office.

President Adams had appointed William Marbury to be a justice of the peace for the District of Columbia. All the paperwork had been completed, but Marbury had not received his commission. Marbury wanted his job and chose to go to court to get it—a decision that caused John Marshall, James Madison, and Thomas Jefferson all kinds of embarrassment and confusion. It became one of the most important milestones in the history of the Supreme Court, the Constitution, and the United States.

Marbury went straight to the top: He filed a lawsuit in the U.S. Supreme Court asking for a special legal document called a *writ of mandamus*—a document requiring a government official to do his job. This writ, addressed to Secretary of State Madison, demanded that Madison turn over Marbury's commission.

Chief Justice Marshall was caught in an impossible dilemma—or so Jefferson and Madison thought. In the first place, Marshall's own failure to deliver the commissions had caused this mess. (In the early days of the federal courts, there were few formal rules requiring judges to disqualify themselves in cases in which they were personally involved.) If Marshall granted Marbury's request for a writ of mandamus, Jefferson and Madison could ignore the writ because the Court seemed so weak and lacking in authority. If he denied Marbury's request, it would look like an admission that the Court had no power. Either way, the Court would look ridiculous. The dilemma became even more troubling when the Republican-dominated Congress passed the Judiciary Act of 1802, repealing the 1801 Act (getting rid

*John Marshall, the fourth and the greatest Chief Justice (1755—1835; term, 1801—1835), did more than anyone else to make the Supreme Court a respected and powerful branch of the national government. His judicial opinions are foundations of American constitutional law.*

of the "midnight judgeships") and suspending the Supreme Court's sessions for 1802. The 1802 Act made it clear that Congress could strangle the federal courts if it wanted to.

On February 24, 1803, John Marshall delivered his opinion for a unanimous Supreme Court in the case of *Marbury v. Madison*. He asked three questions. First, did Marbury have a right to seek help from the federal courts, as Marbury claimed? Yes, the Chief Justice declared, and he took the opportunity to read a stinging lecture to the Jefferson Administration about its duty to obey the law—a duty it had ignored by refusing to deliver Marbury's commission. Second, Marshall asked whether a writ of mandamus was the right remedy for the injury that the Jefferson Administration had caused Marbury. Of course it was. After all, Chief Justice Marshall explained, there are two kinds of things that government officials do:

• First, government officials think about policy and make decisions. The courts cannot control such exercises of discretion.

• Second, government officials do the ordinary, "mechanical" acts that are part of their job, such as delivering judicial commissions.

A writ of mandamus is the right remedy for a government official's refusal to do "mechanical" acts that the law requires.

The third question was trickiest: Was the cure for Marbury's problem a writ of mandamus issued by the Supreme Court? Marshall explained that the Court had limited powers under the Constitution to hear cases brought straight to it, as Marbury had done. The Constitution's term for the class of cases that may be begun in the Supreme Court is *original jurisdiction*. The Constitution, Marshall noted, does not list writs of mandamus as part of the Court's original jurisdiction. But one section of the Judiciary Act of 1789 *did* list writs of mandamus as part of that original jurisdiction. Which should the Court follow: the Constitution or a statue?

According to Marshall, the Constitution is a *fundamental law* that is above ordinary laws. If the Constitution does not authorize the Court to grant a writ of mandamus in its original jurisdiction and the statute does, something must be wrong with the statute. The statute is *unconstitutional* and must be null and void. Therefore, the section of the Judiciary Act of 1789 permitting Marbury to go straight to the Supreme Court for a writ of mandamus was unconstitutional. The Court could not grant Marbury the help that he sought.

Marshall surprised everyone. The Chief Justice had declared that the Court had no power to help Marbury. But he also had shown that the Court had a huge and important power to declare acts of Congress unconstitutional. (Most people had forgotten about the "Carriage Tax Case," or did not realize that the power to uphold a law as constitutional suggested an equal power to throw out a law as unconstitutional.) The Court was the final authority on what the Constitution meant—unless, as in the case of *Chisholm v. Georgia* and the subsequent Eleventh Amendment, the people amended the Constitution to overturn a decision of the Supreme Court.

President Jefferson was furious. He believed that Marshall had declared war on his Administration and would use the power of judicial review as his weapon in that war. But Marshall had done a brilliant job with *Marbury v. Madison*. He had actually denied that the Court had the power to do anything specific about the Jefferson Administration's misconduct in the matter of the "missing commissions." Marshall also had avoided a battle over the repeal of the Judiciary Act of 1801, the law that had created the "midnight judgeships." He clearly understood that those who live and run away will live to fight another day. But Marshall had asserted that the Supreme Court had the authority and the responsibility to control the actions of the other branches of the federal government by interpreting the Constitution.

Jefferson and his allies believed that each branch of the federal government had an equal power and responsibility to interpret the Constitution. They rejected Marshall's argument that the Court should have the last word unless overruled by the people through a constitutional amendment. The President and the Republican-dominated Congress decided that it was necessary to clip the Court's wings.

The Constitution provides that all federal officials, including the President and federal judges, can be impeached (formally accused) by the House of Representatives and tried by the Senate for "treason, bribery, or other High Crimes and Misdemeanors." Impeachment is the Constitution's method for removing federal officials who are corrupt or who abuse their powers.

President Jefferson and the Republican-controlled Congress determined to use the impeachment power to rein in the federal courts. Their first target was a New Hampshire Federalist named John Pickering. Pickering, the federal district judge for New Hampshire, was old, sick, and a drunkard. He had not committed any "impeachable offense," but that did not matter to Congress. The House impeached him and the Senate removed him from office. (Pickering probably had no idea what had happened to him.) The supporters of the impeachment campaign argued that impeachment was just "the enquiry, by the two Houses of Congress, whether the office of any public man might not be better filled by another."

Congress then went after a Supreme Court Justice: old, fat Samuel Chase of Maryland. He had denounced Republicans from the bench during trials under the Sedition Act in his circuit court. The House impeached Chase on the same theory the members had used to oust Judge Pickering. Everyone knew that if Chase was convicted, Chief Justice John Marshall would be the next target.

Chase's trial in the Senate produced an unexpected obstacle to his conviction: Vice President Aaron Burr. Burr had shot and killed Alexander Hamilton in a duel in July 1804 and had been indicted for murder by grand juries in New Jersey and New York. Although Burr was never tried on these charges, his career was almost at an end. In fact, the Republicans had already picked New York's Governor George Clinton to replace Burr as the party's nominee for Vice President in 1804. But Burr had a few months to go in his term as Vice President. The Constitution required that he preside over the trial of Justice Chase, and Burr carried out the task with dignity and fairness, winning the respect even of his political enemies. Chase was acquitted, and the Jefferson Administration's war with the judiciary was at an end.

For the next thirty years, John Marshall presided over the Supreme Court. He delighted John Adams, who said that the Marshall appointment was the best legacy of his Presidency. Marshall still infuriated Thomas Jefferson. Jefferson repeatedly denounced the "twistifications" of the "crafty chief judge" in letters to his friends, but Marshall prevailed.

As the leader and the spokesman of the Supreme Court, Chief Justice Marshall established many principles at the core of American constitutional law. He ruled that the Constitution authorized the Supreme Court to declare state laws unconstitutional and that the states had to obey the decisions of the Supreme Court. He held that a person who lost a case in the highest court of a state could appeal that decision to the United States Supreme Court if the case posed a question of federal constitutional law. He declared that the federal government was the creature of the people of the United States, not the tool of the state governments. It was the supreme authority in the federal system of government, second only to the people themselves.

Many of the Marshall Court's decisions had to do with the *commerce clause* of the Constitution. Article I, Section 8 gives Congress the power to regulate commerce among the states. What does this power mean? How far does it reach? When can states pass laws regulating business? When must the states' power bow to that of Congress? Are there areas where the states may not act, even though Congress has not acted? John Marshall's Supreme Court handed down major decisions on all these questions.

The commerce clause may not seem controversial today, but in the early years of the United States it was a source of great political and constitutional dispute. Many Americans did not trust strong central government; they preferred to have government stay as close to the people as possible. They preferred government to be local and small scale. But Chief Justice Marshall saw that many problems affecting trade and commerce were national problems, not local ones. He remembered that one reason for the movement to write and adopt the Constitution was to give the nation's government the power to establish uniform rules for interstate commerce. He understood that asking for local solutions to national problems would only make the problems worse because there would be too many schemes to solve them, all conflicting with one another and making it nearly impossible for trade to take place across state lines. John Marshall was faithful to this nationalist vision.

Marshall had support on the Court from young Joseph Story. Story was a Massachusetts lawyer and politician who was only thirty-two years old when President James Madison named him to the Supreme Court to succeed William Cushing, who had died in 1810. Story was brilliant and energetic. He wrote many stout commentaries on American law and, as the first law professor at Harvard University, helped to found the nation's oldest law school. He still found time to sit as a Supreme Court Justice and to ride circuit in the New England states. Story was just as enthusiastic for national power and a strong Constitution as was John Marshall. Story looked up to Marshall as if Marshall were his father, and Marshall considered Story almost to be his

Collection of the Supreme Court of the United States

*This rare daguerrotype shows Associate Justice Joseph Story of Massachusetts (1779—1845; term, 1812—1845). Story was Chief Justice John Marshall's loyal ally in constitutional interpretation. He became the first professor of law at Harvard in 1817, laid the institutional foundations of the Harvard Law School, and wrote a dozen learned and influential legal treatises while performing his duties on the Court.*

son. The two men worked side by side for more than twenty years, from 1812 to Marshall's death in 1835.

John Marshall held the office of Chief Justice for thirty-four years, longer than any other man. His tenure spanned the terms of six Presidents. When he died, legend has it that the Liberty Bell hanging in Philadelphia's Independence Hall tolled so loudly and stubbornly in his honor that it cracked. Another great Supreme Court Justice, Oliver Wendell Holmes, Jr., declared in 1901 (the centennial of Marshall's appointment to the Supreme Court) that if one person were chosen to represent American law, that person would be John Marshall.

Holmes thought that Marshall's greatness was partly an accident: "Part of greatness consists in being *there*" (that is, being in the right place at the right time). But Marshall had many talents. He was willing to shoulder the work involved in writing *opinions*, the formal statements of the reasoning of the Court in deciding a case. In writing those opinions, he had a remarkable ability to make a difficult and complex legal argument seem simple and clear. He was also charming, winning over even stubborn men like Justice William Johnson. President Jefferson had appointed Johnson to combat Marshall, but Johnson found the Chief Justice extremely persuasive. Even on those rare occasions when Johnson disagreed with the Chief Justice, he nearly always chose to sit silently as the Chief Justice read the "opinion of the Court" rather than to express his disagreement in a dissenting opinion.

Today, we are used to the idea that when the Supreme Court decides a case, one Justice will write the *opinion of the Court* and any Justice who is outvoted can write a *dissenting opinion* (explaining why he or she disagrees and setting out arguments for this position). But John Marshall invented the opinion of the Court. Previously, as the judges did in England, each Supreme Court Justice had delivered his opinion on the case before the Court. Lawyers could figure out the result by counting up the votes, but they did not have a single clear statement of what the majority of the Justices thought. Marshall's willingness to write opinions for the Court, his skills in writing them so as to command the support of his colleagues, and his practice never to dissent from a Court decision he disagreed with made the opinion of the Court a central feature of the workings of the Supreme Court.

In all these ways—in the substance of the cases that the Court decided under his leadership and in his shaping of the Court's place in the constitutional system and its methods of doing business—John Marshall laid the foundation for the modern Supreme Court.

# CHAPTER THREE

# ROGER B. TANEY

To succeed John Marshall as Chief Justice, President Andrew Jackson appointed his Attorney General, Roger B. Taney (pronounced *tawny*) of Maryland. Many conservatives, including Marshall's friend Justice Joseph Story, were appalled. Taney was a Roman Catholic—and many Americans feared the power of the Catholic Church. Taney had backed Jackson's efforts to crush the Second Bank of the United States. He was also a critic of John Marshall and the Supreme Court. Senator Daniel Webster of Massachusetts, one of the strongest supporters of the Marshall Court, wrote in a private letter, "Judge Story thinks the Supreme Court is *gone*, and I think so too."

Like all other Presidents, Jackson wanted a Supreme Court that would hand down decisions to his liking. He had been suspicious of the Marshall Court and once had refused to enforce one of Chief Justice Marshall's rulings defending the rights of the Cherokee Indians against the greed of the state of Georgia. With a man he could trust in the Chief Justice's chair, Jackson believed that he could rest easier. Besides, Taney was one of the ablest lawyers of his day, a worthy successor to Chief Justice Marshall.

Taney served as Chief Justice for twenty-nine years—a record sec-

*Roger B. Taney of Maryland (1777—1864; term, 1835—1864) succeeded John Marshall as Chief Justice. Although Taney for most of his tenure presided wisely over the Court, he is best remembered for his disastrous opinion in the Dred Scott case (1857), which historians believe helped to cause the Civil War.*

ond only to Marshall's. His tenure spanned the terms of ten Presidents. The Taney Court refined and developed the expansive ideas of federal power and judicial power symbolic of John Marshall. Despite Justice Story's despairing charges in his dissenting opinions, it is likely that Marshall generally would have approved of the work of the Taney Court. One of its most important achievements was to strike a balance between the federal power to regulate interstate commerce and the states' *police powers*, that is, the state governments' power to make laws or take other actions to protect the health, safety, welfare, and morals of their citizens.

If such achievements were the only important legacies of the Taney Court, Roger B. Taney would be generally remembered as one of the greatest Chief Justices. But Americans remember the Taney Court today for the *Dred Scott* case, the single greatest blunder ever committed by a federal court and a terrible stain on American history.

Dred Scott was a slave, born in the slave state of Missouri. His owner had taken him briefly from Missouri into the free state of Illinois, where slavery was illegal by state law and under the terms of the congressional Missouri Compromise of 1820 (by which Congress declared that new states north of a line drawn across the Louisiana Purchase would be free states and new states south of that line would be slave states), and then back to Missouri. Antislavery lawyers and politicians filed a lawsuit on Scott's behalf against John F. A. Sanford, his legal owner. They sought Scott's freedom on the ground that he had become free when his previous owner had taken him into a free state.

The *Dred Scott* case moved quietly through the federal court system. When it reached the Supreme Court, the trouble started. The majority of the Court at first agreed that because Scott was from Missouri, his status should be determined by that state's law. Justice Samuel Nelson began drafting the Court's opinion to state that narrow holding. But Chief Justice Taney and other proslavery Justices egged on antislavery Justice John McLean. McLean was a cantankerous troublemaker who had talked often about running for President. He took the bait and announced to his colleagues that he would write a broad dissent from the case attacking the institution of slavery. To the irritation of Justice Nelson, Chief Justice Taney took the opportunity to write an opinion answering McLean.

Taney had reasons of his own to write a broad opinion analyzing the constitutional issues posed by slavery. He did not personally like slavery—indeed, he had freed his own slaves some years before—but he believed that slavery was protected by the Constitution. The Chief Justice had frowned on the many attempts by Senators and Representatives to work out compromises between North and South to control the spread of slavery into the new states and territories of the United States. The *Dred Scott* case seemed to be the perfect occasion for the Court to resolve the national controversy over slavery and the Constitution once and for all.

In the 1850s, four general positions existed on the slavery issue. The Supreme Court had to choose one of them to decide the *Dred Scott* case:

• *The antislavery view:* Slavery at least should be limited to those states where it had already been established, but eventually it must be abolished throughout the United States. To the extent that the Constitution protected slavery and slaveholders' rights, it was evil—"a compromise with death," as several abolitionists (those who wanted to do away with slavery) called it.

• *The old moderate view:* The issue of slavery could and should be compromised in Congress by Senators and Representatives from the North, South, and West. Congressional "peace treaties" such as the Missouri Compromise of 1820 and the Compromise of 1850 would limit the spread of slavery but not choke it off. This view was developed by an earlier generation of politicians, led by Henry Clay of Kentucky.

• *The new moderate view:* Slavery could be adopted or rejected by the voters of a territory organizing to become a state but otherwise should stay as it was. This view's leading advocate was Senator Stephen A. Douglas (Democrat-Illinois), who called it "popular sovereignty."

• *The proslavery view:* Slavery was a positive good for slave-owners and slaves alike. Slaves were property protected by the Constitution's safeguards of private property. Any attempt to abolish slavery, to limit it, or to keep it out of any part of the Union was a violation of the Constitution.

The *Dred Scott* decision came as a bombshell to the country when the Court announced it on March 6, 1857. But Taney and some of the other Justices on both sides of the case had "leaked" the decision to several politicians, including the new President, James Buchanan of Pennsylvania. In his inaugural address two days before the Court's announcement, Buchanan predicted that the Court would soon produce a definitive, final answer to the slavery controversy, and he urged all Americans to obey it. Buchanan and those who thought as he did believed that the Court's decision would dispose of slavery as a political issue. They were dead wrong.

The Court ruled, seven to two, against Dred Scott's bid for freedom. Although Taney's opinion did not command an absolute majority of the Justices, it drew the most attention because Taney was the Chief Justice. By contrast, Justice Nelson stuck to his narrowly-drawn opinion ruling against Scott on the basis of Missouri law. A few Justices sided with Nelson, but his opinion was generally ignored.

Taney declared that the Constitution clearly protected slavery. Any attempts to limit or choke off slavery's expansion violated the document. Even the old Missouri Compromise of 1820 was unconstitutional. Taney's opinion also killed off the "popular sovereignty" theory of slavery in the territories. He even declared that, in the eyes of the Framers and thus according to the Constitution, black persons were not—and could not be—citizens, and they had no rights that white Americans were bound to respect.

In short, Taney ruled that slavery was valid everywhere and could be taken anywhere in the United States. He even implied that slave-holders could take their slaves into a free state and hold them there as slaves, even though the state's laws prohibited slavery. His opinion read the Constitution as a proslavery charter of government, confirming the worst fears of the abolitionists and frustrating moderate attempts to compromise the issue.

Taney's opinion in *Dred Scott* infuriated opponents of slavery, and they flocked to join the newly organized Republican Party (a party claiming descent from that of Thomas Jefferson). The Republicans maintained that the decision did not settle the slavery issue once and for all. They stepped up their campaign against slavery and promised to work to overturn the *Dred Scott* decision by legitimate means. Many moderates, disappointed by what they saw as a proslavery power grab, also joined the Republicans.

Dred Scott and John Sanford were virtually ignored in the controversy. Scott was freed despite the Court's decision, and he became a porter in a St. Louis hotel, where curious tourists and visitors came to see him. He died of tuberculosis a year or so after the decision. John Sanford (whose name had been misspelled Sandford in the Supreme Court's report of the case) ended his days in an insane asylum—driven mad, some said, by his role in the lawsuit. (Sanford was a New York abolitionist who probably never met Scott—he was involved only as a means to a greater end.)

Taney had delivered a terrible blow to the prestige and authority of the Supreme Court, but he did not realize the damage he had done with his opinion in the *Dred Scott* case. He watched in horror and anger as Republican Abraham Lincoln of Illinois, who had denounced the *Dred Scott* decision as unconstitutional and vowed to find a way to overturn it, won the 1860 Presidential election. In one of the great ironies of American history, Chief Justice Taney had to administer the oath of office to President Lincoln, on March 4, 1861. The two men loathed each other.

As Lincoln led resistance to the Southern states' attempts to leave the Union in 1861, Taney issued decision after decision (from the U.S. Circuit Court in Maryland) declaring each and every one of Lincoln's war measures unconstitutional. The President ignored the decisions. To anyone who claimed that he was violating the Constitution, Lincoln explained that he was trying to *save* the Constitution as a whole in a time of great crisis; it was absurd to let the whole system fall apart to avoid the risk of violating one of its parts.

Chief Justice Taney was convinced that President Lincoln was trying to become a dictator. He expected daily to see federal soldiers storm into his courtroom to arrest him. He would have welcomed arrest—it would have transformed him into a martyr to the rule of law. But Lincoln's refusal to acknowledge Taney's decisions was far more painful to the old Chief Justice. He died, tired and bitter, in 1864, the fourth year of the Civil War. Perhaps the worst pill that Taney had to swallow was the knowledge that Lincoln would get to name the next Chief Justice of the United States.

# CHAPTER FOUR

# SAVING FACE AND SHIFTING GROUND

The Supreme Court was very quiet during the Civil War. The Justices recognized that times of war are not good periods for the rule of law. They did not challenge many of the Administration's sweeping measures to advance the Union cause, though some arguably violated the Constitution. One glaring example was the President's decision to suspend the writ of *habeas corpus*. This legal document is a court order available to any imprisoned person who has a valid reason to argue that his imprisonment is not justified by law. The President acted on his own, though Article I, Section 9 of the Constitution implies that the approval of Congress is needed to suspend the writ. Congress later endorsed the President's decision, but critics of the Administration had their doubts.

Also, President Lincoln and Congress did not treat the Supreme Court well during the Civil War. They decided to expand the Supreme Court to ten members—the largest it has ever been. They did this in part to add a new Justice to handle circuit-riding duties in California and Oregon, but also to make certain that there would be enough votes on the Court to support Administration measures to carry on the war effort. When Chief Justice Taney died, in 1864, Lincoln used the vacancy as a way to get rid of a thorn in his side.

Treasury Secretary Salmon P. Chase of Ohio was an ardent abolition-ist. Time and time again, he had stirred up trouble in Lincoln's Cabi-net, and he seemed likely to challenge the President for the 1864 Republican Presidential nomination. President Lincoln got Chase out of the way by naming him the new Chief Justice, and the Senate confirmed the appointment.

After Lincoln was assassinated in April 1865, a few days after the Union's victory in the Civil War, the Supreme Court handed down a major decision attacking the federal government's measures against Northern opposition to the war. Some Northern Democrats, called "copperheads" after the poisonous snake of that name, had gone be-yond merely denouncing the war. One of them, Lambdin P. Milligan, had led a plot to overthrow the governments of Ohio, Illinois, and Indiana and to release Confederate prisoners of war. A military court arrested and tried Milligan and sentenced him to death. But Milligan was a civilian, not a soldier. He argued that military courts had no power over civilians, and he sued in the federal circuit court in India-napolis, Indiana, for a writ of *habeas corpus* to challenge the authority under which he was being held in military prison.

When the case reached the Supreme Court, the Justices agreed with Milligan. Lincoln's former campaign manager, Justice David Da-vis, delivered the opinion of the Court. If civilian courts were still open—and they were when Milligan was arrested—no one, not even Congress, could authorize military courts to try civilians. The Court declared that it had the authority to decide whether military necessity justified violations of constitutional rights.

The issues raised in the *Milligan* case were related to issues in other cases that the Court never got a chance to decide. These cases dealt with Civil War measures taken by the federal government and with policies adopted by Congress, called *Reconstruction,* to administer the defeated Southern states. Congress passed laws preventing the Court from hearing these cases. Congress exercised this authority under Ar-ticle III, Section 1 of the Constitution to define the federal courts' *subject-matter jurisdiction*—that is, the courts' power to hear various kinds of cases. Chief Justice Chase and his colleagues had to concede that Congress had constitutional power to cut off jurisdiction, even to prevent the Court from hearing a case that had been within its juris-diction when the case began. Congress, dominated by Northern Republicans, was reminding the courts who was boss.

Congress also wanted to remind the President who was boss. Vice President Andrew Johnson had succeeded to the Presidency when

Lincoln was murdered. The new President soon broke with Congress over the government's treatment of the defeated Southern states.

The dispute between the President and Congress over Reconstruction grew into an ugly constitutional crisis which dragged the Court into the middle of the mess. When Justice John Catron died in 1865, Congress abolished his seat and, for good measure, reduced the Court from ten Justices to seven. Justices then sitting would not lose their seats, but Johnson could not replace the next two to die or resign. (The Court actually shrank to eight Justices as a result of the statute and the death in 1867 of Justice James M. Wayne.)

In early 1868, the House of Representatives decided to impeach the President. Some Representatives believed that he had violated the Constitution by refusing to enforce Reconstruction statutes that Congress had passed over his veto. Other Representatives argued that an impeachable offense was whatever a majority of the House and two-thirds of the Senate said it was—thus reviving the understanding of impeachment advocated by President Jefferson's supporters more than sixty years before.

Under the Constitution, the Chief Justice of the United States presides over the trial of a President on charges of impeachment to ensure that the presiding officer is fair. (If the Vice President were to preside over the trial of the President, as he does in other impeachment trials, he might be tempted to influence the trial so that he could become President.) Thus, Chief Justice Chase presided over President Johnson's trial by the Senate. Following the example of Vice President Aaron Burr's handling of the Senate's trial of Justice Samuel Chase in 1805 (the Chief Justice was not related to old Samuel Chase), Chief Justice Chase presided with fairness. He refused to allow the trial to become a partisan brawl. The Senate voted to convict, but the vote was one short of the two-thirds required by the Constitution. Johnson thus stayed in office for the last nine months of his term. Chief Justice Chase's conduct saved the Presidency and helped to restore some of the Supreme Court's lost prestige.

General Ulysses S. Grant was elected President in 1868 to succeed Johnson, who left Washington in a bitter mood, not even waiting for the inauguration. The eighteenth President, a Republican, was popular with Congress and the nation because he had led the Union's armies to victory in the Civil War. Congress was so pleased by Grant's election that they rewarded him by passing a law increasing the size of the Supreme Court to nine Justices. Grant nominated former Secretary of War Edwin Stanton to fill the new seat, and Congress confirmed him. A seat on the Supreme Court had been Stanton's lifelong ambition, but Stanton died before he could accept.

The Civil War left a legacy that became part of the Constitution. In 1868, the Fourteenth Amendment was ratified by the states. This was one of three amendments that historians call the *Civil War Amendments*. The Thirteenth Amendment, ratified in 1865, had abolished slavery. The Fifteenth Amendment, ratified in 1870, recognized the right of American males to vote regardless of their race. The Fourteenth Amendment was, in many ways, the most important because it reshaped the structure of government set up by the Constitution:

1. It put the federal government above the states once and for all. The prewar system of federalism was a source of great controversy because politicians such as John C. Calhoun of South Carolina had argued that the Constitution was a compact, or agreement, among the states and that the federal government was the agent of the states. The Fourteenth Amendment made explicit what the force of the Union Army had already accomplished: The Union was supreme and preeminent.

2. It declared that persons born in the United States or persons who had become citizens of the United States were citizens of the United States *first* (rather than of individual states) and that the rights of citizenship of the United States outranked citizenship of a given state.

3. It declared that state and local governments could not deprive persons of life, liberty, or property without "due process of law" and that state and local governments could not deny persons "the equal protection of the laws."

At least one purpose of the Fourteenth Amendment was to ensure that the Civil Rights Act of 1866, the first law passed by Congress to protect the rights of Americans (specifically the freed slaves) against racial discrimination, was constitutional. It appeared that the Amendment also applied the Bill of Rights to limit the power of state and local governments to violate the rights protected by the first ten Amendments to the Constitution. The Amendment seemed to overturn the 1833 Supreme Court decision in *Barron v. Baltimore* in which Chief Justice John Marshall had ruled that the first ten Amendments limited only the powers of the federal government. But in 1873, in a series of cases known as the *Slaughterhouse Cases*, the Court limited the reach of the Fourteenth Amendment.

The state legislature of Louisiana had adopted as a public health measure a law that required the butchers of New Orleans to use one, and only one, designated slaughterhouse in that city. Butchers in New Orleans denounced the law as setting up a monopoly. Their lawyers tried to persuade the Supreme Court that the law deprived the butchers of private property without due process of law in violation of the Fourteenth Amendment. In effect, they claimed, the Fourteenth Amendment prohibited government from infringing the broad rights of the individual, including the right to conduct business as he or she saw fit.

This was the first major case to interpret the Fourteenth Amendment. The Justices split, five to four. Speaking for the majority, Justice Samuel Miller read the Amendment narrowly. He concluded that the Amendment protected only certain technical rights having to do with citizenship of the United States. Thus, the states were not barred from violating federal constitutional rights listed in the Bill of Rights; those amendments still limited the federal government only. Justice Miller also declared that the Amendment was intended only to protect the rights of the freed slaves. It had no larger purpose. Thus, the Louisiana slaughterhouse law was constitutional.

Justice Stephen J. Field dissented. He argued that private economic rights were indeed part of the "liberty" protected by the Amendment, and that the slaughterhouse law clearly violated that liberty. Field was joined by three other Justices.

One of the major problems with the decision in the *Slaughterhouse Cases* was that it suggested that the Civil War Amendments actually gave the federal government very little power to protect the rights of black Americans from state and local governments. In 1883, in a complex series of cases known to historians as the *Civil Rights Cases*, the Justices let the other shoe drop. In effect, the Supreme Court told black Americans that they were on their own. They should not look to the federal authorities for help in protecting their rights.

Exhausted by his tenure as Chief Justice, Salmon P. Chase died in 1873 after only nine years in office. President Grant appointed the able, hard-working Morrison R. Waite of Michigan to succeed Chase. Waite battled the Justices' rising workload until he himself died, in 1888.

Waite's successor, Melville W. Fuller of Maine, decided to do something about the flood of cases that was wearing out the Supreme Court Justices and federal district judges. (The rising tide of federal litigation resulted from the growth of the national economy and the legal profession, and from the development of new kinds of lawsuits and business deals.) Fuller led the Justices in lobbying Congress. In 1891, Congress passed a new Judiciary Act that reshaped the federal court system. The Act created a whole new set of federal circuit courts and authorized the appointment of dozens of new circuit court judges to staff those courts. Congress finally abolished the century-old practice of circuit riding, which had exasperated and exhausted every Supreme Court Justice from John Jay on.

The last half of the nineteenth century was marked by a major shift in the emphases of American constitutional law. During the years before the Civil War, the part of the American economy devoted to industry became more and more important. So, too, did those parts of the economy that carried out business across state lines. Industry and "interstate commerce" became a principal source of the nation's wealth. The growth of industry and interstate commerce carried with it new questions of law that sooner or later had to come before the Supreme Court.

At the same time, new ideas as to how the American economy should work were gaining popularity. In the 1873 *Slaughterhouse Cases*, Justices Stephen J. Field and Joseph P. Bradley emerged as spokesmen (together with many industrialists and economists) for the doctrine of *laissez faire*. *Laissez faire* is a French phrase meaning "leave it alone." People who believe in *laissez faire* argue that the economy works best when it is left alone to be a *free market*—that is, when buyers and sellers can do business with one another without having to worry about government regulations. Justice Field kept up the fight and began to win other members of the Supreme Court to his views.

In 1877, the case of *Munn v. Illinois* signaled a turning point in the development of constitutional rules governing state power to regulate the economy. The Illinois legislature had adopted a law regulating the rates that operators of grain storage facilities could charge farmers who wanted to store their grain while waiting for railroads to pick it up for shipment and sale in the East. The Justices upheld the Illinois law by the narrowest vote—five to four. Chief Justice Waite ruled that when an economic venture, like a grain storage facility, affects the *public interest*, the state can pass laws regulating it. But the laws had to be reasonably designed to promote the public interest. Justice Field dissented, putting forth his usual *laissez faire* arguments.

Advocates of *laissez faire* were horrified that the Court had upheld a law permitting a state to tell a private businessman how much he could charge for his services. But *Munn* allowed the Court to strike down state laws regulating economic activities that the Justices felt were *unreasonable* or that they believed did *not* advance the public interest. The Justices believed that simply taking Peter's property to give it to Paul was not a reasonable law. Nor did it advance the public interest.

As the nineteenth century came to an end, the Justices more and more often ruled against federal and state laws regulating the economy. The Court informed Congress that because manufacturing (in the Justices' view) took place within one state, it was not "interstate commerce" that Congress could regulate. The Court also declared that a federal income tax, which had been adopted as an emergency measure during the Civil War and revived in the 1890s, was a "direct tax" forbidden by the Constitution.

Many law professors, political scientists, historians, lawyers, and politicians began to attack the Court for defending the established economic system under the guise of protecting the Constitution. Once again, the Supreme Court found itself at the heart of public controversy.

The Court was not *all* serious business in this period. It is hard to imagine the Justices keeping straight faces about one of their 1890 cases: *In re Neagle*. Although a murder was at the heart of this case, it had elements of low comedy bordering on farce.

The story of *In re Neagle* had begun nearly thirty years earlier. Before President Lincoln named Stephen Field to the Supreme Court, Field had been Chief Justice of the California Supreme Court. The previous California Chief Justice was David Terry. Terry was presiding over the court when a beautiful young woman presented her case. She claimed that she had been living with a wealthy Californian as his wife for many years before he died. Somehow they had forgotten to go through the marriage ceremony. She argued that she was what lawyers call the man's "common-law" wife and thus entitled under California law to half of his property as his widow. But, she sobbed, the man's relatives claimed that she was nothing but a floozy trying to cash in on the estate of a man who had supported her handsomely while he lived.

Chief Justice Terry fell in love with the young woman—or with the money she claimed she was entitled to—and resigned from the bench to become her husband *and* her lawyer. Field succeeded him as Chief Justice. Rumors spread that the court would rule against the new Mrs. Terry. Terry publicly swore that he would "get" Field. When Field was ready to announce the court's decision, he ordered the court's marshal to search Terry. The marshal found two pistols, knives, and other weapons. Field ordered Terry thrown out of the courtroom. The decision did indeed go against the newlyweds, and Terry vowed vengeance.

When Field became an Associate Justice of the U.S. Supreme Court, in 1863, he explained the Terry matter to President Lincoln. The President assigned a U.S. Marshal to accompany Justice Field whenever he had to ride circuit in California. More than twenty years passed, but neither Justice Field nor the Terrys forgot the vow.

On the fateful day that gave rise to *In re Neagle*, Justice Field was riding circuit in California. He was having breakfast in a railroad dining car with his current U.S. Marshal, a man named Neagle. Coincidentally, Mr. and Mrs. Terry had boarded the train, and Terry recognized Field. He strode up to Field and struck him across the face. He then reached into his own coat. Neagle later testified that he had spotted a gun under Terry's coat. The Marshal calmly pulled out *his* revolver and shot Terry dead, then went on with his breakfast. Hearing the shot, Mrs. Terry ran into the dining car and threw herself on her husband's body, sobbing hysterically. When she was removed from the scene, a search of the corpse disclosed no gun.

Neagle was arrested and tried for murder under California law. (Mrs. Terry had unsuccessfully begged the California authorities to arrest Justice Field as well.) Neagle defended himself on the ground that he was a federal officer carrying out his lawful duty in an appropriate manner. The case reached the U.S. Supreme Court. It voted, eight to zero, to accept Neagle's argument and throw out the California murder indictment. Justice Field took no part in the decision of the case. In his memoirs, he could not conceal his satisfaction at Terry's fate.

# CHAPTER FIVE

# THE GREAT DISSENTERS

For most of American history, the Supreme Court has been a quiet, little-noticed institution. Most of its cases have been dry and technical. As a result, until modern times, neither the public nor the press paid much attention to most of the cases decided by the Justices.

Occasionally, however, one of the Justices cannot go along with the majority and writes an explanation of his or her views. This written explanation is called a *dissenting opinion*. Other Justices in the minority can join the dissenting Justice's opinion or write dissents of their own. Still others can write opinions explaining why they agree with the majority but how they got to the same result by a different route. These are called *concurring opinions*.

Chief Justice Charles Evans Hughes once explained, in a book he wrote about the Court in the 1920s, that a dissenting opinion was "an appeal to the brooding omnipresence of the law." A dissenting opinion is a Justice's way to put his or her ideas before the nation, to get them thought about and discussed. A dissenting Justice hopes, often with good reason, that a later group of Justices may see the question his or her way and *overturn* the earlier decision of the Supreme Court. In this way, dissenting opinions help to shape the development of our constitutional law.

Some dissents are so eloquent or controversial that they attract the attention of the press and the public. Several Supreme Court Justices became public heroes because of their dissenting opinions. These Justices have been called "the great dissenters."

Justice John Marshall Harlan wrote one of the first and most famous great dissenting opinions in the 1896 case of *Plessy v. Ferguson*. This case challenged a Louisiana law requiring separate railroad cars for black and white passengers. The Southern states in the years after the Civil War had adopted laws, known as *Jim Crow laws*, designed to restrict the rights of black Americans. Southern legislators argued that it was necessary to adopt systems of separation, also called *segregation*, to keep peace between whites and blacks.

A lawyer named Albion W. Tourgée worked long and hard in this period to stand up for the rights of black Americans. He hated the segregation laws and came up with a way to challenge them in court. He got Homer Plessy, a black citizen of Louisiana, to sit in a whites-only railroad car. When the conductor challenged the man's right to sit in the car, Plessy quietly submitted to arrest, as Tourgée had planned. Plessy then challenged the Louisiana segregation law because it violated his right to the equal protection of the laws under the Fourteenth Amendment to the U.S. Constitution.

Tourgée's strategy backfired. The Supreme Court upheld the segregation law by a vote of eight to one. Justice Henry B. Brown wrote for the Court that segregation was not necessarily a violation of the Fourteenth Amendment's Equal Protection Clause. All that the clause required, Justice Brown declared, was that black and white citizens have access to equal facilities. *Separate* facilities *could* be *equal* facilities. In fact, as long as the facilities were equal, separation was not only constitutional, it also was good policy. Justice Brown doubted that black and white Americans could ever live together in peace and friendship.

Justice Harlan's was the only dissenting vote. He declared that segregation was inherently unequal. He pointed out, in one of the most famous sentences ever written by a member of the Supreme Court, "Our Constitution is color-blind." Harlan's dissenting opinion startled many Americans who never would have expected Harlan to think that way. He had been born and raised in Kentucky, a border state. He had owned slaves before the Civil War. When the war broke out, he declared his loyalty to the Union, freed his slaves, and served bravely in the Union Army. Harlan's views stung the consciences of some Americans, but he did not live to see them become the law of

Collection of the Supreme Court of the United States

*Oliver Wendell Holmes, Jr., (1841—1935; term, 1902—1932) was the greatest legal thinker to sit on the Supreme Court. His dissenting opinions inspired generations of lawyers and public servants.*

the land. He died in 1911, more than forty years before the Supreme Court rejected the *Plessy* doctrine of "separate but equal."

In 1902, President Theodore Roosevelt appointed a second "great dissenter" to the Supreme Court. Oliver Wendell Holmes, Jr., was born in Massachusetts in 1841, the son of a great poet and literary figure, Dr. Oliver Wendell Holmes. The younger Holmes was graduated from Harvard College and served in the Union Army in the Civil War. The Justice enjoyed telling the following story about his war service: When President Lincoln once visited the front lines and was caught standing in the open as the Confederate army opened fire, young Captain Holmes bellowed at the President, "Get down, you old fool!" Holmes himself was wounded three times. When his tour of duty ended, he returned home to study law at Harvard Law School. After several years in private practice as a lawyer, he became a law professor at Harvard, then a member of the Massachusetts Supreme Judicial Court, and eventually Chief Justice of that court.

Justice Holmes was a great legal scholar. His book *The Common Law* (1881) is one of the most influential books on legal history and legal thought ever published in the English-speaking world. He declared on the book's first page that "the life of the law has not been logic—it has been experience." By this observation, which Holmes backed up through several hundred pages of careful research and argument, he showed that the law is not some mystical constellation of ideas, waiting somewhere in space for judges to discover its terms. Rather, it is a growing and living thing that judges and legislators must adapt to changing problems and circumstances. These ideas sound natural to us today, for we live in the shadow of Justice Holmes. In the 1880s and 1890s, however, they were revolutionary ideas that changed the way that judges and legal scholars thought about law for generations.

Justice Holmes brought to the U.S. Supreme Court his remarkable store of legal knowledge and his equally remarkable knack for writing short, eloquent, pithy opinions. He gathered around him the brightest young minds in politics and government. Judge Learned Hand was a cherished friend. So was Louis D. Brandeis, the crusading Boston reformer and the best lawyer in the United States. And so was Holmes's protégé and disciple, the young Professor Felix Frankfurter of Harvard Law School.

Professor Frankfurter sent Justice Holmes a new Harvard Law School graduate each year. This young man—he was male and unmarried, by the rules of the Court at that time—would serve as Justice Holmes's secretary and research assistant, or "law clerk." Many of Justice Holmes's law clerks went on to become leaders of the legal profession, distinguished law professors, and judges. (This system remains today. Clerking for a Supreme Court Justice is a prestigious position, sought by top law students after graduation.)

Justice Holmes disliked his colleagues' attempts to read their personal views into the Constitution. He argued that the people and their elected representatives had a right to run the government in any way they saw fit as long as it did not clearly violate the Constitution. He reminded the Justices over and over again that the word *unconstitutional* does not mean *unwise*. The Supreme Court should not strike down laws that were merely silly or half-baked or poorly drafted. The power of judicial review, Holmes taught, should be used sparingly. *That* was the way to preserve the Court's prestige and authority. It was also the way to make certain that the government of the United States and the government of each state would be democratic and not dominated by a group of unelected judges.

Chief Justice Fuller understood and tolerated Holmes's dissents.

When Fuller died in 1910, his successor, Edward D. White of Louisiana, also understood and accepted Holmes's need to express his views. Chief Justice White had fought as a Confederate soldier. His appointment, by President William Howard Taft, an Ohioan, was seen as a symbolic gesture linking North and South. The two Civil War veterans, Chief Justice White and Justice Holmes, enjoyed talking over their memories of the war and speculating on whether they had faced each other in battle.

In 1916, fourteen years after the appointment of Justice Holmes, President Woodrow Wilson stunned the nation and the legal community by naming Holmes's friend Louis D. Brandeis to the Supreme Court. Brandeis was the first Jewish nominee to the Supreme Court. He had made many enemies because he placed his brilliant legal mind at the service of reformers who wanted the government to regulate the economy. As was the custom in that era, Brandeis did not appear in person before the Senate Judiciary Committee to answer questions about his background and views. After a bitter confirmation fight, the Senate voted to confirm Brandeis.

Brandeis was the ideal colleague for Holmes. The two men complemented each other perfectly. Holmes was a master of philosophy; Brandeis was an unsurpassed master of economic and social facts and details. They also had close ties with Professor Felix Frankfurter, who began to send clerks for Justice Brandeis as well as for Justice Holmes.

Holmes and Brandeis joined forces on the Court. They repeatedly dissented from decisions of the Court that struck down federal and state laws regulating the economy. The pair argued that those laws *were* constitutional. Brandeis explained that the states were "laboratories of reform," which had the authority under the Constitution to experiment with new ways to solve society's problems. Their opinions were publicized and quoted across the nation and found respectful hearings in the nation's foremost law schools.

In the years during and after the First World War, several cases concerning issues of free speech reached the Supreme Court for the first time. The federal government and many of the states had passed laws restricting what people could say or publish in criticizing government policy. Some of these laws were based on the lawmakers' fears of violent revolution, like the Bolshevik Revolution in November 1917 that had imposed a Communist government on Russia.

One day in 1918, a man named Abrams and several of his friends wrote, printed, and distributed handbills urging young men not to take part in the draft of men to become soldiers in the U.S. Army. The handbills were written in Yiddish and thus could not be read by most of their intended audience. Abrams and three friends threw the handbills out of open windows in office buildings in lower Manhattan; only a few reached the people they were written for. Even so, the United States prosecuted Abrams and his friends for the crime of *sedition* under a new Sedition Act enacted that year. The four were found guilty and sentenced to be *deported*—that is, shipped out of the country.

The U.S. Supreme Court had already upheld the Sedition Act in an opinion written by Justice Holmes in 1918. In *Schenck v. United States*, Holmes had declared, "The most stringent protection of free speech would not protect a man who falsely shouted fire in a crowded theatre, causing a panic." Justice Holmes believed that he had marked out a clear line between most kinds of speech, which *were* protected by the First Amendment, and the single type of speech that the government could outlaw and punish: speech that clearly threatened to cause immediate action to break the law and endanger the nation.

Although Holmes and Brandeis had helped to uphold the Sedition Act, they were appalled by the majority decision in *Abrams v. United States*. They did not believe that Abrams's actions, or those of his friends, had posed a serious threat of immediate peril to the nation, so they agreed to dissent from the majority opinion. Justice Holmes wrote a noble dissent for himself and Justice Brandeis: "The ultimate good desired is better reached by free trade in ideas. . . . The best test of truth is the power of the thought to get itself accepted in the competition of the market, and . . . truth is the only ground upon which [people's] wishes [for "the ultimate good"] safely can be carried out. That at any rate is the theory of our Constitution." Justice Holmes spelled out one more time, as clearly as he could, what kind of speech was *not* protected under the First Amendment: "It is only the present danger of an immediate evil or an intent to bring it about that warrants Congress in setting a limit to the expression of opinion where private rights are not involved."

For half a century, the Court did not heed the Holmes-Brandeis dissent in *Abrams*. Indeed, in 1925, in the case of *Gitlow v. New York*, it proposed another test for illegal speech: whether the speech in question had a "bad tendency." This is an extremely vague test, and Holmes and Brandeis joined in attacking it. But there was one feature of the *Gitlow* case that made it a landmark in constitutional law: For the first time, the Court held that the Fourteenth Amendment imposed at least some of the terms of the U.S. Bill of Rights to limit the powers of state and local governments.

Holmes and Brandeis continued their lonely crusade to protect both individual freedom and the government's power to pass laws to solve social and economic problems. They vexed and infuriated the new Chief Justice, former President William Howard Taft, who went on the bench in 1921. (Ironically, Taft was succeeding the late Chief Justice White, whom he had appointed Chief Justice eleven years earlier. To become Chief Justice had been the greatest ambition and dream of Taft's life. Taft is the only person to be President and a Justice.) Fearful that more liberal judges would rise to the Court, the conservative Taft put enormous pressure on President Warren G. Harding to appoint only those judges whom Taft himself approved. Thus, Taft managed to block the appointments to the Supreme Court of

Collection of the Supreme Court of the United States

*William Howard Taft of Ohio (1857—1930) is the only person who has been both President (1909—1913) and Chief Justice of the United States (1921—1930). During his tenure as Chief Justice, he persuaded Congress to restructure the federal court system and to give the Supreme Court a home of its own.*

Learned Hand, another of Holmes's friends, and Benjamin N. Cardozo, the Chief Judge of the New York Court of Appeals.

In 1925, Justice Harlan Fiske Stone joined the Court and entered the ranks of the "great dissenters." Born in Vermont and educated with the young Calvin Coolidge at Amherst College in Massachusetts, Stone had become a distinguished legal scholar. He was Dean of Columbia Law School when President Coolidge appointed him Attorney General and ordered him to investigate the scandals left over from the Administration of the late President Warren G. Harding. President Coolidge rewarded Stone's vigorous efforts to clean up the "Teapot Dome" scandals with a seat on the Supreme Court. Stone soon infuriated Chief Justice Taft by joining Holmes and Brandeis.

Still another case where the "great dissenters" spoke over the heads of their colleagues to the nation and the future involved both a pressing legal problem and a new way to fight crime. In 1920, the Eighteenth Amendment had become part of the Constitution. This new provision banned the sale or interstate transportation of alcoholic beverages. It is popularly known as Prohibition. For over ten years, the federal government had fought a grim and determined battle against illegal manufacturers of liquor in the United States and smugglers of liquor brought in from Canada, Mexico, and Europe. One of the new weapons the government used against these bootleggers was the *wiretap*, by which the government could listen in on bootleggers' telephone conversations.

In a case that reached the Supreme Court in 1928, a bootlegger named Olmstead challenged the introduction into evidence at his trial of transcripts from a government wiretap. He declared that the government had violated his rights under the Fourth Amendment by tapping his phone and "bugging" his place of business without a warrant. The lower courts had rejected Olmstead's argument, and the Supreme Court agreed with them. Chief Justice Taft wrote an opinion for the majority in which he argued that the Fourth Amendment prohibited only "unreasonable searches and seizures." He declared that installing a wiretap or bugging device was not a "search" and that information gathered by a wiretap or bugging device was not "seized" in a way that the Fourth Amendment covered.

Justices Holmes and Brandeis again dissented. Holmes wrote a short opinion declaring wiretapping and bugging to be a "dirty business" and endorsing the reasoning of his friend Brandeis. Brandeis produced perhaps his most important judicial opinion—a long, scholarly, eloquent explanation and defense of the right to privacy, "the right most valued by civilized men." Justice Brandeis pointed out that all sorts of technological devices might be invented that could not have been imagined in 1789 by the framers of the Fourth Amendment but would destroy the right to privacy that the Revolutionary generation of Americans sought to protect. He also pointed out that government should not break the law in order to enforce it. If government did break the law (the Constitution) to enforce the law (Prohibition), Brandeis warned, the government would "invite contempt for law" throughout the society. It would thus destroy the rule of law. It took decades for Brandeis's point of view to persuade a later group of Justices. The 1928 *Olmstead* case was not overruled by the Supreme Court until *Katz v. United States* (1967) was decided.

There were some subjects that all nine Justices did agree on. In 1925, the Court, led by Chief Justice Taft, lobbied Congress for yet another Judiciary Act. The 1925 Judiciary Act was nicknamed "the Judges' Bill" because the Justices of the Supreme Court took an active role in getting Congress to adopt it. This law gave the Supreme Court control over the kinds of cases that it had to hear.

Previously, the Court had had to hear any case that fit within the law defining the Court's *appellate jurisdiction*—that is, the Court's power to hear certain kinds of cases brought to it from lower courts. The Judges' Bill created a procedure by which the Justices could decide which cases they would or would not hear. Except for a narrow class of cases, most people who want the Court to take their case have to file a request with the Court, explaining why their case is important enough for the Court to hear it. This request is called a *petition for a writ of certiorari*. At least four Justices must agree that a case is important enough for the Court to take it by issuing this writ.

The Judges' Bill also adjusted the structure of the federal court system to the shape it has today. At the lowest level, the trial courts are the U.S. District Courts. At the intermediate level are the U.S. Courts of Appeals. At the top of the pyramid is the U.S. Supreme Court.

Still another subject that the Justices could agree on was that their quarters were too small. While the President had the White House and Congress had the Capitol, the Supreme Court had to be content for most of its history with the small, overcrowded Old Senate Chamber in the depths of the Capitol. Chief Justice Taft and his colleagues persuaded Congress to consider building a new structure just for the Court.

Chief Justice Taft never lived to see the building completed; he died in 1930. His successor, Charles Evans Hughes, led the Court into the magnificent Supreme Court Building, which opened, gleaming with marble, in 1935. One Justice supposedly remarked, "By Heaven, we'll be nine black beetles in the Temple of Karnak!"

# CHAPTER SIX

# CHARLES EVANS HUGHES

The Supreme Court experienced several important changes between 1930 and 1933. Old faces departed, and new faces joined the company. These changes are important because they fashioned a critical stage in the life of the Supreme Court and the constitutional system.

When Chief Justice Taft died in early 1930, he left behind a massive legacy—a Supreme Court dominated by conservative Justices who would defend rights of private property against experiments by federal, state, or local governments. Taft himself had appointed a few of these men during his Presidency. As a former President, he also had had tremendous influence with Presidents Harding and Coolidge on the subject of judicial appointments. But Taft would not have been pleased by the man the new President, Herbert Hoover, chose to succeed him.

Charles Evans Hughes had had a distinguished career in politics, law, and diplomacy. He had been an enlightened governor of New York. President Taft had appointed him to the Supreme Court in 1910. He resigned his office in 1916 to become the Republican Party's near-victorious Presidential candidate in 1916 against President Woodrow Wilson. (Hughes has been the only Supreme Court Justice to be a major party's Presidential nominee.) From 1921 to 1929, he served Presidents Harding and Coolidge as Secretary of State. Some liberal Senators, such as the old Progressive George W. Norris of Nebraska, opposed Hughes's nomination to the Court because they believed that the former Wall Street lawyer was a tool of big business. Norris later apologized publicly to the new Chief Justice.

Hughes was a tall, imposing man with a well-trimmed beard. Some lawyers said that he looked the way they had always imagined God to look. He presided over the Court with dignity and firmness. He was a perfectionist who was so strict about the time limits on lawyers' arguments before the Court that he once supposedly stopped a lawyer in the middle of the word *if*. He commanded the respect of all the other members of the Court except for crusty old James McReynolds.

No one could abide McReynolds, whom President Wilson had named to the Court in 1914 to extract him from the Cabinet. McReynolds hated Jews, blacks, women, and any man who disagreed with him. He refused to sit next to Brandeis on the bench or even when the Justices posed for their annual photograph. Hughes must have sighed more than once, thinking about his prickly colleague.

The Chief Justice also had difficulty with McReynolds's three allies —George Sutherland, Pierce Butler, and Willis Van Devanter. These four conservative Justices were determined to uphold Chief Justice Taft's legacy of respect for the rights of private property. They consistently voted to strike down federal and state laws regulating the economy and providing government help to those in need. Reporters dubbed them the "Four Horsemen of the Apocalypse." The name comes from the New Testament's *Book of the Revelation of St. John*, which describes Pestilence, War, Famine, and Death as four horsemen taking part in the final confrontation between Good and Evil.

A Justice who had voted frequently with Taft and the "Four Horsemen" died on the very same day that Taft died. Justice Edward Sanford was known as "Taft's shadow" because he had been recommended by Taft and had always voted with Taft. Now he had died with Taft. President Hoover appointed Owen J. Roberts to succeed Sanford. Roberts was a moderate who shunned the extremes of liberalism and conservatism. He kept his own counsel, but his fellow Justices soon realized that they should not underestimate him. The quiet Roberts would make a difference when he chose to.

A second change of personnel on the Court meant the departure of one of the giants of American law. Justice Holmes had turned ninety in 1931. Chief Justice Hughes every now and then had had to nudge him awake during oral arguments. Holmes finally admitted that he was too old to continue in office and wrote out a brief letter of resignation in January 1932. He lived four more years, dying in early 1935, a beloved figure.

President Hoover had the task of appointing Holmes's successor. He looked at one name on the list over and over again—Chief Judge Benjamin Nathan Cardozo of the New York Court of Appeals. Cardozo was Jewish, and so was Justice Brandeis. The President worried whether the country would tolerate two Jewish Supreme Court Justices serving at the same time. But he also knew that the legal community unanimously considered Cardozo to be the greatest judge in the United States. He finally decided that the country needed Cardozo on the Court. Instead of the outcry he expected, the President was deluged with praise for the appointment by everybody, including former Justice Holmes. Only Justice McReynolds disapproved. He

*The Hughes Court in 1931, with the "Great Dissenters" (GD) and the "Four Horsemen" (FH): left to right, standing, Harlan Fiske Stone (1872—1946; term, 1925—1946) (GD); George Sutherland (1867—1942; term, 1922—1938) (FH); Pierce Butler (1866—1939; term, 1923—1939) (FH); Owen J. Roberts (1875—1955; term, 1930—1945); left to right, sitting, James C. McReynolds (1862—1946; term, 1914—1941) (FH); Oliver W. Holmes, Jr. (1841—1935; term, 1902—1932) (GD); Chief Justice Charles Evans Hughes (1862—1948; term, 1930—1941); Willis Van Devanter (1859—1941; term, 1910—1937) (FH); Louis D. Brandeis (1856—1941; term, 1916—1939) (GD).*

read a newspaper during Cardozo's swearing-in ceremony to show the world what *he* thought of the matter.

Cardozo was a quiet, gentle man who looked far older than his sixty-two years. His father, Judge Albert Cardozo of the New York State Supreme Court, had been forced off the bench in disgrace when investigations disclosed that he had been a party to the corruption of New York City's Tammany Hall Democratic organization. Young Benjamin was permanently scarred by his father's disgrace. He never married and never showed any interest in anything but the law. He had a distinguished record in college and law school at Columbia University and soon stepped forward as a successful reform candidate for a New York City Civil Court judgeship. Cardozo soon won election to the state's highest court, the Court of Appeals (New York State's Supreme Court is actually its trial court), and then became Chief Judge of that court. He was famous throughout the nation and the rest of the Western world for his scholarship and his elegant writing style. His lectures and essays about jurisprudence, which were published as *The Nature of the Judicial Process, The Growth of the Law, Paradoxes of Legal Science,* and *Law and Literature,* are classics of the philosophy of law. He succeeded Holmes as a member of the liberal bloc on the Court, joining Justices Brandeis and Stone.

President Hoover was defeated for re-election in 1932 by Democrat Franklin D. Roosevelt, a towering figure in the history of American politics. Hoover was the victim of the American people's desire for a government that would do *something* about the Great Depression, which had begun in 1929, and of the people's demand for the repeal of the Eighteenth Amendment (Prohibition).

President Roosevelt was determined to experiment with government to combat the Depression and aid Americans in want. He was not afraid to propose government programs that President Hoover had felt might violate the Constitution. In 1933, Congress and the American people were eager to back up anything that President Roosevelt suggested. Congress even voted to adopt New Deal laws that many of its members had not read through. Many of these laws had been poorly drafted, however, and some of them were clearly unconstitutional. Court cases challenging these laws began to make their way up the federal judicial ladder.

The most famous of these cases was brought by the Schechter Poultry Corporation. The Schechter brothers, who ran a chicken business in New York City, found themselves confronted by the centerpiece of the first New Deal laws: the National Industrial Recovery Act, which created the National Recovery Administration (NRA), symbolized by the famous "blue eagle." The NRA was based on the idea that economic competition was a major reason for the Depression. Competition had caused rival companies to undercut each other to win more business. Runaway price cutting and massive employee layoffs had helped to bring about the Depression. The NRA organized each industry, including the poultry industry, and authorized the leading companies in each industry to issue a code, or set of rules, that governed prices, quality of product, and other matters. The codes had the force of law. The poultry industry accused the Schechter brothers of violating the poultry industry code—specifically by selling sick chickens. The Schechters decided to fight the government's attempt to prosecute them.

The "sick chicken" case (as it became known) reached the Supreme Court in 1935. The Justices were unanimous in their decision for the Schechters and against the NRA. Even liberals Brandeis, Cardozo, and Stone went along. (In fact, even before the case reached the federal courts, Justice Brandeis tried to warn the President that the NRA would be declared unconstitutional if it ever came before the Court. But Brandeis's message, carried by his and Roosevelt's friend Professor Felix Frankfurter, fell on deaf ears.) The NRA, the Court ruled, violated the Constitution. Congress had *delegated*, or given, its authority to make laws not just to an executive agency but to the private companies that the law authorized to write the codes for each industry. Congress could not delegate this lawmaking power to the executive branch. It certainly could not give it to private companies.

President Roosevelt secretly did not mind too much about the death of the "blue eagle" because the NRA was not bringing the economy out of the Depression. But the *Schechter* decision angered Roosevelt because the Supreme Court seemed not to be interested in helping the country shake off the Depression. The President feared that the Court would cause more problems for the New Deal—and he was right.

The Justices struck down several more New Deal laws. In these cases, they were not unanimous, however. The "Four Horsemen" were able to win over Justice Roberts, and sometimes even Chief Justice Hughes, to strike down one law after another. Justices Brandeis, Cardozo, and Stone filed a series of eloquent and angry dissenting opinions, but they were cold comfort to the President. It seemed that the Court was throwing out New Deal measures almost as fast as Congress and the President could pass them.

In 1936, President Roosevelt won a smashing victory in his bid for a second term, carrying forty-six of the forty-eight states. As part of his campaign, he had attacked the conservative decisions of the Supreme Court. His landslide triumph gave him an idea: Why should the Court stand alone against the mandate that Roosevelt had won from the people?

In early 1937, Roosevelt dropped a bombshell. He gave a speech announcing that he had come up with a "Court reorganization bill." In the radio speech he delivered explaining the bill, he sought the people's backing for his proposal. The Justices, he pointed out, were old. They were not retiring because the government had no pension system that would permit them to retire. No wonder they were staying on the bench into their seventies and eighties; they had to stay active to earn money to support themselves and their families. But because they were so old and tired, the Justices could not keep up with their workload. Even more important, Roosevelt insisted, the Justices could not keep up with the changing times: "Little by little, new facts become blurred through old glasses fitted, as it were, for the needs of another generation." The Court needed help, the President declared.

President Roosevelt described a bill that he was about to send to Congress to solve the Court's problems. For every Justice over seventy who chose not to retire, Roosevelt suggested that the President be allowed to appoint an additional Justice to help carry the workload of the Court. There would be a maximum of six new justices—not by coincidence, the exact number of members of the Court over seventy.

The bill sounded simple, but the Justices realized what it was: a measure to permit the President to "pack" the Court with Justices who would support his programs. Eighty-year-old Justice Brandeis was hurt and outraged. Although he was the oldest Justice, he had also voted to support most of the New Deal laws struck down by his colleagues. More important, he had tried repeatedly to warn the Administration to be more careful in drafting its bills. Now, it seemed, he was being punished and humiliated.

The American people also realized what the bill was designed to do. They were angered by the Court's decisions, but that did not mean that they were ready to injure the Court's independence. Many Americans thought that the Supreme Court was the equivalent of the Constitution. The President's proposal seemed to be a slap at the Constitution—a badly timed one in the Constitution's 150th year.

The President discovered that he did not have the people behind him this time.

The Court-packing controversy was the first to enmesh all three branches of government in eighty years—since the *Dred Scott* case of 1857. For months, Congressional debate raged over the Court-packing bill. Democrat Joseph Robinson of Arkansas, the Majority Leader in the Senate, supported the bill—but he had set a price for his support: Roosevelt had to promise him the first new seat on the Court. Roosevelt and other liberals were not pleased with this necessary bargain. Robinson was a very conservative Democrat, and they feared he might not be faithful to the New Deal as a Justice.

Democrat Burton K. Wheeler of Montana, a leading Senatorial opponent of the Court reorganization bill, had an idea and wrote to Chief Justice Hughes. Was the Court really overworked? Was the bill necessary?

Chief Justice Hughes *was* opposed to the bill. He had grumbled to friends that "if Congress wants me to preside over a convention, I can do it." But he believed that the dignity and independence of the Court would not permit him to oppose the bill actively. Wheeler's letter presented an opportunity to work against the bill without seeming to work against it. Hughes consulted with Justice Brandeis, of the liberal bloc, and Justice Van Devanter, of the conservative Four Horsemen, on a response, which Wheeler read to the Senate.

No, the Chief Justice declared, the Court was not overworked. In fact, it was ahead of its work at that point. Besides, he pointed out, the Court reorganization bill would actually make *more* work for the Court: There would be more Justices to consult, more to write opinions, more to decide, more to debate.

The Hughes letter took the wind out of the sails of the Court-packing plan. But Senator Robinson was stubborn. He wanted that seat on the Court. He continued to fight for the bill. Then the second shoe dropped.

In a surprise decision, the Justices upheld a major New Deal law, the National Labor Relations Act of 1935. The vote in the case of *National Labor Relations Board v. Jones & Laughlin Steel Corp.* was five to four. Justice Owen Roberts, the quiet Pennsylvanian who had previously tended to vote with the Four Horsemen, had provided the needed fifth vote to uphold the National Labor Relations Act as constitutional. Labor unions applauded, for they regarded the law as "labor's Bill of Rights." The country heaved a sigh of relief, calling Justice Roberts's vote "the switch in time that saved nine"—that is, the nine Justices. For the rest of his life, Roberts maintained that the Court-packing controversy had had nothing to do with his vote; he sincerely believed that the labor law was constitutional. But there was no doubt that his vote to uphold the law had shown that the Court would be receptive to New Deal measures that were constitutional.

The Four Horsemen were furious. Justice Sutherland, their intellectual leader, read his entire dissenting opinion from the bench. He was red-faced and angry. One reporter noticed that his remarks from the bench were even more pointed and furious than his written opinion. Everyone saw that the power of the Four Horsemen was at an end.

Two more events helped to kill the Court-packing plan. The first was the retirement of Justice Willis Van Devanter. Congress had finally provided a pension system for the Justices, and Van Devanter stepped down to take advantage of it. For the first time in his Presidency, Roosevelt had a chance to appoint a new Justice. The second event was the unexpected death of Senator Robinson, who collapsed on the floor of the Senate, still fighting for the bill and his dream of a seat on the Court.

The President decided to abandon the Court-packing bill. It was his first major defeat in Congress, and he was not happy about it. He had invested much of his energy and prestige in the bill, and he hated ending up with egg on his face. But the country was happy to see the controversy blow away, and Roosevelt realized it. Besides, he now had the opportunity to appoint Justices to the Court. Thus, he could help to reshape American constitutional law.

Chief Justice Hughes was privately delighted with the downfall of the Court-packing plan. He had managed to preserve the independence of the Court without getting it involved in the rough-and-tumble of politics, which would have destroyed the Court's independence and prestige. He also had managed to change the Court's direction so that it would not be a rigid opponent of the Administration's attempts to solve the problems of the American economic system. And he had ensured that the debate over the Court-packing bill would be a high-level debate about the Constitution and the system of government it created.

Historians have agreed that Hughes's careful statesmanship saved the Court and the Constitution's system of checks and balances. Thanks to the Chief Justice's efforts, the Supreme Court was preserved to help the nation deal with the pressing problems awaiting it in the years ahead.

# CHAPTER SEVEN

# PROBLEMS OF WAR AND PEACE

In late 1937, President Roosevelt nominated his first Supreme Court Justice. He was still smarting from his defeat in the Court-packing controversy, and he wanted to "punish" the Court by appointing a hard-and-fast supporter of the bill. He also wanted to name a loyal advocate of the New Deal. And he wanted to make certain that the Senate would confirm his nominee. He chose Senator Hugo L. Black of Alabama, knowing that the Senate would be hard-pressed to turn down one of their own colleagues. He was right.

Justice Black had been born and raised in rural Alabama. He had served briefly as a police court judge and had piled up a record as a Senator who frequently used an iron hand in conducting Congressional investigations. He was an ardent New Dealer who seemed to be a truly liberal Southerner—a combination that Roosevelt thought would be ideal for the Court. Black celebrated his confirmation by taking a vacation in Europe.

Soon after Justice Black's departure, newspaper reporters stumbled over a sensational story: Justice Black had been a member of the racist Ku Klux Klan. This organization was born in the defeated South in the 1860s and 1870s, following the end of the Civil War. Dressed in white sheets and pointed hoods to hide their faces, Klansmen tarred and feathered and lynched black men who had sought to exercise their constitutional right to vote and white politicians who had tried to help the freed slaves. The original Klan had been put down by the Union Army, but the Klan had revived throughout the nation in the 1920s. The new Klansmen denounced Catholics, Jews, immigrants, and blacks with equal force and nastiness. The Klan had been a major issue in the Democratic conventions of 1924 and 1928 when Al Smith, a Catholic, denounced the Klan, and his political opponents in the party found themselves forced to tolerate the Klansmen. Now, it seemed, the white hood and sheet of the Klan were lurking under the black robes of a Supreme Court Justice.

Justice Black met the issue head-on when he returned home. In a dramatic radio address, the soft-voiced Alabaman admitted, "I *did* join the Klan." He explained that anyone who had hoped to succeed in Alabama politics—or, indeed, in politics anywhere in the South— had either to join the Klan or to agree not to oppose it. He affirmed that he was free of any kind of racial or other prejudice and pledged to the nation that he would deal fairly with Americans of any race, color, religion, or sex who came before the Supreme Court.

Despite some calls for his resignation, Justice Black stayed on the Court and proved that he had meant every word of his radio speech. He won respect as a defender of the Constitutional rights of black Americans and as an ardent defender of freedom of religion, speech, and press.

President Roosevelt ultimately filled eight of the Court's nine seats. In 1941, when Charles Evans Hughes decided to retire, Roosevelt moved Harlan Fiske Stone up from the post of Associate Justice to succeed Hughes—a decision that pleased Hughes. Three of the other Justices appointed by Roosevelt stand out: Felix Frankfurter, William O. Douglas, and Robert H. Jackson.

Felix Frankfurter was overwhelmed when President Roosevelt decided that he should succeed the late Justice Benjamin Cardozo, who had died in July 1938. Frankfurter had been convinced that Roosevelt would never name him to the Court because his strident advocacy of liberal causes made him far too controversial. Besides, he was Jewish, and anti-Jewish feeling in America was still widespread. But Roosevelt decided that Frankfurter belonged on the Court—both because Frankfurter was a valued friend and because he probably knew more about the Supreme Court than any other living person. The short, dynamic, eloquent Harvard Law School professor dazzled the Senate

Judiciary Committee with his wide-ranging knowledge of the Court and of American constitutional law. He won confirmation easily.

Three weeks after Justice Frankfurter joined the Court in early 1939, Justice Brandeis decided it was time to step down. President Roosevelt appointed as his successor one of the youngest men ever to be named to the Supreme Court: forty-year-old William O. Douglas, the chairman of the Securities and Exchange Commission. Douglas had taught law at Columbia and Yale law schools, and he was renowned for his understanding of the economic system and for his mastery of difficult and technical questions of law and fact. Brandeis was delighted with Roosevelt's choice of Douglas to succeed him. Douglas was a lonely, difficult, brilliant man. He had been born in the small town of Yakima, Washington, and was imbued with the fiercely independent spirit of the Northwest.

Robert H. Jackson had been one of Roosevelt's toughest and most reliable allies in the Court-packing fight. He had been one of the greatest occupants of the office of Solicitor General—the government's chief lawyer, who supervises the government's appearances in cases in the federal courts, especially the Supreme Court. Jackson had become Attorney General, but his eye was on a seat on the Supreme Court, perhaps even the post of Chief Justice. He was miffed in 1941 when Roosevelt chose Harlan Fiske Stone to succeed Chief Justice Hughes, but the President promised Jackson the next vacancy on the Court and soon kept his promise.

Stone was a better Associate Justice than a Chief Justice. Lacking Hughes's gift for managing conflict, he could not prevent the drawing of lines between Justices Black and Douglas, on the one hand, and Justices Frankfurter and Jackson, on the other.

Frankfurter and Jackson resisted using the powers of the Court in a free-swinging fashion to vindicate individual rights. They invoked the tradition of Justices Holmes and Brandeis. The Court, they declared, was an undemocratic institution in a democratic system of government. It should use its powers only when absolutely necessary. It should not play St. George looking for dragons to kill and wrongs to right. Black and Douglas disagreed. They maintained that the Court had long ignored individuals' claims for protection for their constitutional rights. It was up to the Justices now to repair that balance.

Personal differences added venom to the differences in judicial philosophy between the Black-Douglas wing of the Court and the Frankfurter-Jackson wing. Justice Frankfurter still behaved as if he were a Harvard Law School professor. He tended to lecture his colleagues as if he were still running a constitutional law seminar at Harvard and they were backward law students. Black especially resented and resisted Frankfurter. Douglas was also irritated by Frankfurter, for he too had been a brilliant law professor and considered himself to be at least as intelligent as Frankfurter was. (These divisions persisted into the 1960s.)

As the Court entered the 1940s, it faced several thorny cases raising issues concerning the Bill of Rights. Two sets of cases stand out.

The United States has spawned many unusual religious groups, but none more so than the Jehovah's Witnesses. One of the Witnesses' central beliefs got them into trouble repeatedly with the federal and state governments: They argued that all governments were not only illegitimate but evil. The Witnesses recognized no government but that of God. They thus refused to comply with many government requirements, such as the draft, because they refused to acknowledge the authority of government.

In the late 1930s, the Gobitis family of Minersville, Pennsylvania, tangled with the local school board because the family were Jehovah's Witnesses. The Gobitis children refused to salute the American flag and recite the Pledge of Allegiance because they believed that saluting the American flag was the same as worshipping an idol, which the Bible commanded against. When the children were expelled from school, their parents sued the town's board of education.

The case reached the Supreme Court in 1940. The Gobitises claimed that their freedom of religious belief under the First Amendment had been violated. The Justices ruled, eight to one, that the school board could constitutionally require pupils in school to pledge allegiance and salute the flag. Justice Frankfurter delivered the Court's opinion. He argued that in those troubled times, when Europe was falling to the forces of Nazi Germany and Fascist Italy, the government could encourage feelings of patriotism even though the measures might offend the religious views of some Americans. Justice Stone was the lone dissenter. He accepted the Gobitis family's arguments about their freedom of religion and scolded his colleagues on the Court for agreeing to encourage patriotism by means that denied the freedoms that America stood for.

The *Gobitis* case raised a major outcry. The nation's newspapers loudly denounced the Court and Justice Frankfurter. Several of the Justices were sensitive to public opinion and began to wonder if they had made a mistake in *Gobitis*. Also, as old Justices retired and new ones joined the Court, it became clear that the Supreme Court might reconsider its holdings in *Gobitis*. And it did, within three years.

In the 1943 case of *West Virginia Board of Education v. Barnette*, the Supreme Court abandoned its earlier position in *Gobitis*. In this new case, the vote was also eight to one, but this time Justice Frankfurter found himself alone in dissent. Justice Jackson explained in his opinion for the Court that the Justices were upholding the freedom of conscience of the individual. Forcing everyone to agree on an idea, even one so noble as patriotism, achieved only "the unanimity of the graveyard." Justice Frankfurter wrote an impassioned dissenting opinion. He explained that if his purely personal views were at stake, he would of course agree with the majority. After all, he was Jewish, and the Jewish people had long been targets of persecution all over the world. But he was a Justice of the Supreme Court, and his personal views had nothing to do with his beliefs as a Justice about what was constitutional or unconstitutional.

In another civil liberties controversy, Japanese-Americans were not so lucky as the Jehovah's Witnesses. When Japan's navy and air force bombed American military bases at Pearl Harbor, Hawaii, on December 7, 1941, the United States was drawn into the Second World War. Many Americans feared—without reason—that Japanese-Americans (both those who had emigrated from Japan years or decades before and those who had been born in the United States) would secretly work for Japan to sabotage the American war effort. Their fears were largely the result of racial prejudice.

President Roosevelt signed Executive Order No. 9066, authorizing the War Department to take necessary measures to prevent such domestic sabotage. The War Department rounded up over 110,000 Japanese nationals and naturalized citizens living in the United States and their children, who were American citizens by birth. The Army forced them to give up their property, businesses, and careers, and herded them into "relocation centers" in the Western deserts. Although these "relocation centers" were nothing like the Nazi death camps, which murdered millions of Jews, Gypsies, and others in Europe during the war, they *were* concentration camps by the definition of that term then in use throughout the world.

Several young Americans of Japanese ancestry sued in federal court to challenge the government's internment measures. The Justices upheld the measures as valid wartime acts of the federal government. It took forty years for a series of lawsuits by brave and determined lawyers to overturn this blot on American justice. Even so, in late 1987 the Supreme Court refused their pleas that the United States be required to compensate the Japanese-Americans for their lost property. In the spring of 1988, the government enacted a statute providing $20,000 in monetary compensation for each of the surviving internees.

Chief Justice Stone died suddenly in 1946, as he was reading a dissenting opinion from the bench. By this time, a new President was in the White House, Harry S Truman. He consulted former Chief Justice Hughes, even inviting the old man to return to the Court, but Hughes turned him down, recommending that the President appoint Justice Jackson to succeed Stone. Jackson was in Europe at the time. He was the chief American member of the Nuremberg War Crimes Tribunal, which was trying former Nazi officials for "crimes against humanity." In his absence, Justices Black and Douglas apparently took the opportunity to lobby the Administration against appointing Jackson to succeed Stone. Jackson got wind of their efforts and issued a blast of his own, vigorously denouncing Black for supposed improprieties in a case called *Jewell Ridge*, in which Black had not disqualified himself even though his former law partner had argued the case before the Court. The issue was far from clear-cut, and Jackson went overboard in his attack on Black. The controversy threatened to split the Court beyond repair. President Truman decided not to appoint Jackson or any other current member of the Court. Instead, he turned to his old friend, Secretary of the Treasury Fred M. Vinson of Kentucky.

If Stone had been a weak Chief Justice, Vinson was even worse. He had been a fine Senator and a good Cabinet official, but he was at best a mediocre lawyer and judge. He was a fish out of water on the Court. The other Justices had no respect for him. One day at lunch, they discussed the possibility that there be no separate office of Chief Justice and that the title instead could rotate from Justice to Justice if the Court so chose. Vinson managed to get on well with only the three other Justices whom Truman was to appoint: Harold H. Burton of Ohio, who was praised by his colleagues and everyone else who knew him as the fairest man ever to sit on the Court; Tom Clark of Texas, a former Attorney General, whom Truman later labeled "the biggest mistake I ever made"; and Sherman Minton of Indiana, one of the most colorless men ever to sit on the Supreme Court.

The Vinson Court continued divided and quarrelsome. The Justices split repeatedly on civil liberties issues and on other vital cases. Perhaps the most important case of Vinson's Chief Justiceship emerged from the Korean Conflict (1950–1953).

At the height of the Korean Conflict, the nation's steel mills were about to be shut down by a major strike. Neither management nor labor would budge. Because uninterrupted steel production was vital to the war effort, President Truman invoked his "war powers" under the Constitution and seized the steel mills. He then drafted the steel workers into the Army and ordered them back to work. One manufacturer, Jones & Laughlin Steel Corporation, challenged the President's executive orders. The federal court system sped the case through the pipeline to get it before the Supreme Court. The Justices agreed with the steel company and declared the President's orders unconstitutional. A clear majority of the Justices rejected Truman's claims of inherent Presidential war powers: The President, they held, had invaded the legitimate powers of Congress. Truman was furious, but agreed to abide by the Court's decision. It was a major victory for the rule of law.

Under Chief Justice Vinson, the Court had to deal more and more with questions of individual rights. Congressional investigating committees and the Justice Department mounted campaigns against current and former members of the Communist Party. These men and women, government investigators charged, were secretly supporting the Soviet Union, America's adversary in the "Cold War." Targets of these investigations claimed that their activities were protected by the First Amendment from criminal punishment or from congressional harassment, but the government persisted. These individuals tried to persuade the Justices to recognize that the First Amendment protected individuals' rights to say and think as they wished and to join organizations without penalty. But most of the Justices agreed with the government that the Communist Party posed a threat to the national security. Thus, the government was free to make membership in the Communist Party a crime. The government was also free to fire a government employee for being even a former member of the Party. These issues were to persist into the 1950s.

# CHAPTER EIGHT

# EARL WARREN AND THE "WARREN REVOLUTION"

In the summer of 1953, Chief Justice Vinson died suddenly. The Supreme Court was in the middle of hearing arguments on a major series of cases brought by black Americans challenging state laws segregating public school systems. Vinson had been clearly unfriendly to the challengers. Justice Felix Frankfurter, who wanted the Court to strike down segregation laws as unconstitutional, had been deeply worried about Vinson's likely opposition. Frankfurter also detested Vinson. As he was dressing for the Chief Justice's funeral, Frankfurter told his law clerk that Vinson's death was the first proof he had ever had of the existence of God.

The new Republican President, Dwight D. Eisenhower, cast about for Vinson's successor. Although he had promised the first Court vacancy to Governor Earl Warren of California, he resisted naming the Governor to be Chief Justice. Warren had challenged Eisenhower for the 1952 Republican Presidential nomination; also, the two men did not like each other. Eisenhower viewed his pledge as a political consolation prize; to give Warren the Chief Justiceship was more than his due. But Warren successfully insisted that the President honor his promise.

Warren was confirmed, although liberals were distressed by the ap-

*Earl Warren of California (1891—1974; term, 1953—1969) is regarded as one of the three greatest Chief Justices (John Marshall and Charles Evans Hughes are the other two). A veteran politician, he used his political skills to unite the Court behind the sweeping series of judicial decisions usually dubbed "the Warren Revolution." Most Americans remember him as chairman of the Warren Commission, appointed in 1963 by President Lyndon B. Johnson to investigate the assassination of President John F. Kennedy.*

pointment because of Warren's support for harsh measures against Japanese-Americans during the Second World War. But Warren, whom the Court's law clerks soon dubbed the "Superchief," amazed everyone, including the President who had appointed him, because of his deep commitment to the cause of civil rights.

Warren worked with the tireless Felix Frankfurter to ensure that all nine Justices would line up behind a decision striking down school segregation. He himself wrote a carefully phrased, deliberately low-key opinion that all the Justices could accept. And he prepared himself and his colleagues for what he expected to be a firestorm of criticism.

The Supreme Court announced its unanimous decision in *Brown v. Board of Education* on May 17, 1954. It was the first of two decisions, known to historians as *Brown I*. This opinion held that separation of blacks and whites is inherently unequal. The Court silently rejected the 1896 decision in *Plessy v. Ferguson,* which stood for the rule that separate treatment of blacks and whites does not violate the Fourteenth Amendment's requirement of "equal protection of the laws." The second case, known as *Brown II,* was announced a year later. *Brown II* dealt with the way to repair, or remedy, the wrongs resulting from the segregation systems struck down by *Brown I.* The Supreme Court ordered that desegregation take place "with all deliberate speed."

Many Southern states and cities vowed to resist *Brown.* They accused the Supreme Court of *usurping* power from the states. Proposals were introduced in Congress for a constitutional amendment to strip the Court of power over civil rights cases. Southern Senators delayed for nearly a year the vote to confirm President Eisenhower's nomination to the Court of federal Judge John Marshall Harlan—the grandson of the Justice who had declared in 1896 that "our Constitution is color-blind"—to succeed the late Justice Robert H. Jackson. (Jackson was the last Justice to die in office.)

But the nation agreed with Chief Justice Warren, and *Brown* was a great victory for civil rights and a landmark in American history. In 1967, the black lawyer who had led the victorious team of civil rights attorneys, Thurgood Marshall, became the first black Justice of the U.S. Supreme Court. He was appointed by President Lyndon B. Johnson, a Texan.

*Brown* was only the first of many cases in which Chief Justice Warren led what several historians have dubbed the "Warren Revolution." He was quickly recognized as one of the most forceful Chief Justices ever to hold the office. Under his leadership, the Supreme Court stepped forward as the guardian of individual rights and racial equality.

For example, the Warren Court ruled that Congress's power to regulate interstate commerce authorized the federal government to ban segregation in private places, such as restaurants and motels. The Court also applied federal constitutional standards to the rules that states used to define the rights of people accused of crimes. The Justices ruled that the Fourth Amendment to the Constitution, which prohibits "unreasonable searches and seizures" of private homes, restricts the powers of state and local governments as well as the federal government. They held that a person accused of a serious crime who is too poor to afford a lawyer has a right to a lawyer appointed by and paid by the government, because of the Sixth Amendment to the

Constitution. They limited the powers of the federal and state governments to punish persons for left-wing political views. They argued over the limits on the government's power to regulate or prohibit pornography and whether pornography is protected by the First Amendment's guarantees of freedom of the press. They reminded the states that the First Amendment's religion clauses protect separation of church and state, and they struck down laws and rules requiring prayer or Bible reading in the public schools.

Chief Justice Warren declared that the most important decisions of the Warren Court had to do with the way that states run elections for their legislatures. State legislatures divide the states into legislative districts, a process called *apportionment*. Often, the people in charge of drawing the borders of these districts have tried to make sure that they will stay in power. They have drawn boundaries giving the people of a large city the same number of representatives in the state

*These nine men—the Warren Court—were the center of swirling nationwide controversy and attacks in the mid-1960s: left to right, standing, Abe Fortas (1910—1982; term, 1965—1969); Potter Stewart (1915—1985; term, 1958 —1981); Byron R. White (1917—; term, 1962—1993); Thurgood Marshall (1908—1993; term, 1967—1991); left to right, sitting, John Marshall Harlan II (1899—1971; term, 1955—1971); Hugo L. Black (1886—1971; term, 1937—1971); Chief Justice Earl Warren (1891—1974; term, 1953—1969); William O. Douglas (1898—1980; term, 1939—1975); William J. Brennan, Jr. (1906—; term, 1956—1990).*

Collection of the Supreme Court of the United States

legislature as a handful of people in a rural county. They have made certain that black voters are underrepresented in state and local legislatures.

In 1963, the Supreme Court invalidated Tennessee's apportionment of its state legislature, which watered down the votes of the people of Memphis, the state's largest city. The Court declared that the Constitution embodies a principle of "one person, one vote." States must ensure that their legislative districts are so marked out that this principle is a reality.

Again, controversy raged. Again, many politicians called for a constitutional amendment cutting back the powers of the Supreme Court. They were joined by some legal scholars who were concerned about what the Court was doing. These scholars agreed with Justice Felix Frankfurter. They taught that the Court is not a democratic branch of government; if it were too eager to strike down laws passed by democratically-elected federal and state legislatures or actions ordered by democratically-elected federal and state executives, the Court would be in danger of losing its authority and prestige. They also worried that a too-active Supreme Court would cause people to forget how to govern themselves through the democratic processes of legislation and elections.

The defenders of the Warren Court replied that the democratic branches of government had been far too slow to defend individual rights and racial equality. It took the Court to win these victories and to make the elected officials of the federal and state governments live up to their responsibilities to *all* Americans. The Court was merely acting as the conscience of the nation. The debate continues to this day.

Some right-wing Americans mounted a demand to impeach Chief Justice Warren. Some even accused him of being a Communist agent. Warren chose to ignore these charges. He did his best to give effect to the fundamental values that he believed were at the heart of the Constitution even when the text did not state them clearly.

On November 22, 1963, President John F. Kennedy was shot and killed as he rode in a motorcade in Dallas, Texas. As the country reeled, the new President, Lyndon B. Johnson, appointed a commission to investigate the assassination. He asked Chief Justice Warren to preside over the commission. Warren at first did not want to accept. He believed that the Chief Justice had a responsibility to the nation and the Court that could not be put aside. Eventually, he gave in to the President, for he believed that the crisis was so special and the need to reassure the nation so great that he had to put aside his other obligations.

The Warren Commission worked for nine months. Its *Report* declared that a sullen lone gunman, Lee Harvey Oswald, had slain the President for reasons unknown and that Oswald's murder two days later by Jack Ruby, a Dallas nightclub owner, was a bizarre crime, also by a loner. The Warren Commission *Report* sparked a controversy that still is lively three decades later. Chief Justice Warren publicly and privately refused to speculate on the web of conspiracy theories that still surrounds the case.

The most famous Warren Court decision may well be *Miranda v. Arizona*, handed down in 1966. In this case, Chief Justice Warren first spelled out the substance of the famous "Miranda warnings" that police officers must read to criminal suspects before questioning them:

> You have the right to remain silent. If you choose to give up the right to remain silent, anything you say can be used in evidence in a court of law. You have the right to have an attorney present during questioning. If you so desire, or cannot afford one, an attorney will be appointed for you by the court.

The Chief Justice believed that these warnings were the best way to make sure that suspects knew their rights under the Constitution. At first, police officers resented the *Miranda* decision, but in recent years they have accepted it because it makes police officers better at their job. If the police follow the guidelines in *Miranda*, they guard against the possibility that a court will throw out a case because a defendant's rights were violated.

When Earl Warren determined to retire in 1968, President Johnson tried to promote an old friend, Justice Abe Fortas, to become the nation's first Jewish Chief Justice. Conservative Senators blocked the appointment, asking harsh questions about Fortas's financial dealings. Fortas withdrew his name and, in 1969, was forced to resign from the Court. Warren had to remain as Chief Justice until Johnson's successor, President Richard M. Nixon, appointed Judge Warren E. Burger of Minnesota as the nation's fifteenth Chief Justice, in the summer of 1969. Nixon and Warren, both Californians, had detested each other since 1952, when Nixon abandoned Warren's campaign for the Republican Presidential nomination to back Dwight Eisenhower, who rewarded Nixon with the Vice Presidential nomination. Nixon had won the Presidency in 1968 running on a "law-and-order" ticket that had harshly criticized the Warren Court's decisions on the rights of criminal suspects. Thus, it was ironic that President Nixon nominated Chief Justice Warren's successor.

When Earl Warren left office, most of the criticism of the Warren Revolution abated. He died in 1974, mourned by the entire nation. He will live on as a symbol of the idea that the law should be responsive to the powerless and the weak in society, and that judges should be able to use the law creatively to help prod society and government into solving major social problems.

# CHAPTER NINE

# THE BURGER COURT

Federal Judge Warren E. Burger of Minnesota was known as a tough-minded conservative—precisely what President Nixon wanted the new Chief Justice to be. Nixon dubbed Burger a *strict constructionist*—a judge who reads and applies the Constitution as written, rather than one who tries to find new rights lurking in the language of the document.

When Justice Fortas resigned, President Nixon wanted to name a strict constructionist Justice who would cement Southern support for his Administration. But his nominee, federal Judge Clement Haynsworth of South Carolina, ran into trouble. Liberal Senators accused him of having been a member of segregated social clubs and of financial misconduct. Haynsworth was defeated by the Senate. Nixon tried again, naming Judge G. Harrold Carswell of Florida, but Carswell also was defeated. Even moderate Republicans could not stomach a nominee who had a clear record of racist and pro-segregation activity in the 1940s and 1950s. Finally, Nixon appointed Judge Harry A. Blackmun of Minnesota, a childhood acquaintance of Chief Justice Burger and an able federal appellate judge. Blackmun answered reporters' questions whether he was a strict constructionist by saying, "I don't know what that means." (Burger and Blackmun were briefly dubbed "the Minnesota Twins.")

Some constitutional scholars hailed the Burger Court as a sign that the days of the free-wheeling Warren Court were over. Others fretted that the new Chief Justice would lead a wholesale attack on the landmarks of the Warren era. Neither side proved to be correct. The Burger Court consolidated advances made by the Warren Court—trimming some Warren Court precedents and reasserting others. In fact, some Burger Court decisions went beyond anything expected from the Warren Court.

In 1971, a former Pentagon employee, Dr. Daniel Ellsberg, decided to act against U.S. involvement in the Vietnam Conflict. He had helped to write a secret Defense Department history of decision making in that war. Now, he decided he would leak his copy of that history to *The New York Times*. The *Times* began publishing a series of articles in the spring of that year. Its page-one exclusives were accompanied by extensive extracts and documents from the secret "Pentagon Papers." When the government tried to suppress further publication of the Pentagon Papers, the *Times* decided to fight. So, too, did the *Washington Post*, to which Ellsburg leaked the history after a federal court in New York City issued an order blocking the *Times* from publishing more excerpts. When the government sought to restrain the *Post*, the *Boston Globe* began its own series. The story spread beyond the government's power to choke it off.

The case reached the Supreme Court in record time—less than a month after the first story appeared in the *Times*. The Court issued a terse, unsigned opinion rejecting (by a vote of 6–3) the government's claim of authority to suppress the Pentagon Papers stories. Each Justice wrote a separate concurring or dissenting opinion in the case. Three Justices—Hugo L. Black, William O. Douglas, and William J. Brennan, Jr.—argued that the government could never act to suppress such a story in a newspaper. Three Justices—Potter Stewart, Jr., Byron R. White, and Thurgood Marshall—maintained only that the government had not made a strong enough argument to justify suppressing newspaper stories in this case. And three Justices—the new Chief Justice and Justices John Marshall Harlan and Harry A. Blackmun—dissented, saying that the Pentagon Papers articles threatened the nation's security.

The retirements of Justices Black and Harlan in the summer of 1971 gave President Nixon two more chances to reshape the Court. He nominated a quiet, scholarly Virginian, Lewis F. Powell, Jr., and a brilliant, young, combative Justice Department lawyer, Assistant Attorney General William H. Rehnquist. Powell had no trouble winning Senate approval, but Rehnquist's road to the Court was rocky. Nevertheless, Rehnquist was confirmed. Rehnquist fulfilled the President's hopes that he would be a strict constructionist Justice, but Powell soon became one of the Court's pivotal members. He often decided cases by spelling out the competing interests at stake and then "balancing" them to decide which way he would vote.

In 1973, the Supreme Court tackled perhaps the most emotional and controversial constitutional issue since the Civil War: abortion. In the case of *Roe v. Wade*, a deeply divided Court ruled that in most circumstances, under the constitutional right of privacy identified and explained by the Warren Court, a woman has the right to control her body and to decide whether to go through with a pregnancy. The opinion, written by Justice Blackmun, struck its critics as more radical than anything the Warren Court had attempted. It was as far removed from "strict construction" as one could get. Over the years the Supreme Court has held firm, ruling again and again that *Roe v. Wade* is still good law and that the constitutional right of privacy exists even though the word does not specifically appear in the Constitution.

In 1974, to President Nixon's astonishment, *his* Supreme Court played a pivotal role in driving him from office. At issue were tape recordings of Presidential conversations in the Oval Office of the White House about the break-in at Democratic Party offices in the Watergate apartment complex in Washington, D.C., by employees of President Nixon's re-election committee. A specially appointed federal prosecutor in the case claimed that the grand jury investigating the scandal needed the tape recordings to determine who should be indicted and brought to trial for federal crimes. The President replied that the doctrine of *executive privilege* required him to keep the tapes secret to preserve the aura of confidentiality that would enable Presidential advisers to give their real opinions without having to worry about disclosure and public reaction.

The Court voted, eight to zero, against the President. (Justice Rehnquist chose not to take part in the case because he had helped develop the President's argument for executive privilege when he was still at the Justice Department in the years before Watergate.) Chief Justice Burger, writing for the Court, agreed that executive privilege is part of American constitutional law. However, he ruled, it cannot stand as an absolute bar against the great public need for the administration of justice and the investigation of crimes. Burger ruled that, when a grand jury wanted Presidential tapes, documents, or testimony, and the President asserted executive privilege, the judge should be allowed to see or hear the material at issue in his or her own office —*in camera* is the Latin phrase lawyers use—and to decide which parts should be protected by executive privilege and which should be turned over to the court. This decision forced President Nixon to turn over tapes and transcripts that made his impeachment and removal from office a certainty. He resigned before the House of Representatives could impeach him.

Yet another great controversy arose during the era of the Burger Court. Many civil rights advocates believed that it was not enough just to say to black Americans, "You're equal now. Go compete." Black Americans labored under major disadvantages and needed special treatment to make their chances truly equal. Some scholars and public officials came up with an idea called *affirmative action*. Affirmative action permits admissions offices of colleges or graduate schools and government departments to give preference to qualified candidates who are also members of racial or ethnic minorities over qualified candidates who are not members of such minorities. Some other government officials came up with a different sort of plan—a *quota system* that sets aside a specific number of places for members of those minorities.

Allan Bakke, a white candidate for medical school, was turned down by the University of California at Davis even though he was qualified. All the places for non-minority-group students had been filled in the entering class, and Bakke, because he was white, was not allowed to claim one of the places held for minority-group students. He sued, claiming that his right to equal treatment under the Fourteenth Amendment and the federal civil rights laws had been violated by the UC-Davis plan.

The Supreme Court split again. Four Justices held that the Davis plan had violated the federal civil rights laws; Bakke should be admitted to the medical school for that reason only. Four Justices held that the Davis plan was not only legal but constitutional and that Bakke should lose. Justice Powell cast the deciding vote. He ruled that it was not enough to evaluate the UC-Davis plan under the federal civil rights laws—the question was whether the plan was constitutional. He then ruled that the UC-Davis plan was unconstitutional. Thus, he rejected the quota system. But he also ruled that an affirmative action plan *can* take race into account under the Constitution and the civil rights laws.

Collection of the Supreme Court of the United States

*In this 1981 photograph, Chief Justice Warren E. Burger (1907—; term, 1969
—1986) administers the oath of office to Associate Justice Sandra Day
O'Connor of Arizona (1930—; term, 1981—), the first woman to be named
a member of the nation's highest court. Her husband, attorney John O'Connor,
holds the Bible.*

The affirmative action controversy continues to this day. Its opponents denounce it as "reverse discrimination"; its supporters claim
that it is the only fair way to remedy centuries of racial and ethnic
discrimination.

Chief Justice Burger stepped down in 1986 after seventeen years as
Chief Justice, during which he worked hard to improve the quality
and administration of the federal judicial system. He explained that
he wanted to devote his energies to leading the national commission
appointed to commemorate the bicentennial of the U.S. Constitution. (Burger shares a birthdate with the Constitution; its 200th
birthday, on September 17, 1987, was his eightieth birthday.) Aside
from judicial landmarks, his tenure as Chief Justice was notable because, in 1981, Sandra Day O'Connor became the first woman to be
appointed to the Supreme Court. Justice O'Connor, who was a class-
mate of Justice Rehnquist at Stanford Law School, was appointed by
President Ronald W. Reagan to succeed Justice Potter Stewart, who
had retired.

There is as yet no clear legacy of the Burger Court. The Justices cut back on some major landmarks of the Warren era, such as the decisions outlining the doctrine of separation of church and state and restricting the use in criminal trials of evidence seized in violation of the Fourth Amendment. They built on and extended other Warren Court decisions, however, notably in the field of racial equality. In essence, the Burger Court was a period of marking time, of consolidating the bold advances of the Warren era, much as the Taney Court largely consolidated, developed, and preserved the experiments of the Marshall Court.

# CHAPTER TEN

# THE REHNQUIST COURT

To succeed Chief Justice Warren E. Burger, President Reagan named Justice William H. Rehnquist. Rehnquist ran into opposition from liberal Senators again but managed to win confirmation as the sixteenth Chief Justice. The Senate's vote to confirm—sixty-five to thirty-three—was the closest that any Chief Justice-designate has had since 1835, when the Senate confirmed Roger B. Taney (twenty-nine to fifteen). To fill the seat left vacant by Justice Rehnquist's promotion, President Reagan nominated and the Senate soon confirmed Judge Antonin Scalia, the first Italian-American to sit on the Court.

One early indication of the future development of the Rehnquist Court was the controversy stirred up by the announcement in the summer of 1987 that Justice Lewis F. Powell, Jr., would retire from the Court for reasons of poor health. Justice Powell had long been the "swing" vote on the Court. His position on constitutional issues was often critical in the many five-to-four decisions that the Burger Court handed down in the early 1980s.

President Reagan had long awaited the chance to appoint a Justice who would tip the scales to a conservative jurisprudence more to his liking. His first choice to succeed Justice Powell was a learned and controversial former law professor, Judge Robert H. Bork. Immediately, critics of the Bork nomination organized to oppose his confirmation by the Senate. Most observers doubted that Bork's opponents had a chance to stop a nominee who was highly qualified to sit on the Court and who was also the first choice of a powerful and popular President.

Bork found his hearings before the Senate Judiciary Committee to be very rough going. In these televised sessions, he described for the Senators—and for the American people—his views on constitutional law. This was a major departure for a nominee. Previous nominees had declared that they could not talk about their views on constitutional law in any but the most general terms—dealing in specifics would compel them to prejudge issues that they might have to decide if they were confirmed. Bork took this step because he had written extensively about constitutional issues for law reviews and leading

*The Supreme Court, October Term, 1986: left to right, standing, Sandra Day O'Connor (1930—; term, 1981—); Lewis F. Powell, Jr. (1907—; term, 1972—1987); John Paul Stevens (1920—; term, 1975—); Antonin Scalia (1936—; term, 1986—); left to right, sitting, Thurgood Marshall (1908—1993; term, 1967—1991); William J. Brennan, Jr. (1906—; term, 1956—1990); Chief Justice William H. Rehnquist (1924—; term, 1972—1986, as Chief, 1986—); Byron R. White (1917—; term, 1962—1993); Harry A. Blackmun (1908—; term, 1971—).*

political magazines, and many Senators wanted to know if he still held the provocative opinions set forth in those articles. Judge Bork troubled moderate Senators because he seemed to backtrack on his views in order to persuade the Senate to vote to confirm him. This worry about "confirmation conversion," combined with both the Reagan Administration's surprisingly halfhearted efforts on Bork's behalf and the harsh and occasionally unfair anti-Bork campaign, led the Senate to reject Bork's nomination by a vote of fifty-six to forty-four, the largest vote to reject a nominee to the Court in American history.

The President cast about for another candidate. His second choice, Judge Douglas H. Ginsburg, seemed to many critics to be too inexperienced for elevation to the Supreme Court. The issue turned out to be moot. Judge Ginsburg withdrew his name under pressure from Reagan Administration officials after the news media reported that the nominee had smoked marijuana in violation of the law when he was a

Collection of the Supreme Court of the United States

*When, on July 20, 1990, ill health forced Associate Justice William J. Brennan, Jr., to retire from the Court, his admirers and his critics agreed that he had been one of the most influential Justices in the nation's history. Brennan combined a devotion to liberal judicial views, deep learning, a clear and eloquent writing style, and a remarkable talent for building consensus among the Justices.*

young professor at the Harvard Law School. (Ironically, it turned out that the Administration never formally submitted Judge Ginsburg's nomination to the full Senate.)

The President's third nominee, Judge Anthony M. Kennedy, had been frequently mentioned in the news media as a leading candidate for the Court. His views apparently echoed those of centrist Justice Powell. Judge Kennedy easily won unanimous confirmation by the Senate and became the 104th Justice, in February 1988.

Two more changes in the membership of the Court, in 1990 and 1991, had a profound effect on the institution and on the American people's perceptions of it.

In the summer of 1990, Justice William J. Brennan, Jr., suffered a serious stroke and announced his decision to retire from the Court. Throughout the 1970s and 1980s, he had been the leading liberal Justice. Widely praised for his ability, his congeniality, and his talent for building consensus, Brennan had been the most important factor in heading off the conservative counter-revolution that many right-wing critics of the Court had hoped for under Chief Justices Burger and Rehnquist.

President George Bush nominated David H. Souter of New Hampshire, a new member of the U.S. Court of Appeals for the First Circuit, to succeed Brennan. Like Brennan, Souter was a graduate of Harvard College and Harvard Law School; also like Brennan, Souter had been a respected member of his state's supreme court. Observers nicknamed Souter the "Stealth nominee," because he had no record on many of the most pressing constitutional issues likely to come before the Court.

When the shy, reclusive Souter appeared before the Senate Judiciary Committee, he declined, as had most previous nominees, to state his positions on issues such as abortion; he explained that he was unwilling even to appear to prejudge such issues. Despite the frustration that Souter's comments sparked among liberal Senators, his impressive qualifications and the reasonableness he projected in his testimony led to his swift confirmation.

One year later, Justice Thurgood Marshall stunned the nation by announcing his retirement. In a spirited press conference, Marshall explained his decision by saying, "I'm old. I'm old and tired and falling apart." When one reporter asked him what he would do in retirement, Marshall snapped, "I'll sit on my rear end."

Marshall, a symbol of the civil rights struggle, was the only member of the Court to have argued death-penalty cases as a lawyer or to have

Collection of the Supreme Court of the United States

*The death (on January 24, 1993) of former Associate Justice Thurgood Marshall marked the end of an era in American history. Acclaimed as one of the great lawyers of the twentieth century for his work in civil rights, Marshall was the first African-American to be named to the Supreme Court.*

experienced racial discrimination first-hand. He used his great gifts for story-telling to lead his colleagues down paths of life they had had no opportunity to explore. Marshall had declared that he had been appointed to the Court for life and that he intended to serve his entire term. He sometimes joked, "The only way I will leave the Court will be feet first." But Brennan's decision to retire left Marshall feeling lonely and isolated, the only forthright liberal on the Court. His dissents from the majority's increasingly conservative decisions on such issues as the death penalty (which he opposed) grew more and more eloquent, passionate, and frustrated, and he occasionally expressed harsh public criticism of the civil rights policies of Presidents Reagan and Bush. (Justice Marshall died in January 1993; he was mourned as one of the greatest American lawyers, a champion of social justice, and a symbol of civil rights.)

President Bush chose forty-three-year-old Clarence Thomas, another federal appellate judge, to succeed Marshall. Bush stressed

Thomas's origins in poverty in Pinpoint, Georgia, and described his life as an "American success story." The President insisted that he had named Thomas to succeed Marshall not because both men were African-Americans, but because Thomas was "the best qualified" candidate for the job.

A graduate of Holy Cross College and of Yale Law School, Thomas had served in the Department of Education and as chairman of the Equal Employment Opportunity Commission (EEOC). At EEOC, he denounced affirmative-action policies and other government programs designed to aid members of minority groups and victims of discrimination. He claimed that the only lasting way to combat discrimination was to rely on one's own efforts to succeed. Like Souter, Thomas had no clear judicial record on many vital issues facing the Court. Unlike Souter, however, Thomas had expressed clear views on affirmative action (as a policy, not a matter of law) and had made statements that could be read as hostile to the landmark abortion decision, *Roe v. Wade*. Also unlike Souter, Thomas's record was undistinguished; the American Bar Association's committee on judicial appointments gave him its lowest qualified rating. Many critics ridiculed Bush's argument that Thomas was "the best qualified" candidate by listing dozens of judges and legal scholars from all over the intellectual spectrum who, they insisted, were far more qualified to sit on the Court.

The Senate Judiciary Committee pressed Thomas to declare his views on key issues such as abortion, but he refused. At one point, he prompted gasps of disbelief (even from some of his supporters) when he declared that he had never discussed *Roe v. Wade* with anyone— friends, family, or law-school classmates. One noted scholarly critic of the Thomas nomination pointed out, "Having an open mind does not mean having an empty mind."

Thomas withstood often bitter criticism from civil-rights organizations and groups representing the interests of women and the elderly. He seemed well on his way to an easy confirmation when, one week before the Senate was to vote on his nomination, he, the Administration, the Senate, and the nation were stunned by unprecedented charges against a Supreme Court nominee.

National Public Radio and *Newsday* reported that University of Oklahoma law professor Anita Hill, who had worked for Thomas in the early 1980s at the Department of Education and EEOC, had submitted an affidavit to the Senate Judiciary Committee charging that Thomas had sexually harassed her. The accusations were detailed, explicit, and appalling. Though Hill was careful to note that Thomas had never physically molested her, she alleged that he had repeatedly attempted to date her and that he had often subjected her to explicit descriptions of pornographic films, sexual comments, and off-color jokes and remarks.

These revelations put the Thomas nomination into question. Were the charges true? If so, were they relevant to Thomas's qualifications for the Court? Why had Hill come forward after eight years of silence? How had the news media learned about her charges? Had the Senate confirmation process been tainted beyond repair? How should the Senate proceed?

The Senate postponed its planned vote for a week to permit Hill

Collection of the Supreme Court of the United States

*Few nominees to the Court have had so difficult a time winning confirmation as Associate Justice Clarence Thomas (1948—; term, 1991—), whom President George Bush named in 1991 to succeed Justice Thurgood Marshall. Despite controversies over his qualifications, his claims that he hadn't yet formed an opinion on such controversial constitutional issues as abortion, and the charges of sexual harassment leveled against him by Professor Anita Hill, the Senate voted to confirm Thomas's nomination—but by only a four-vote margin, the smallest in over a century.*

and Thomas to testify before the Judiciary Committee. The televised hearings held the nation spellbound. They demonstrated what most women had known for years: sexual harassment was a widespread problem for working women—yet a problem that most men tended to ignore. During Hill's testimony, Republican Senators were courteous to her, but they closed ranks behind Thomas and mounted vigorous, occasionally vindictive attacks on Hill's credibility. Democratic Senators appeared disorganized and hesitant, and Thomas and his supporters took full advantage of the situation. In his dramatic appearance before the committee, Thomas angrily denied all the charges, professed himself bewildered as to why Hill had testified against him, and denounced the committee's proceedings as "a high-tech lynching of an uppity black man" who dared to think for himself. Again, however, Thomas stunned the committee and the nation—this time, when he declared that he had not seen or read Hill's testimony.

Thomas and Hill were intelligent, accomplished, and highly credible; each had a parade of supportive witnesses. Neither the committee nor the nation could determine which was telling the truth; opinion polls shifted based on who had last appeared in the public eye. After a day of acrimonious debate, the Senate confirmed Thomas by a vote of 52 to 48—the narrowest percentage for a Supreme Court nominee in the nation's history. (In 1888, the Senate confirmed Stanley Matthews, also by a four-vote margin, 32–28.)

The Thomas confirmation sparked a short-lived but inconclusive debate over how the confirmation process should work. Senators urged that the Senate should play a more active role in the choice of nominees, but the President rejected this view. He and his aides insisted that the key questions were how FBI screening reports on nominees should be kept secret and how best to examine sensitive allegations against a nominee.

The issues that confronted the Court in the 1980s and 1990s emphasized how important the Court's membership continues to be. Three clusters of decisions proved especially divisive: those striking down statutes against burning the American flag as violations of the First Amendment's protection of free speech; those limiting the rights of criminal suspects and defendants; and those upholding federal, state, and local laws and regulations restricting access to abortion.

*The Flag:* In 1984, the leftist activist Gregory Lee Johnson burned an American flag during a protest at the 1984 Republican National Convention in Dallas; he and other protestors danced around the burning flag, chanting, "Red, white, and blue/We spit on you." Texas authorities prosecuted Johnson under a state flag-desecration law. On appeal, they argued that the statute was needed to protect a cherished American symbol. In 1989, the Court reversed Johnson's conviction by a vote of 5 to 4; Justice Brennan wrote the majority opinion in *Texas v. Johnson*. The majority declared that First Amendment rights were more important to the nation than the mere symbol of those rights. During the oral argument of the case, Justice Scalia underscored Justice Brennan's point, pointing out that burning the flag only underscored its role as a national symbol in public debate.

*Texas v. Johnson* provoked a flurry of rage. President Bush and members of both parties in Congress demanded a constitutional amendment authorizing laws barring flag-burning. Congress enacted a flag-desecration statute as a half-way measure. Another left-wing activist, Sara Eichman, publicly burned an American flag the day the new statute went into effect. As she hoped, she was arrested and convicted under the new law, and her appeal became a test case. In 1990, the Justices decided *United States v. Eichman*, which upheld *Texas v. Johnson* and struck down the federal law under the First Amendment. Again, the Court's 5-to-4 decision touched off protests and demands for a flag amendment, but the furor died down without action in Congress or the state legislatures.

*Criminal Procedure:* The Rehnquist Court continued to cut back Warren Court precedents interpreting the criminal-procedure provisions of the Bill of Rights. The Justices also sought to restrict the availability to convicted defendants of federal appeals challenging state-court convictions. In January 1993, for example, the Justices decided *Herrera v. Collins*, holding that a criminal defendant does not have a constitutional right to present newly-discovered evidence tending to clear him after he has been convicted beyond a reasonable doubt. Court-watchers wondered how far the Supreme Court would go in limiting federal constitutional protection of the rights of criminal suspects and defendants.

*Abortion:* In June 1989, the Court decided *Webster v. Reproductive Health Services*, the most controversial abortion decision since *Roe v. Wade*. The Justices made clear that they were not overturning *Roe v. Wade*, but they permitted states (in this case, Missouri) to adopt severe new abortion restrictions that gutted the first-second-third trimester system marked out in the 1973 case. Pro-choice groups denounced *Webster*; pro-life organizations hailed it as a partial victory and hoped for more decisions that would chip away at *Roe v. Wade*.

In 1991, the Justices decided *Rust v. Sullivan*, which seemed again to narrow the scope of *Roe v. Wade*. The Court upheld federal regulations that prohibited hospitals, doctors, and family-planning clinics receiving federal funds from mentioning abortion as an option to their pregnant patients. Even if a patient asked the doctor to talk about abortion, the doctor's sole permissible response was, "Abortion is not an approved method of family planning." The dissenting Justices pointed out that the regulations damaged doctors' ability to give their patients the best possible professional advice by limiting the options they could discuss. They insisted that, in the conflict between the general federal objective to promote access to health services and the specific policy goal of discouraging abortion, the general objective

*The Supreme Court of the United States, October Term 1992. First row (left to right): Associate Justices John Paul Stevens (1920—; term, 1975—) and Byron R. White (1917—; term, 1962—1993), Chief Justice William H. Rehnquist (1924—; term, 1971—1986, as Chief, 1986—), Associate Justices Harry A. Blackmun (1908—; term, 1971—) and Sandra Day O'Connor (1930—; term, 1981—). Second row (left to right): Associate Justices David H. Souter (1939—; term, 1990—), Antonin Scalia (1936—; term, 1986—), Anthony M. Kennedy (1936—; term, 1988—), and Clarence Thomas (1948—; term, 1991—).*

had to prevail. (On January 22, 1993, the twentieth anniversary of *Roe v. Wade*, President Bill Clinton signed an executive order rescinding the regulations upheld in *Rust v. Sullivan*.)

The Court's 1992 abortion ruling, *Planned Parenthood of Southeast Pennsylvania v. Casey*, rocked pro-choice and pro-life groups. Court analysts noted that, while the Justices upheld some restrictions on abortion adopted by the state of Pennsylvania, they struck down others. Justices Souter, O'Connor, and Kennedy emerged as a moderate core for a Court majority unwilling to disturb *Roe v. Wade*. Just as significant, the 1992 decision signalled that the Court was becoming increasingly resistant to the "chipping away" strategy of pro-life legislators.

It was not clear, as twelve years of Republican dominance of the White House came to an end, what effect the new administration of President Clinton would have on the Supreme Court. No Democrat had appointed a Justice to the Court since 1967, when Lyndon B. Johnson appointed Thurgood Marshall; the only Justice still on the Court in 1993 who had been named by a Democrat was Byron R. White, whom John F. Kennedy had appointed in 1962.

Court-watchers speculated about which Justices might retire during Clinton's term of office. Linda Greenhouse of *The New York Times* noted that any change in the Court was necessarily gradual and piecemeal. She pointed out that the Clinton Administration would have a more direct effect on the federal judiciary by appointing judges to vacancies on the federal district and circuit courts and by altering the legal strategy of the federal government at all levels of the federal court system. She concluded, "Mr. Clinton can probably take his time formulating his approach to the Court. The future, indistinct though it may be, is now on his side." (See pp. xi–xii.)

The Supreme Court today is a powerful and universally respected institution, however controversial specific decisions might be. Except for an occasional proposed constitutional amendment to overturn a specific decision by the Court, there is general agreement that the Court performs its duties and fulfills its responsibilities under the Constitution.

The only major controversy having to do with the structure of the federal judicial system revolves around the proposal to add a fourth level of federal courts between the present Courts of Appeals and the Supreme Court. Former Chief Justice Burger and several current Justices have contended that the Supreme Court is badly overworked—that it cannot decide all the cases that it must decide. They want to create an *intercircuit tribunal*, a special court to which the Justices would refer cases in which different federal Courts of Appeals or state supreme courts dealing with federal issues have reached differing decisions on the same principle of law. The Supreme Court would review decisions of this intercircuit tribunal as a last resort, but the proposed new court would act as a safety valve to give the Justices more time to decide the cases that the Court should decide. Opponents of the idea claim that the new court would actually make more work for the Justices. In addition, a major study of the Court's workload directed by New York University Law School Professors Samuel Estreicher and John Sexton indicates that the Court is not really overworked at all—thus striking a major blow at the case for the intercircuit tribunal. The proposal was shelved in the late 1980s.

The Court is the guardian of the Constitution—subject only to the decision by the people to adopt a constitutional amendment overturning a decision of the Justices. The Court's decisions on whether laws or other government actions are constitutional remind Americans at regular intervals of the values and principles at the core of the Constitution. The arguments before the Court, the briefs submitted to it, and the decisions and opinions handed down by the Justices are accessible to all. The Court also stands as the supervisor or manager of the federal judicial system, reaching out when it has to in order to promote coherence and consistency in federal law.

Justice Oliver Wendell Holmes, Jr., once wrote of the Court, "It is quiet here, but it is the quiet of a storm center." That is as true as ever.

# CONCLUSION:

# HOW THE SUPREME COURT WORKS TODAY

In many ways, the U.S. Supreme Court is the most public of the three branches of government. This is how the Court does its job.

1. The Supreme Court chooses which cases it will hear. In nearly every instance, an individual or organization who wants the Court to hear his, her, or its case will file a *petition for a writ of certiorari*. This petition sets forth all the legal reasons for the Court to hear the case. The petition asks for a special document issued by the Court to the lower court saying, "Send the record of this case to us. We want to look it over." Whoever won in the decision of the lower court files a *brief in opposition*, a legal argument that the Court should *not* hear the case. The Justices read these petitions and briefs. Each Justice assigns one of his or her law clerks—top-ranked law school graduates who work for the Justice—to write reports on the petitions explaining the arguments and recommending which way the Justice should vote. Then the Justices meet in their conference room to vote. These sessions are private.

The Chief Justice has prepared a list, called the "discuss list," of the cases that he thinks are important enough for the Justices to talk about. He speaks first, explaining each case and his reasoning about it. Each Justice then has a chance to speak, with the senior Justice going first and the newest Justice speaking last. Then they vote in reverse order, with the newest Justice voting first. If at least four Justices want to hear the case, the petition is granted. These votes are kept secret, but the announcements of which cases the Court accepts for review and which cases the Justices turn down are made public as soon as possible. Of about 2,000 to 3,000 cases the Court is asked to review each year, the Justices grant review in about 160 to 200. Sometimes several cases present the same questions. The Justices will put them together—a process that lawyers call *consolidating* cases for review.

2. At the next stage of the Court's work, the question is not whether the Justices should hear the case, but how they should rule on the issue the case presents. Lawyers call this stage *hearing the merits of the case*. Both sides file *briefs*—more legal arguments on the major issues in the case. The Justices and their clerks read these briefs carefully, as well as the documents setting forth the record of the case in the lower courts. Sets of briefs in each case are available in the Supreme Court Clerk's office for the news media, the legal community, and the public to read.

3. The Justices then listen to the lawyers for each side and other lawyers they sometimes invite to present arguments. These sessions, called *oral arguments*, are held in public. The Justices have the right to interrupt the lawyer who is arguing the case at any time to ask questions about the case. The lawyer is not there to make a speech, but to answer the Justices' questions. The best arguers, or *oral advocates*, know how to break their argument, answer the question, and finish a coherent presentation to the Court.

4. The Justices and their clerks consider what they have heard and read. In another conference, the Justices talk about the case and then vote on it. If the Chief Justice is in the majority, he decides either to write the *opinion for the Court*—the essay explaining the Court's reasoning—or to assign it to another Justice. If there is a split, the Justices in the minority may write dissenting opinions. If the Chief Justice is in the minority, the Associate Justice who has been on the Court the longest assigns the writing of the opinion for the Court.

5. The Justices show one another drafts of their opinions. This stage of the process—*circulating opinions*—sometimes changes the ways that the Justices think about the case. The author of the opinion for the Court can answer points from the dissenting opinion or opinions in his or her draft. Sometimes a Justice in the majority likes the result but has different reasons for voting that way. He or she may write a concurring opinion explaining these different reasons. Some-

times a concurring opinion becomes the opinion for the Court as Justices change their minds and votes. Sometimes a dissent can become the opinion for the Court, and the draft opinion for the Court can become a dissent. This whole process is secret.

6. On the days that the Court announces its decisions, the Justices meet the press and the public in the Supreme Court chamber, and the Justices read the decisions for each day, one by one. The Supreme Court print shop has already printed up copies of the opinions for distribution at that time to the winning and losing sides and to the news media. Special newsletters for lawyers and law professors publish the opinions in full. Eventually, unofficial series of reports issued by law book companies and the official *United States Reports* publish the Court's decisions for all to read. Law professors and students write articles in magazines called *law reviews* analyzing the Court's decisions and opinions, offering praise or criticism. The process of developing constitutional law continues until the next round of cases.

# PRINCIPAL AND CHECKING POWERS OF THE CONGRESS, THE PRESIDENCY, THE SUPREME COURT

## The Principal Powers of the Congress

- Passes federal legislation (for final approval by the President)
- Submits the federal budget, establishes taxes
- Passes laws regulating foreign, interstate commerce
- Declares war (after the President's request)
- Raises and supplies the military
- Can authorize the borrowing of money by the sale of federal bonds

## The Congress's Checking Power over the President

- Can override a President's veto by a two-thirds majority of both houses
- Can impeach (House) and try (Senate) the President and other officials of the Executive Branch
- Votes (Senate only) to ratify or reject any treaty the President makes
- Votes (Senate only) to confirm or reject Presidential nominations, such as for ambassadorships, judgeships, Cabinet members, and other principal offices

- Controls spending by rejecting Presidential budget requests
- Can investigate and reorganize departments of the Executive Branch

## The Congress's Checking Power over the Supreme Court

- Can propose amendments to the Constitution to override a Supreme Court ruling
- Must approve (Senate) nominees to the Supreme Court
- Can impeach (House) and try (Senate) federal judges
- Decides jurisdiction of courts
- Can change the size of the Supreme Court
- Can create new federal courts or shut down existing federal courts below the level of the Supreme Court

## The Principal Powers of the President

- Acts as head of state
- Signs into law legislation passed by Congress
- Administers U.S. laws
- Proposes the federal budget
- Is Commander-in-Chief of the armed forces
- Makes and signs treaties with other nations
- Nominates Supreme Court Justices, federal judges, ambassadors, thousands of other federal officials

## The President's Checking Power over the Congress

- Can veto laws passed by Congress
- Can order special sessions of Congress
- Can urge members of his or her political party to vote a certain way (not defined by the Constitution, but this power has evolved over time)
- Can appeal directly to citizens to pressure their Representatives and Senators to vote the way he or she wants them to (not defined by the Constitution, but this power has evolved over time)

## The President's Checking Power over the Supreme Court

- Nominates Supreme Court Justices and lower federal-court judges for Senate confirmation

- Can grant pardons to persons convicted of violating federal laws

## The Principal Powers of the Supreme Court

- Makes final review of lower federal-court rulings and state courts' decisions when federal law or Constitutional issues are involved
- Is the first, and final, court to hear cases involving foreign ambassadors
- Settles law disputes between the states
- Supervises administration of the federal court system

## The Supreme Court's Checking Power over the President

- Can declare that the President or other members of the Executive Branch acted unconstitutionally, exceeding their authority under law
- Can interpret laws and treaties signed by the President and regulations issued by agencies or departments of the executive branch
- Can issue special orders (injunctions) preventing the President or other government officers from acting or making them do specific things

## The Supreme Court's Checking Power over the Congress

- Can rule that legislation passed by Congress and signed into law by the President is unconstitutional, therefore void

# FOR FURTHER READING

[An asterisk indicates that a paperback edition is available.]

## GENERAL

The definitive reference work on the Constitution is Leonard W. Levy, Kenneth L. Karst, and Dennis J. Mahoney, eds., *The Encyclopedia of the American Constitution* (New York: Free Press/Macmillan, 1986 with 1991 Supplement). A good introduction to the Constitution's principles and history is John Sexton and Nat Brandt, *How Free Are We? What the Constitution Says We Can and Cannot Do* (New York: M. Evans, 1986)*; a more unconventional and very accessible treatment is Jerome Agel and Mort Gerberg, *The U.S. Constitution for Everyone* (New York: Perigee/Putnam, 1987; 16th ed., 1992).*

An excellent short general history of the United States is Allan Nevins, Henry Steele Commager, and Jeffrey B. Morris, *A Pocket History of the United States*, 8th ed. (New York: Washington Square Press, 1992). See also Samuel Eliot Morison, Henry Steele Commager, and William E. Leuchtenburg, *The Growth of the American Republic*, 7th ed. (New York: Oxford University Press, 1980); Samuel Eliot Morison, Henry Steele Commager, and William E. Leuchtenburg, *The Concise History of the American Republic*, 2d ed.

(New York: Oxford University Press, 1983)*; Alan Brinkley, *The Unfinished Nation: A Concise History of the American People* (New York: Alfred A. Knopf, 1993); the volumes in the *New American Nation* series, edited by Henry Steele Commager and Richard B. Morris and published by Harper & Row, and in the American Century series, edited by Eric Foner and published by Hill & Wang. Readers should also follow *Constitution*, a magazine on American constitutional history and law for the general reader published by the Foundation for the American Constitution.

Two authoritative constitutional histories of the United States are Alfred H. Kelly, Winfred A. Harbison, and Herman Belz, *The American Constitution: Its Origins and Development*, 7th ed. (New York: W. W. Norton, 1991), and Melvin I. Urofsky, *A March of Liberty* (New York: Alfred A. Knopf, 1988).

The best study of the Federal Convention of 1787 is Clinton L. Rossiter, *1787: The Grand Convention* (New York: W. W. Norton, 1987).* Richard B. Bernstein with Kym S. Rice, *Are We to Be a Nation? The Making of the Constitution* (Cambridge, Mass.: Harvard University Press, 1987)*, presents an overview (based on the latest scholarship) of the era of the American Revolution, emphasizing the Americans' experiments in constitution-making and political building. Richard B. Bernstein with Jerome Agel, *Amending America: If We Love the Constitution So Much, Why Do We Keep Trying to Change It?* (New York: Times Books/Random House, 1993), examines the ways the American people have changed the Constitution by using the amending process, describes the thousands of failed amendments, and analyzes the effects of the amendments on American development and national identity.

## CONGRESS
Other than highly technical political science monographs, the handful of good general books on Congress includes Richard A. Baker, *The Senate of the United States: A Bicentennial History* (Malabar, Fla.: Robert E. Krieger, 1988)*; James Currie, *The U.S. House of Representatives: A Bicentennial History* (Malabar, Fla.: Robert E. Krieger, 1988)*; and Alvin M. Josephy, Jr., *On the Hill* (New York: Simon & Schuster, 1979). A modern classic is John F. Kennedy, *Profiles in Courage* (New York: Harper, 1956)*. A valuable collection is Paul F. Boller, Jr., *Congressional Anecdotes* (New York: Oxford University Press, 1991).* Lonnelle Aikman, *We the People: The Story of the United States Capitol*, 11th ed. (Washington, D.C.: United States

Capitol Historical Society with National Geographic Magazine, 1978 and regularly updated)* is an excellent history of the building that includes extensive historical discussion of Congress as well.

Thomas P. O'Neill with William Novak, *Man of the House* (New York: Random House, 1987),* is a rewarding memoir. Allen Drury's novel *Advise and Consent* (Garden City, NY: Doubleday, 1959)*, is worth reading. Brooks Jackson, *Honest Graft: Big Money and the American Political Process*, rev. ed. (Washington, D.C.: Farragut Publishing, 1990)*, is essential for anyone who wants to understand the plight of the modern Congress.

## THE PRESIDENCY

Classic studies include: Edward S. Corwin, Randall W. Bland, Theodore T. Hindson, and Jack W. Peltason, *The President: Office and Powers*, 5th rev. ed. (New York: New York University Press, 1984)*; Thomas M. Cronin, *The State of the Presidency*, rev. ed. (Boston: Little, Brown, 1980)*; Marcus Cunliffe, *The Presidency* (New York: American Heritage Books/Houghton Mifflin Co., 1986)*; Louis W. Koenig, *The Chief Executive* (New York: Harcourt Brace Jovanovich, 1981); William E. Leuchtenburg, *In the Shadow of FDR* (Ithaca, N.Y.: Cornell University Press, 1983)*; Richard M. Pious, *The American Presidency* (New York: Basic Books, 1979)*; George Reedy, *The Twilight of the Presidency*, rev. ed. (New York: Mentor/New American Library, 1987)*; Clinton L. Rossiter, *The American Presidency*, rev. ed. (1960; Baltimore: Johns Hopkins University Press, 1987)*; and Arthur M. Schlesinger, Jr., *The Imperial Presidency*, rev. ed. (Boston: Houghton Mifflin, 1990)*.

First-rate studies of presidential elections include Theodore H. White, *The Making of the President 1960* (New York: Atheneum, 1961)*; Lewis Chester, Godfrey Hodgson, and Bruce Page, *An American Melodrama: The Presidential Campaign of 1968* (New York: Dell, 1970); and Richard Ben Cramer, *What It takes* (New York: Random House, 1992)*.

Other studies include Stanley I. Kutler, *The Wars of Watergate* (New York: Alfred A. Knopf, 1990)*; J. Anthony Lukas, *Nightmare: The Underside of the Nixon Years* (New York: Viking, 1989)*; Herbert Abrams, *"The President Has Been Shot!"* (New York: W. W. Norton, 1992); and Lonnelle Aikman, *The Living White House* (Washington, D.C.: White House Historical Association with National Geographic Society, 1982 and regularly updated).* Bob Woodward and Carl Bernstein, *All the President's Men* (New York: Simon & Schuster,

1974)* and *The Final Days* (New York: Simon & Schuster, 1975)*, are highly readable.

Some of the best of the thousands of Presidential biographies are: Robert F. Jones, *George Washington* (New York: Rose Hill Books/Fordham University Press, 1986)*; Peter Shaw, *The Character of John Adams* (Chapel Hill, N.C.: University of North Carolina Press, 1975)*; Noble E. Cunningham, Jr., *In Pursuit of Reason: The Life of Thomas Jefferson* (Baton Rouge: Louisiana State University Press, 1987)*; Robert V. Remini, *The Life of Andrew Jackson* (New York: Harper & Row, 1989)*; Stephen B. Oates, *With Malice Toward None: The Life of Abraham Lincoln* (New York: Harper & Row, 1977)*; Gabor S. Boritt, ed., *Lincoln: The War President* (New York: Oxford University Press, 1992); Garry Wills, *Lincoln at Gettysburg: The Words that Remade America* (New York: Simon & Schuster, 1992)*; William J. Cooper, Jr., *The Warrior and the Priest: Theodore Roosevelt and Woodrow Wilson* (Cambridge, Mass.: Harvard University Press, 1980); James MacGregor Burns, *Roosevelt: The Lion and the Fox* (New York: Harcourt Brace, 1956)*; James MacGregor Burns, *Roosevelt: The Soldier of Freedom* (New York: Harcourt Brace Jovanovich, 1970)*; Frank Freidel, *Franklin D. Roosevelt: A Rendezvous With Destiny* (Boston: Little, Brown, 1990)*; William E. Leuchtenburg, *Franklin D. Roosevelt and the New Deal, 1932–1940* (New York: Harper & Row, 1963)*; David McCullough, *Truman* (New York: Simon & Schuster, 1992)*; Herbert S. Parmet, *Eisenhower and the American Crusades* (New York: Macmillan, 1972); Herbert S. Parmet, *Jack: The Struggles of John F. Kennedy* (New York: Dial Press, 1978); Herbert S. Parmet, *JFK: The Presidency of John F. Kennedy* (New York: Dial Press, 1980); Robert Dallek, *Lone Star Rising* (New York: Oxford University Press, 1991) (the first of two volumes on Lyndon B. Johnson)*; Garry Wills, *Nixon Agonistes* (Boston: Houghton Mifflin, 1970); Herbert S. Parmet, *Richard Nixon and His America* (Boston: Little, Brown, 1990); Lou Cannon, *President Reagan: The Role of a Lifetime* (New York: Simon & Schuster, 1991)*; and Garry Wills, *Reagan's America* (New York: Doubleday, 1988)*. The University Press of Kansas is midway through a valuable series of historical studies of each President.

Two valuable collections are Paul F. Boller, Jr., Presidential Anecdotes (New York: Oxford University Press, 1981)*, and Paul F. Boller, Jr., *Presidential Campaigns* (New York: Oxford University Press, 1984)*.

## THE SUPREME COURT

Kermit H. Hall, ed., *The Oxford Companion to the Supreme Court of the United States* (New York: Oxford University Press, 1992), is an authoritative one-volume reference work. Robert G. McCloskey, *The American Supreme Court* (Chicago: University of Chicago Press, 1960)*, is a classic treatment in great need of updating. A far more recent study of very high quality is William M. Wiecek, *Liberty Under Law* (Baltimore: Johns Hopkins University Press, 1988)*. Students will enjoy Mary Ann Harrell and Burnett Anderson, *Equal Justice Under Law: The Supreme Court in American Life*, 4th ed. (Washington, D.C.: Supreme Court Historical Society with National Geographic Magazine, 1982 and regularly updated).*

Three brief, graceful studies by Archibald Cox also stand out: *The Warren Court* (Cambridge, Mass.: Harvard University Press, 1968)*, *The Role of the Supreme Court in American Government* (New York: Oxford University Press, 1976)*, and *Freedom of Expression* (Cambridge, Mass.: Harvard University Press, 1981)*. Professor Cox's more general study, *The Court and the Constitution* (Boston: Houghton Mifflin, 1987)*, builds on his earlier works and is a good introduction to the more theoretical side of constitutional law. See also Harry H. Wellington, *Interpreting the Constitution* (New Haven: Yale University Press, 1990)*, and Laurence H. Tribe and Michael Dorf, *On Reading the Constitution* (Cambridge, Mass.: Harvard University Press, 1991)*. David G. Savage, *Turning Right: The Rise of the Rehnquist Supreme Court* (New York: Wiley, 1992)* is an excellent journalistic account, far better than the better-known but more sensationalized Bob Woodward and Scott Armstrong, *The Brethren: Inside the Supreme Court* (New York: Simon & Schuster, 1979)*.

Two fine collections of biographical studies are G. Edward White, *The American Judicial Tradition*, rev. ed. (New York: Oxford University Press, 1988)*, and Allison Dunham and Philip B. Kurland, eds., *Mr. Justice* (Chicago: University of Chicago Press, 1964). See also Richard B. Morris, *John Jay, the Nation, and the Court* (Boston: Boston University Press, 1967); Francis N. Stites, *John Marshall: Defender of the Constitution* (Boston: Little, Brown, 1981)*; Leonard Baker, *John Marshall: A Life in Law* (New York: Macmillan, 1974)*; R. Kent Newmyer, *Supreme Court Justice Joseph Story: Statesman of the Old Republic* (Chapel Hill, N.C.: University of North Carolina Press, 1985)*; Liva Baker, *The Justice from Beacon Hill: The Life and Times of Oliver Wendell Holmes* (New York: HarperCollins, 1991); Alpheus Thomas Mason, *Brandeis: A Free Man's Life* (New York: Viking,

1946); Lewis J. Paper, *Brandeis* (Englewood Cliffs, N.J.: Prentice-Hall, 1983); Alden L. Todd, *Justice on Trial: The Case of Louis D. Brandeis* (New York: McGraw-Hill, 1964)\*; Melvin I. Urofsky, *Louis D. Brandeis and the Progressive Tradition* (Boston: Little, Brown, 1981)\*; Alpheus Thomas Mason, *Harlan Fiske Stone: Pillar of the Law* (New York: Viking, 1956); James F. Simon, *Independent Journey: The Life of William O. Douglas* (New York: Harper & Row, 1980); James F. Simon, *The Antagonists: Hugo Black, Felix Frankfurter and Civil Liberties in Modern America* (New York: Simon & Schuster, 1989)\*; and G. Edward White, *Earl Warren: A Public Life* (New York: Oxford University Press, 1982).\*

Of the many histories of leading constitutional cases, the best include: Don E. Fehrenbacher, *Slavery, Law, and Politics* (New York: Oxford University Press, 1981)\*, an abridged edition of *The Dred Scott Case* (New York: Oxford University Press, 1978); Peter Irons, *Justice at War* (1983; new ed., Berkeley: University of California Press, 1993)\*; Richard Kluger, *Simple Justice* (New York: Alfred A. Knopf, 1976)\*; Anthony M. Lewis, *Gideon's Trumpet* (New York: Random House, 1964)\*; Anthony M. Lewis, *Make No Law* (New York: Random House, 1991)\*; and Sanford J. Ungar, *The Papers and the Papers* (New York: Dutton, 1972)\*.

# INDEX

# ABOUT THE AUTHORS

RICHARD B. BERNSTEIN, adjunct associate professor at New York Law School, has written or edited twelve books on American constitutional history, including *Are We to Be a Nation?: The Making of the Constitution* (with Kym S. Rice) and the three-book set *Into the Third Century: The Congress, The Presidency, The Supreme Court* (with Jerome Agel), from which *Of the People, By the People, For the People* has been updated and expanded. A graduate of Amherst College and the Harvard Law School, he has served on the faculty of Rutgers University, Newark. He has been co-curator of the New York Public Library's Constitution Bicentennial Project, historian of the New York City Commission on the Bicentennial of the Constitution, co-curator of the Congress Bicentennial Project of the Library of Congress, and research director of the New York State Commission on the Bicentennial of the U.S. Constitution. He serves as assistant editor of *The Papers of John Jay* and is completing a history of the First Congress. He lives in Brooklyn, New York.

JEROME AGEL has written and produced more than fifty books, including collaborations with Carl Sagan, Marshall McLuhan, R. Buckminster Fuller, and Isaac Asimov. His works include *The U.S.*

Constitution for Everyone; Why in the World: Adventures in Geography; Between Columbus and the Pilgrims: the Americas 1492-1620; The Making of Kubrick's 2001; From Many, One: Your 50 United States; and the nonfiction novels 22 Fires and Deliverance in Shanghai.

The most recent Bernstein-Agel collaboration was Amending America: If We Love the Constitution So Much, Why Do We Keep Trying to Change It?